THE TRADING WORLD OF
THE TAMIL MERCHANT

Ports of the Southern Coromandel c. 1700

- Masulipatnam
- Motu Palli
- Nizampatnam / Petapoli
- Armagon
- Pulicat
- Madras
- San Thome
- Covelong
- Sadras
- Kunimedu
- Pondicherry
- Teganapatnam, Ft. St David (Cuddalore)
- Porto Novo
- Tranquebar
- Karikal
- Nagore
- Nagapatnam
- Patmadoer
- Kilacare
- Tuticorin
- Kayalpatnam
- Manapadu
- Cape Comorin

COROMANDEL COAST

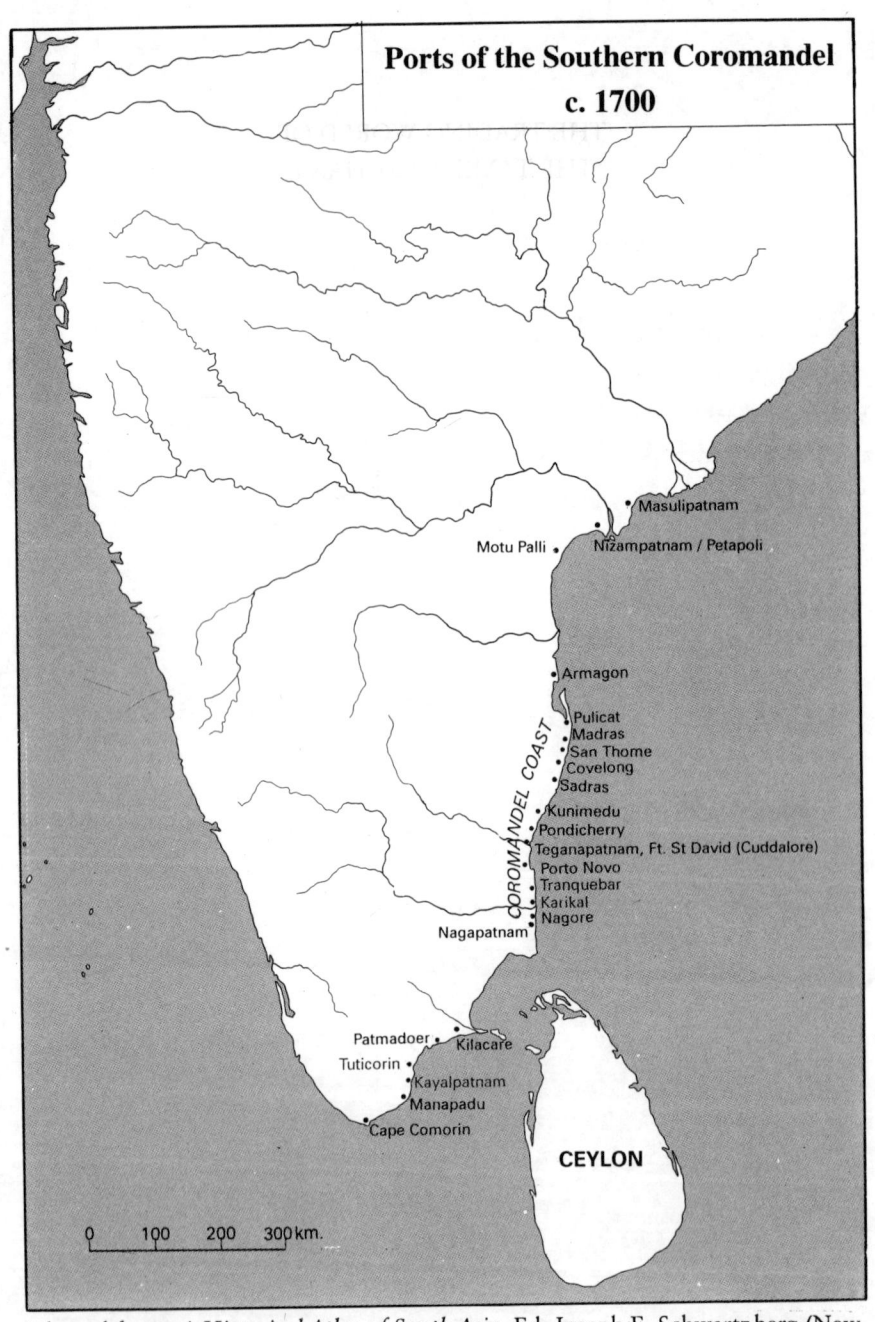

CEYLON

0 100 200 300 km.

Adapted from: *A Historical Atlas of South Asia*. Ed. Joseph E. Schwartzberg (New York: Oxford University Press, 1992), plate VI.B.2., p.50.

THE TRADING WORLD OF THE TAMIL MERCHANT

Evolution of Merchant Capitalism in the Coromandel

KANAKALATHA MUKUND

Orient Longman

ORIENT LONGMAN LIMITED

Registered Office
3-6-272 Himayatnagar, Hyderabad 500 029 (A.P.), India

Other Offices
Bangalore / Bhopal / Bhubaneshwar / Calcutta / Chandigarh
Chennai / Ernakulam / Guwahati / Hyderabad / Jaipur
Lucknow / Mumbai / New Delhi / Patna

© Orient Longman Limited 1999

ISBN 81 250 1661 9

Typeset by
OSDATA
Hyderabad 500 029

Printed in India at
Novena Offset Printing Co.
Chennai 600 005

Published by
Orient Longman Limited
160 Anna Salai
Chennai 600 002

The coastline of India as depicted in the map is neither correct nor authentic.

Time past and time present
Are both perhaps present in time future
And time future contained in time past.

T. S. Eliot, "Burnt Norton", *Four Quartets*

CONTENTS

List of Illustrations and Tables	viii
Acknowledgments	ix
Introduction	xi
List of Abbreviations	xiv
1. Merchant Capitalism: Theory and Context	1
2. Trade, Merchants and the Urban Setting: The Sangam Period (50–400 C.E.)	13
3. Temples, Urbanisation and the Development of Trade in the Medieval Period (900–1300)	25
4. Trade and Merchants: The Vijayanagar Period (1400–1600)	42
5. Merchants Capitalists in the Early Decades of the East India Companies (1600–1670)	53
6. Textile Trade (1670–1750): Structurally Fragmented Markets and Prices	76
7. Textile Trade (1670–1750): Merchant Capitalism at its Zenith	103
8. Merchant Capitalists as a Social Class	144
9. Conclusion	168
Glossary	183
Appendix	188
Bibliography	189
Index	200

ILLUSTRATIONS AND TABLES

Graphs

1.	Grain Prices at Madras, 1693–1750	87
2.	Prices of Longcloth at Madras, 1674–1750	90

Tables

3.1	Donations to Temples by Classes	33
3.2	Borrowers of Temple Funds by Classes	34
6.1	English Textile Trade in Southern Coromandel	81
6.2	Prices of Paddy in Madras and Fort St David	84
6.3	Cotton Prices, 1670–1742	84
6.4	Years of Grain Shortage in Madras	85
6.5	Conditions of Cotton Supply, 1672–1746	86
6.6	Pattern of English Textile Trade, 1672–1750	88
6.7	Silver Prices in Madras, 1680–1750	88
7.1	Terms of Sale of Broadcloth at Madras	136
7.2	Calendar of Losses Reported by Merchants	138
9.1	Respondentia Interest Rates at Madras	173

ACKNOWLEDGMENTS

To write a history of the Coromandel merchants has been a long-cherished dream of mine. I have been able to translate this dream into reality through the help of many institutions and individuals, to whom I owe deep gratitude and whose support I would like to acknowledge.

The Indian Council of Social Science Research awarded me a Senior Fellowship which made it possible for me to undertake this study.

Dr R. Radhakrishna, Vice-Chancellor, Andhra University, (then Director of the Centre for Economic and Social Studies (CESS), Hyderabad), extended his support to me in many ways, not the least by providing the institutional affiliation of the Centre during the tenure of the fellowship.

N. Krishnaji, Senior Fellow of CESS, N. Subba Reddy, Honorary Senior Fellow, and G. Vijay Kumar, Librarian, have helped me in more ways than they perhaps realise. I would also like to acknowledge the generous help of Dr G. K. Mitra whenever I needed to use the computers at CESS.

Most of the work for this study was done in the Tamil Nadu State Archives. The staff, especially Sivakumar, Ravi, Loganathan, Augustin and Vijaya Kumar (of the Library), by their ungrudging cooperation, made my work much easier.

I have used several other libraries and institutions whom I would like to thank:

> The Librarian and staff of University of Bombay Library, with a special word of thanks to Mrs Joseph.
> The Government Oriental Manuscripts Library, Chennai.
> The Director and Librarian, Department of Archaeology, Government of Andhra Pradesh.
> The Archaeological Survey of India, Chennai.
> Father John Correia-Afonso and the Librarian of the Heras Institute of Indian History and Culture, St Xavier's College, Mumbai.

Acknowledgments

The U. V. Swaminatha Iyer Library, Chennai.
The Maraimalai Adigal Library, Chennai.

Fellow scholars, especially Lalitha Iyer who listens to my interminable theories with interest and sympathy, have helped with suggestions and references.

Most of all, I could never have written this book without the total support of two people—my husband Jagannathan Mukund, and my mother Janaki Narasimhan who has set standards of excellence which have been a source of inspiration and intimidation since my childhood.

INTRODUCTION

This was orginally intended to be a study of the evolution of merchant capitalism and mercantile institutions in the Coromandel region between 1500 and 1750. In a region with as long a history of commercial activity as the Coromandel, it soon became clear that to appreciate better the dynamics of development and change, it would be necessary to go back to the earliest periods of history, so that the evolution of trade and institutions could be understood as a holistic and historical process. The region referred to as the Coromandel is considered to comprise almost all of South India from Visakhapatnam down to the tip of the peninsula. In the seventeenth century, the Dutch began to refer to the northern Coromandel, that is the region around Masulipatnam, and the southern Coromandel, roughly south of Madras, the latter corresponding to much of present-day Tamil Nadu.

Very soon into the study it also became evident that to cover the whole of the Coromandel region would be a near impossible task, particularly in view of the constraint imposed by my own lack of knowledge of Telugu. I therefore decided to concentrate on the Tamil areas alone, hoping that what was lost by making an artificial boundary between the Tamil and Telugu regions would be compensated for by the more extensive treatment that the southern Coromandel would receive.

The study is based on the hypothesis that merchants in the Coromandel had evolved over the centuries into a distinct class of merchant capitalists, with a conscious perception of their identity (and aspirations) both as an economic and as a social class. The coverage of trade and merchant groups is thus selective, since the emphasis is on the merchant capitalists. Similarly, the state and forms of administration, revenue collection and appropriation of surplus by the ruling classes are treated as a given. The emphasis is more on mercantile institutions and social relationships.

Many aspects of South Indian society, economy and the state have received the attention of scholars, both Indian and foreign.

Introduction

Obviously, the views from within and without would differ in terms of perspective, context and the audience being addressed. While acknowledging the great contributions made to our understanding of social relationships by the analytical insights of foreign scholars, I have deliberately avoided using certain theoretical terms which have been coined to explain the interaction of various institutions and structures in Tamil society. The interplay of religion, society, the state and the economy through the development of institutions like temples, the composite nature of patronage, rights and obligations which marked the relationship between the upper classes and the lower classes are all tenuous strands which make up the social fabric of Tamil culture. The laboured use of triangular diagrams to explain these relationships or of terms like "theatre state" to describe the patronage extended to performing arts which was an intrinsic feature of the behaviour of ruling elites, to me, seem to impose an artificial categorisation, determined by alien norms, on values which are internalised in the culture and ethos of Tamil society.

Different kinds of source materials have been used for exploring the different periods of history. For the earliest period, I have depended almost exclusively on classical Tamil literature. For the medieval period, temple inscriptions are the main source of information. As the centuries advance, travel accounts and, later, the records of the European companies constitute the information base. The nature of the data sources also imposes several limitations in terms of the areas studied and the patterns of mercantile activity. All the material in Tamil—literary works, inscriptions as well as other contemporary documents—has been translated by me, unless a translated version is specifically indicated. No diacritical marks are used, and the standardised form of transliteration (used by scholars like Karashima, Stein and others) has been adopted, with words spelt in English as they are pronounced (rather than as they are written) in Tamil.

This study is organised in three parts, arranged chronologically. The first part examines the analytical origins of the theory of merchant capitalism, and also outlines the evolution of trade and institutions in the Tamil country till the medieval period. The second part describes the functioning of merchants and trade in the period prior to the establishment of Madras and the early forms of colonial administration. The last part deals with the full efflorescence of merchant capitalism in the Coromandel in the context of the

Introduction

interaction of the local merchants with the European companies. The narrative halts at the point where the first signs of decay begin to appear with greater control and penetration of European power. The conclusion synthesises all the strands of the evolution of merchant capitalism in the Coromandel until 1750.

ABBREVIATIONS

DR	*Dagh Register genhouden in't Casteel Batavia*
EFI	*English Factories in India*
FSDC	Fort St David Consultations, Records of the South Arcot District
PC	Public Consultations, Fort St George Records
SII	*South Indian Inscriptions*
SITI	*South Indian Temple Inscriptions*

ONE

Merchant Capitalism: Theory and Context

India's mercantile community provides one of the strongest links of continuity in the economic history of the country, and a study of the former will provide a clearer understanding of developments and changes in the economic structure of India over the centuries. In the pre-industrial and largely agrarian economy, merchants provided the impetus for the increase in production beyond subsistence, i.e., for exchange, and thus made possible the diversification of economic activity. Their trade, which extended beyond localised exchange to interregional and international markets, succeeded not only in creating a more integrated market at a supralocal level, but also enabled the growth of non-agricultural production beyond the limitations of local demand. In terms of organisational forms also, a hierarchy of intermediary agents who provided subsidiary services to make possible the smooth flow of commerce has survived and continues to be important even in the present-day economy.

In South Indian ethos, trade is recognised as one of the most important economic activities after agriculture and crafts, which also signifies the sequence in which the economy diversifies into more specialised activities beyond subsistence. Trade is always associated with maritime trade. Against this background, the aim of this study is to trace the evolution of mercantile activity and organisation in South India from its first recorded origins, and especially in the two centuries and a half before the beginning of the colonial period. The focus here is not just on trade, but on the development of a socio-economic phenomenon of "merchant capitalism". This is used to denote a system in which merchants were not merely the agency in effecting the distribution of goods between different markets and regions, but had accumulated sufficient reserves of capital to control and dominate commodity production and artisan producers and, in the process, had further accumulated capital and tightened their control over the production process.

Role of trade and merchant capital: Theoretical framework

There is an extensive body of literature, both theoretical and historical, which has explored the role of trade in transforming traditional societies and older economic organisations. It analyses not only the institutions connected with trade and the endogenous and exogenous factors which contribute to the process of transformation, but also the implicit meanings of the terms used in this context. Words like exchange, market and so on, lend themselves to a variety of interpretations in different disciplines which also have implications for the processes which are being described.

While trade and trading capital do not, as such, find a place in Marx's schema of historical evolution from primitive accumulation to capitalism, he does discuss in brief the nature of commercial capital, and its implications for the overall development of an economic system.[1] Some forms of exchange and trade—and a separation between the functions of production and trading—have always existed in all societies, from the most primitive to the advanced capitalist. But there is also a specific, identifiable stage when trading becomes a specialised activity, mediating between producers (especially, non-agricultural manufacturers) and widely dispersed consumers and markets, which in turn generates the accumulation of capital in the hands of a merchant class.

Marx comments that *"Within* [emphasis added] the capitalist mode of production ... commercial capital appears simply as capital in a *particular* function. In all earlier modes of production, however, commercial capital rather appears as the function of capital *par excellence"*. He goes on to add that the existence of commercial capital and "its development to a certain level is itself a historical precondition for the capitalist mode of production", because it signified both the concentration of wealth, and production not for consumption but for a market, to be traded.[2] This thus indicates the

---

1. Karl Marx, *Capital*, Penguin ed., intro. Ernest Mandel, trans. David Fernbach (London: Penguin Books, 1976–81), vol. 3: chs. 16–20; all subsequent citations are to this edition.

evolution of specialised functions in the economy in which the agent of production and the agent of circulation are distinct and merchant capital is autonomous of the other functions of industrial capital.[3] While this would indicate that merchant capitalism was a natural stage of economic evolution and would be the precondition for the further development of an economy into full-fledged capitalism, Marx argues that "this development, taken by itself is insufficient to explain the transition from one mode of production to the other", and essentially regards the domination of commercial capital as an indication of the relative underdevelopment of that particular society.[4]

This framework has, in fact, dominated the work of almost all Marxist scholars, based on the generalised argument that commercial profits were derived from either piracy or plunder, and by creating artificial conditions of monopoly which enabled merchants to accumulate large profits. Dobb also argues that primitive technology in communications and transportation created highly segmented markets which merchants were able to exploit to further their monopoly control and profits. He concludes, "For this reason also, while the influence of commerce as a dissolvent of feudal relationships was considerable, merchant capital remained nevertheless in large measure a parasite on the old order", and did not lead to the development of capitalism.[5] Sweezy's alternative explanation, drawing on the work of Henri Pirenne, which stresses the role of trade as the crucial external agent in the transition from feudalism to capitalism in western Europe, by and large, has not been accepted by other Marxist historians.[6] After an extensive analysis of the economy of Mughal India, Habib also concludes: "What we know of the Mughal-Indian economy largely tends to confirm Marx's judgment that merchant capital, through its own development, cannot lead to industrial capital."[7]

2. Ibid., p. 444.
3. Ibid., p. 386 ff. It is worth noting that Marx does not see in this stage of commercial capitalism any domination of the producer by the merchant capitalist.
4. Ibid., pp. 444–445.
5. Maurice Dobb, *Studies in the Development of Capitalism*, paperback ed. (London: Routledge and Kegan Paul, 1963), pp. 88–89.
6. Rodney Hilton, ed., *The Transition from Feudalism to Capitalism*, Verso ed. (London: Verso, 1978).
7. Irfan Habib, "Potentialities of Capitalistic Development in the Economy of Mughal India", *Enquiry* (new series) 3, no. 3, 1971, pp. 52–53.

This negative view of merchant capital could have its roots in three factors. The first is the instinctive disapprobation of an activity—and the individuals involved in that activity—which earns profits without in any way creating value or surplus value.[8] It has also been argued that this sentiment was probably the reason why in most societies, as spatially dispersed as ancient Greece and Tokugawa Japan and in medieval Christian Europe, merchants were regarded as a low class of people.[9] The second is the view that trade is merely an activity which buys a commodity where it is cheap and sells it where it is dear, and has its historical origins in plunder and piracy. Since petty commodity production rarely produces enough surplus for trade, commercial capital can be accumulated only through international trade in luxuries.[10] Thirdly, this perception is probably an expression of the historical experience of western Europe where industrial capital did not have its genesis in merchant capital.

In striking contrast is the central place given to trade and especially the market in Hicks' theory of economic history. Hicks characterised a primitive economy and society as one organised on the basis of custom and command, and not on market principles, where the rise of the market is the force which transforms the primitive economy. Hicks also addresses himself to the tricky question of the origin of the specialised trader and how he began to trade. Rejecting the "piracy" or "brigandage" theory, he suggests that the alternative route to specialised trade and the development of a market had its origins in the regular trading, however rudimentary, which goes on in all communities, until it evolves into specialised trading—incorporating several institutions which are also essential for the further growth of the market. These include legal and business institutions which ensure the smooth functioning of trade and the market.[11]

Polanyi's discussions of marketless trade add further dimensions to the concept of markets and trade. Here, trade can be "gift" or "administered" trade—exchange being regulated by mechanisms other than the price mechanism—and equivalencies are established

---

8. Marx, *Capital*, vol. 3: p. 395.
9. Philip D. Curtin, *Cross-Cultural Trade in World History* (Cambridge: Cambridge University Press, 1984), p. 6.
10. Ernest Mandel, *Marxist Economic Theory*, trans. Brian Pearce (London: Merlin Press, 1968), pp. 102–106.
11. John Hicks, *A Theory of Economic History* (London: Oxford University Press, 1969), ch. 3.

by custom, statute or proclamation. In non-market trade and exchange, Polanyi points out, a crucial factor is the absence of risk. Or, conversely, one of the most important characteristics of the market is the risk factor which merchants must take into account in their judgments of what and how much to buy, and where and when to sell.[12] Sociologists and anthropologists also emphasise the fact that markets are not the abstract, aspatial mechanism of economics, but located in space, often hierarchically structured, with social, economic, cultural, political and other ramifications.[13] Chaudhuri integrates all these parameters and defines a market as a form of economic behaviour which has both static—namely, its location in space—and dynamic, time-related dimensions, and is also a sociological phenomenon.[14] Braudel's description of the growth of trade in Europe demonstrates the importance of the physical structure of markets and their organisation— as for instance, stockyards, shops, weekly markets, special fairs and so on—in the process of economic development in pre-industrial societies.[15]

All this literature also delineates the several changes which take place in an economy both prior to, and simultaneous with, the evolution of trade and markets. Among the endogenous changes, the most important ones are population growth and urbanisation. Changes in technology are also important. As trade becomes more specialised and complex, many institutions and organisational forms also grow. To begin with, the economy shifts from barter to a money-based system of exchange. Money changing, banking, and even the early stock markets, all facilitate the process of investment and create a market for capital and credit. Merchants begin to organise themselves into guilds to protect their trade and other common interests, which ultimately evolve into monopolistic organisations, restricting open access and individual freedom. Legal

12. Karl Polanyi, "Marketless Trading in Hammurabi's Time" and "The Economy as Instituted Process", in *Trade and Market in the Early Empires,* ed. Karl Polanyi, C. M. Arensberg and H. W. Pearson (Glencoe: Free Press, 1957).
13. Cyril S. Belshaw, *Traditional Exchange and Modern Markets* (New Delhi: Prentice Hall, 1969), p. 8.
14. K. N. Chaudhuri, "Markets and Traders in India during the Seventeenth and Eighteenth Centuries", in *Economy and Society,* ed. K. N. Chaudhuri and C. J. Dewey (Delhi: Oxford University Press, 1979) p. 145.
15. Fernand Braudel, *The Wheels of Commerce,* vol. 2, *Civilization and Capitalism, Fifteenth to Eighteenth Century,* trans. Sian Reynolds (London: Fontana, 1982), pp. 26–114.

institutions which protect property, enforce law and order, and contractual obligations are necessary for the steady functioning of commerce, and also serve to redefine the role of the state.

Change can also be induced through exogenous factors, notably war and external trade. In western Europe, the Crusades were considered a major exogenous factor in the development of trade after the twelfth century, since they opened the closed society of Europe to the influences of eastern cultures and nations.

To what extent such analytical generalisations based on the historical experience of western Europe can be applied to other cultures is difficult to determine. India, especially South India, has an economic past which has very little in common with the West. At the same time, arguably, economic specialisation and behaviour evolve along certain recognised, common patterns in most pre-industrial societies. While allowance must be made for variations in patterns which arise because of socio-economic differences across regions, the experience of any particular region cannot be treated as sui generis, entirely unrelated to patterns in other regions.

Maritime trade in the Coromandel: Some issues

This study will consider one such region, that of southern Coromandel, corresponding roughly to modern Tamil Nadu. This region is distinctive because of the cohesion given to its culture by the Tamil language, and from which it derives its social and cultural identity. As an economic region it has its own specific history, with a long tradition of maritime trade. Down the centuries, even in folklore and popular aphorisms, overseas trade is assumed to be the way to amass riches. The history of this trade and the trading network of the Indian Ocean, of which the Coromandel was a part, also belies the conception—especially of the Marxists—that trade capital originated from the booty of piracy and brigandage, and that long-distance trade was carried on only in luxuries which served the vanity of the ruling elite, making it irrelevant and trivial. In line with this understanding, earlier historians had invariably characterised trade in the Indian Ocean as "splendid but trifling".

Recent historiography, however, has revised this formulation, and the focus on luxuries, it is argued, is distorted, ignoring as it does "the more regular and mundane maritime trade in cargoes of necessities which underpinned the passage of luxuries destined for select clients."[16] Given the region's long tradition of commerce, the role the merchant community played in the dynamics of the economy and society, its level of interaction with the state and ruling classes, the institutions which developed to diversify and expand trade, and the endogenous and exogenous factors which shaped the development of the merchant class, all these assume great significance and require an extended study.

As a broad generalisation it can be said that the interest of economic historians of India in merchants and their activities has tended to be sporadic. It is only necessary to look at the *Cambridge Economic History of India*, volume one, to bear out this statement. The result is that several gaps exist in the historiography of mercantile organisation and activities. In the context of South Asia, a related area of interest which has received more attention from scholars has been the commerce of the European East India companies. This has been a strong focus of research, and these studies of the trade of the Asian region within the framework of the European companies provide the backdrop for further work on the traditional circuits of trade and exchange in Asia. Among these studies, we could include the works of van Leur, Meilink-Roelofsz, Furber, Boxer, Glamann, Feldbaek and Chaudhuri.

Even an ethnocentric study of merchant classes which rigidly tries to avoid the European bias cannot afford to neglect the nature and ramifications of European participation in Asian trade between 1500 and 1750. This is only partly a historical imperative, considering the long-term implications of the European presence as colonial powers in the region. More important is the fact that their records give the most comprehensive and continuous information on the local economies and these constitute our main sources of information.

Moving to the arena of issues, we find that while new debates are being started, the old controversies still continue to be discussed, and given the lack of conclusive quantitative data, these are not likely to be resolved. The older notion that the European "impact" (now decried as a value-loaded word) changed indigenous commercial institutions quite significantly has been strongly refuted, and all modern historians are agreed that it was the Europeans who adapted to the indigenous commercial institutions and practices.

16. Kenneth McPherson, *The Indian Ocean: A History of the People and the Sea* (Delhi: Oxford University Press, 1993), pp. 78–82.

Nevertheless, the steady expansion of European demand for Indian textiles did have an impact on the local merchant class and the economy. On the Coromandel coast where the two dominant ports of the latter part of the seventeenth century were the European ports of Madras and Pondicherry, the power that their growing trade gave the Europeans, even before the age of colonial empires, was probably much more critical than in Gujarat.[17] Subsumed within this statement are several issues which still need to be debated regarding the role of the state and the nature of the interaction between the worlds of the merchants and local politics, on the one hand, and the emerging character of the European companies, on the other.

There is no unanimity about the effect of the increased exports on the Indian economy either. The Aligarh school of historians argues that the return imports in precious metals, especially silver, resulted in a general inflation in the Mughal economy. On the other hand, Om Prakash has pointed out that the expansion of trade would result in the fuller employment of underutilised resources in the economy, resulting in export-led growth.[18]

In the specific context of the Coromandel, Sanjay Subrahmanyam, adopting the framework of Braudel, has argued that external trade should be treated as only one of the variables which influenced the indigenous economy. According to him, it has to be studied together with other endogenous factors like overall trends in productivity, demography and urbanisation to gain a more comprehensive understanding of the changes induced by trade.[19] Since his study ends in 1650, well before the dramatic increase in exports to Europe, the applicability of his analysis to the eighteenth century would have to be examined in depth.

The more recent orientation of research, especially on trade, has been to project the Indian Ocean as a holistic, interconnected trade region. Such an approach is also heavily influenced by Braudel's treatment of the Mediterranean region as a total economic entity, defined by the sea. Arasaratnam, a major contributor to the historiography of the

---

17. Ashin Das Gupta, "Indian Merchants in the Age of Partnership, 1500–1800", in *Business Communities of India*, ed. Dwijendra Tripathi (New Delhi: Manohar, 1984), p. 32.
18. Om Prakash, *The Dutch East India Company and the Economy of Bengal, 1630–1720* (Delhi: Oxford University Press, 1988), pp. 239–240, 256–258.
19. Sanjay Subrahmanyam, *The Political Economy of Commerce: Southern India, 1500–1650* (Cambridge: Cambridge University Press, 1990), pp. 343–365.

Merchant Capitalism: Theory and Context

Coromandel and its commerce and merchants, is also an enthusiastic proponent of this framework. His study integrates the hinterland of the Coromandel with the coast, stressing the backward linkages (agrarian and commodity production, commercial channels and mercantile network) of trade.

Arasaratnam also argues that the second half of the seventeenth century was a period of growth in the commerce of the region, and links the decline in the eighteenth century to the decline of local states and political chaos in the region.[20] This, of course, is a major hypothesis for the decline of Surat in the eighteenth century, and Das Gupta has consistently argued that this happened as a result of the weakening of the Mughal state and authority.[21] Historians led by Perlin, Bayly and others have disagreed with this view which, in their judgment, overemphasises the role of *pax Mughalica*. They have put forward the hypothesis that the smaller successor states to the Mughals had a revitalising effect on local trade and economy. The applicability of such a hypothesis to southern Coromandel, where the Mughals ruled with some authority for only a few decades, and the manner in which the unstable political situation affected the local merchants need to be re-evaluated.

The two other major works for the period with reference to the Coromandel essentially devote more space to northern Coromandel, that is the port of Masulipatnam and the area under the jurisdiction of Golkonda. Tapan Raychaudhuri's work deals exclusively with the establishment of the Dutch East India Company on the Coromandel coast. Besides strongly arguing that local merchants successfully competed with and even outcompeted the Dutch in intra-Asian trade in the seventeenth century, Raychaudhuri also believes that rapacious local officials and an extortionate political system were important factors which hindered trade.[22] To what extent this conclusion is valid if more extensive evidence is examined, also remains a question.

Brennig's unpublished dissertation also concentrates on northern Coromandel, which he argues was distinct from the southern region in terms of local political conditions and the socio-economic

---

20. S. Arasaratnam, *Merchants, Companies and Commerce on the Coromandel Coast, 1650–1740* (Delhi: Oxford University Press, 1986).
21. Ashin Das Gupta, *Indian Merchants and the Decline of Surat, c. 1700–1750* (Wiesbaden: Franz Steiner Verlag, 1979).
22. Tapan Raychaudhuri, *Jan Company in the Coromandel, 1605–1720* (The Hague: Martinus Nijhoff, 1962).

background of the merchants.[23] (In contrast, Subrahmanyam argues that the distinction between the northern and southern regions of the Coromandel is artificial, since the common characteristics would unite the region into a single whole.[24] Against this, the choice of southern Coromandel as a specific region for study, based on historical and cultural factors, in addition to economic and political characteristics, also needs to be stressed once again.) Brennig's analysis of the linkages between textile production, merchants and the Dutch is of particular interest in the context of this study.

For the earlier periods, other than general histories, Appadorai's work was the first which focussed on the economic history of South India.[25] Though analytically weak, his work is based on the extensive use of inscriptional evidence. Burton Stein's work on South India[26] began a new debate on the nature of the state, which he characterised as "segmentary", in contradistinction to the highly centralised administrative system postulated by earlier historians like Nilakanta Sastri. Karashima's work, with much greater authority and depth in the use of inscriptional sources in the original Tamil, has proposed that there was a well-developed bureaucratic machinery in charge of revenue administration.[27] For the later Vijayanagar period, Stein has revised his original theory of the continuance of the segmentary state and has now argued in terms of both a patrimonial and a military state which necessitated conquest and expansion to supply the necessary financial and manpower resources to support the state. Karashima, on the other hand, argues that under Vijayanagar rule much of South India was organised under local military chieftains or *nayakas,* and the state which emerged was essentially feudal in nature.[28]

23. J. J. Brennig, "The Textile Trade of Seventeenth Century Northern Coromandel: A Study of a Pre-Modern Asian Export Industry" (Ph.D. diss., University of Wisconsin, 1975).
24. Subrahmanyam, *Political Economy of Commerce,* p. 314.
25. A. Appadorai, *Economic Conditions in Southern India, 1000–1500 A.D.* 2 vols. (Madras: University of Madras, 1936).
26. Burton Stein, *Peasant, State and Society in Medieval South India* (Delhi: Oxford University Press, 1980).
27. Noboru Karashima, *South Indian History and Society: Studies from the Inscriptions,* A.D. *850–1800* (Delhi: Oxford University Press, 1984).
28. Burton Stein, *Vijayanagara.* The New Cambridge History of India, vol. 1–2 (Cambridge: Cambridge University Press, 1989). Also, "Vijayanagara and the Transition to Patrimonial Systems", in *Vijayanagara: City and Empire,* ed. Anna L. Dallapiccola and Stephanie Z. A. Lallemont (Stuttgart: Steiner Verlag, 1985), vol. 1: pp. 73–87. Noboru Karashima, "Nayaka Rule in North and South Arcot Districts",

Merchant Capitalism: Theory and Context

Though the debate on the nature of the state may not be of direct relevance for a study of merchants, it serves to situate merchants as a class within the local administrative framework and in the context of the rulers' perceptions about commerce and the economic role of the state. For the later medieval period also, the relationship between the state and merchants and the degree of politicisation of the latter become important issues. Subrahmanyam has introduced the new concept of "portfolio capitalists", that is, individuals who combined mercantile interests with political activity and ambitions, and therefore bridged the gap between commercial capitalism and political capitalism.[29] All these debates also serve to emphasise the degree of continuity in economic life and organisations in pre-industrial societies, so that we can see the past in its totality.

Kenneth Hall's work on medieval South India highlights the role of trade in linking agricultural production and the rural economy with urban settlements and economy. Hall's central proposition is that each peasant region, or *nadu*, had one market centre or *nagaram*, and the region's economy was also characterised by a hierarchy of markets with the higher-level markets performing more central-place functions.[30] Meera Abraham's study of merchant guilds of South India describes the institutional developments in commercial organisation,[31] while Champakalakshmi's work on early medieval South India highlights the necessary links between urbanisation, overall economic development and diversification, and trade.[32] We are again

---

"Changes in Vijayanagar Rule in the Lower Kaveri Valley", and "Nayakas in Chingleput Inscriptions", in *Towards a New Formation* (Delhi: Oxford University Press, 1992).
29. Subrahmanyam, *Political Economy of Commerce*, p. 298 ff. Also, Sanjay Subrahmanyam and C. A. Bayly, "Portfolio Capitalists and the Political Economy of Early Modern India", *Indian Economic and Social History Review* 25, no. 4, 1988, pp. 401–424.
30. Kenneth R. Hall, *Trade and Statecraft in the Age of Colas* (New Delhi: Abhinav Publications, 1980).
31. Meera Abraham, *Two Medieval Merchant Guilds of South India* (Delhi: Manohar, 1988).
32. R. Champakalakshmi, "Urbanisation in Medieval Tamil Nadu", in *Situating Indian History*, ed. Sabyasachi Bhattacharya and Romila Thapar (Delhi: Oxford University Press, 1987), pp. 34–105; "Urban Processes in Early Medieval Tamil Nadu", in *The City in Indian History*, ed. Indu Banga (New Delhi: Manohar Publications and Urban History Association of India, 1991), pp. 47–68; *Trade, Ideology and Urbanization: South India 300 B.C. to A.D. 1200* (Delhi: Oxford University Press, 1996).

reminded of Braudel's analysis from these glimpses of the evolution of trade and corporate forms of organisation.

On comparing the patterns of economic change in pre-industrial South India with those in pre-industrial Europe, we thus see that there are similarities as well as strong contrasts and differences. Trade played the central role in pre-industrial societies. Since it was the main agent of change—not merely as an endogenous factor, but also as the medium for transmitting external influences—merchants, who were the principal actors in commerce, will be the exclusive focus of this study. When the study is devoted to the specific region of southern Coromandel, it incorporates the region-specific factors into the general theory of economic transition and historical analysis, to illuminate a very specialised aspect of Indian history.

TWO

Trade, Merchants and the Urban Setting: The Sangam Period (50–400 C.E.)

The Coromandel region has a long tradition of trade going back more than two thousand years when trade and mercantile activity had already become specialised economic functions, and the region had developed much beyond the subsistence economy and localised trade which characterised early agrarian settlements. Correspondingly, the spatial organisation of the region in this period was also more specialised as evident in the large towns/cities and ports exhibiting more distinctive urban characteristics.

Patterns of trade

The antiquity of the trade itself, especially the trade with Rome, which is attested to by archaeological and other historical evidence, has been long recognised by scholars.[1] A noteworthy feature of the trading history was the dominance of maritime trade and the visible presence of merchants of diverse ethnic groups in ports and other urban centres.[2] The fact that the economic and cultural life of the region was strongly centred in maritime activities is also evident from the early coinage of the local dynasties, which often had two masted

---

1. Walter Elliot, *Coins of Southern India* (1886; reprint, Delhi: Cosmo Publications, 1975), H. G. Rawlinson, *Intercourse between India and the Western World*, 2d ed. (New York: Octagon Books, 1971), K. V. Subrahmanya Aiyer, *Historical Sketches of Ancient Dekhan* (1917; reprint, New Delhi: Cosmo Publications, 1980) to name just a few of the earliest works. More often cited is E. H. Warmington, *The Commerce Between the Roman Empire and India*, rev. ed. (New Delhi: Vikas, 1974).
2. R. Champakalakshmi states that maritime trade was the most crucial factor in urbanisation in the Sangam period, i.e., up to the fourth century C.E. "Urban Processes", p. 48.

· 13 ·

ships, fish or crabs—all emblems signifying close links with a lifestyle dominated by the sea.[3]

The resource base of the economy which supported this trade, and the links between agriculture and trade, on the one hand, and internal and overseas trade, on the other, are not so easy to establish. Champakalakshmi identifies two kinds of resource areas—the river valleys which supported agriculture and the coastal regions which supported trade. Each of the local rulers of the Sangam period—the Cholas, Pandyas and the Cheras—had "dual centres of political authority", one in their administrative capital and the other in their main port, which enabled them to control both the resource areas in their respective kingdoms.[4] There was also a conscious effort by the rulers to increase their power base by attacking the other major chiefs and minor chieftains *(velir)* and capturing their resource regions.[5]

Early literary works in Tamil, especially the corpus of ten poems comprising the *Pattuppattu* (c. first century), the epics *Silappadikaram* and *Manimekalai* (both dating to the second century),[6] and other works referred to in secondary literature are the main sources of information for our exploration of trade and merchants in an urban setting in this period. While earlier agriculture and manufacturing were regarded as the main economic activities, as trade began to expand, agriculture and trade came to be considered the primary economic activities. Craft-based production and the arts now began to take second place.[7] The linking of agriculture with trade is a clear

---

3. Elliot, *Coins*, Plate I, nos. 36, 37, 38 which Elliot identifies as Pallava or Kurumba (for Kalabhra?) coins; Plate II, no. 45, an early Andhra coin. Rajan Gurukkal, however, argues that "there is no clear evidence of the people of contemporary Tamilakam organizing maritime trade or external long distance trade." The argument is that the region itself did not have any shipping. "Forms of Production and Forces of Change in Ancient Tamil Society", *Studies in History* 5, no. 2, 1989, p. 172.
4. Champakalakshmi, "Urban Processes", p. 48.
5. *Maduraikkanchi,* lines 55 ff., especially the reference to the conquest of the port of Saliyur by Pandiyan Neduncheliyan (lines 87–88).
6. While it is generally agreed that the *Pattuppattu* belong to the last Sangam age and were composed between the first and second century, there are diverse opinions as to the dates of *Silappadikaram* and *Manimekalai*. *The Encyclopaedia of Tamil Literature*, vol. 1 ([Madras: Institute of Asian Studies, 1990], p. 81) accepts that the works date to the second century, which is the opinion of U. V. Swaminatha Iyer, who has edited and published the two epics. The *Encyclopaedia* also notes that other authorities regard the works as belonging to the post-Sangam period, written any time between the fourth and eighth centuries.

Merchants and the Urban Setting: The Sangam Period

indication of the mobilisation through trade of the surplus which was primarily generated in agriculture, the latter being the dominant economic activity.

Agricultural products traded in the market included not only grains (referred to as comprising eight, sixteen or eighteen varieties), but also black pepper, areca nuts and other commercial crops like white sugar, eaglewood, sandalwood and so on. These goods were transported to the port towns to be exchanged for goods brought from overseas and also to be sent up and down the coast on small craft. There were thus three patterns of trade in the region: first, the overland movement of agricultural and non-agricultural products (most important among the latter being textiles, beryls and gems from the western hills, and salt, pearls, dried fish and conchs from the coastal areas); second, the coastal trade, for which the ports of southern Coromandel acted as entrepôts; and third, the overseas trade, both from the East and the West, the latter generally categorised as "yavana desa".[8]

Among the imports, the most important commodities were gold and horses from the West, in addition to wine, dye pigments and coral. The *Pattinappalai* gives a graphic description of the several trade channels which converged at the port of Puhar (Kaverippattinam), "which had an abundance of horses brought over the water, sacks of black pepper brought [overland] in carts, gemstones and gold from the northern mountains, and sandalwood and eaglewood from the western hills, pearls from the southern seas and coral from the eastern seas, grains from the regions of the Ganga and Kaveri, foodgrains from Ceylon, and the products of Burma and other rare and great commodities."[9] The trade to South and Southeast Asia from South India has tended to be overshadowed by the preoccupation of earlier historical works with the trade with the West, especially with

---

7. *Maduraikkanchi*, lines 120–121. Similar ideas are also echoed in the *Divakaram*, quoted by M. Raghava Aiyangar, "The Ancient Dravidian Industries and Commerce", in *Tamilian Antiquary*, ed. D. Savariroyan, vol. 1, pt. 8 (1910; reprint, Delhi: Asian Educational Service, 1986), pp. 78–79.

8. The following composite picture is mostly drawn from *Maduraikkanchi* and *Pattinappalai* of the *Pattuppattu*, and *Periplus of the Erythrean Sea* (trans. and ed. Wilfred H. Schoff [1912; reprint, Delhi: Oriental Reprint, 1974.]). (Hereafter, *Periplus*). The trade in textiles is inferred from the several references to textile production in the *Pattuppattu* and *Silappadikaram*, as well as from the references to cloth exports from the Chola country, in the *Periplus*.

9. *Pattinappalai*, lines 185–192.

Rome. But this reference *(Pattinappalai)* indicates an equally important trade in coral, foodgrains and other products with the littoral islands and coastal regions of South Asia.[10]

The directions of overland trade are also clearly indicated by these literary references. From the coast to the interior, the main commodity was salt, while from the interior—especially the region of the Western Ghats—to the coast, pepper was the main commodity, transported primarily on pack oxen and donkeys. Foodgrains were transported both overland and on boats along the coast, and, as the preceding quotation shows, foodgrains were both imported from and exported to the other South Asian countries. There is an interesting allusion to a pattern of coastal trade—of boats coming in with grain which was exchanged for white salt at Puhar—which, in fact, remained in evidence till quite recent times.[11] The coastal craft were probably small boats, while the ships coming from overseas would have been much bigger and came flying large flags.[12] The Sangam poems have strongly evocative descriptions of ships anchored along the beach in coastal towns, with the images of dark clouds shadowing turbulent seas, and ships at anchor resembling towering hills or elephants or tethered horses, creating a very vivid visual portrayal of shipping activity all along the coast of Tamil Nadu.

Mercantile activity and organisation

In contrast, the portrayals of merchants tend to be far more stylised and idealised and do not really lend themselves to any analysis.[13] It is nevertheless possible to piece together a composite picture of mercantile activity and organisation. Merchants, by and large, specialised

---

10. This is also corroborated by the statement in the *Periplus*, p. 44–45, no. 56. K. A. Nilakanta Sastri (*A History of South India*, 4th ed. [Madras: Oxford University Press, 1975], p. 141) cites Schoff who commented that the trade with the Far East employed larger ships and in greater numbers than the trade with Egypt.
11. *Pattinappalai*, lines 29–30.
12. *Pattinappalai*, lines 172–175; *Maduraikkanchi*, lines 82–83. Based on the information from the *Periplus*, Nilakanta Sastri (*South India*, p. 140) identifies three kinds of craft which were seen on the east coast. In addition to the two mentioned above, there were also large boats made of logs bound together.
13. For instance, *Pattinappalai* (lines 206–212) paints a highly glorified and sanitised picture of the merchants of Puhar who were straightforward and truthful, and so honest in their dealings that they neither overvalued what they sold, nor undervalued what they bought, and openly declared their profits. *Maduraikkanchi* (lines 500–506) praises their virtuous behaviour as householders.

in trading in single commodities.[14] They were generally either itinerant merchants conveying their goods overland from one region to another, or they were city-based traders, selling their goods to the urban consumers. In either category, there does not seem to have been a differentiation between the manufacturer and the trader. The salt merchants who are always mentioned as a distinct class of merchants, also manufactured salt, transported it on carts drawn by bullocks,[15] and travelled with their families as a caravan.[16] In urban centres, there were several artisan-merchants (banglemakers working on conchs, oilmongers, coppersmiths and brasssmiths, toddy tappers and others) selling their products directly to local customers.[17] At the lower levels of the economic hierarchy, thus, trade was not distinguished from production, and concomitantly, nor was there a mercantile or commercial capital distinct from the commodity capital of the producers. Travelling merchants also had to internalise the costs of protecting themselves from attacks by robbers on the trade routes and organised their own defence. They travelled armed with swords and protected with leather coats (as armour), and were praised as brave warrior merchants.[18]

But a range of more specialised functions of trade also coexisted with more primitive organisational forms. In agricultural products and textiles, there was evidently a clear distinction between the trader and the producer/manufacturer. The weavers/artisans *(karugar)* were quite distinct from the merchants *(aruvai vanikan)* and produced a great variety of fabrics which were major exports. The *Periplus* mentions the "Argaratic" muslins which were exported from the Coromandel coast, while the literary works refer to delicate fabrics

---

14. Merchants are generally referred to only as single-commodity (salt, cloth, etc.) merchants. This is also supported by the ancient inscriptions of Alagarmalai, which mention specifically, cloth, salt, toddy, grain, iron and gem merchants. I. Mahadevan, "Tamil Brahmi Inscriptions of the Sangam Age", in *Proceedings of the Second International Conference of Tamil Studies* (Madras: International Association of Tamil Research, 1968), vol. 1: pp. 99–100.
15. *Perumpanarruppadai*, lines 59–65.
16. *Sirupanarruppadai*, lines 51–55.
17. The description of the market streets of several towns has been taken from *Silappadikaram* and *Manimekalai*. Puhar, *Silappadikaram*, Canto I, ch. v; Madurai, ibid., II, ch. xiv; Kanchipuram, *Manimekalai*, ch. xxviii. For both texts, reference is to the editions edited by U. V. Swaminatha Iyer: *Silappadikaram*, 5th ed. (Madras: U. V. Swaminatha Iyer, 1950) and *Manimekalai*, 7th ed. (Madras: U. V. Swaminatha Iyer Library, 1981).
18. *Perumpanarruppadai*, lines 66–76.

of silk, cotton and wool (generally stated to be wool from rats), and especially to extremely transparent and fine cottons with flowered patterns.[19] There seems to be some evidence that the corporate organisation of merchants into guilds, which was a prominent institution in the medieval period, was also important in this (the early) period.[20]

Urban areas were centres of consumption as well as of production and trade, and attracted a great number of trades, services and traders catering to the needs of the urban population. Again, in many cases, production and retailing were not distinct occupations, especially for those dealing in food products (cooked fish, raw and roasted meat, toddy, and other food products), and for tailors, carpenters, copper-, brass- and gold-smiths, dealers in precious stones, perfumes and fragrant substances, wig makers and so on.[21] Some were clearly itinerant traders selling their wares door to door, while others operated from regular shops, and a great variety of retailing practices were in existence.

At the upper end of the hierarchy were the rich merchants, involved in long-distance trade. Three classes—*ippar, kavippar* and *perunkudi*—are mentioned in the old texts. The distinction was supposedly based on the extent of their wealth,[22] which would indicate a possibility of social mobility from one class to another. More probably, the three groups were endogamous caste groups, as can be inferred from the fact that in *Silappadikaram*, Kovalan and Kannagi were both from Perunkudi merchant families. It is clear, however, that these merchants had amassed great wealth, which was

---

19. *Periplus*, pp. 46, no. 59 and 241–242. For an exhaustive list of literary references, see Raghava Aiyangar, "Ancient Dravidian Industries", pp. 82–84. The commentary of *Silappadikaram* also lists various kinds of cotton and silk fabrics.

20. Champakalakshmi ("Urban Processes", p. 50) and Moti Chandra, (*Trade and Trade Routes in Ancient India* [New Delhi: Abhinav, 1977]) both interpret the name of Kovalan's father Masattuvan (in *Silappadikaram*) as *maha-sartha-vaha* or the great caravan leader when merchants belonging to the guild would organise themselves in a caravan. See also, R. C. Mazumdar, *Corporate Life in Ancient India* (reprint, Calcutta: Firma K. L. Mukhopadhyaya, 1969), ch. 1, for the prevalence of corporate organisation in economic life.

21. From the description of Puhar and Madurai in *Silappadikaram*, I, v, and II, xiv, and of Kanchipuram, in *Manimekalai*, xxviii.

22. "If the wealth of the merchant of each class was piled around and the merchant stood under an umbrella on an elephant/bull/in his footwear (respectively), they could not see each other." Quoted from the *Jeevasambodanai* by Raghava Aiyangar, "Ancient Dravidian Industries", p. 90. This explanation is also quoted in all the commentaries.

Merchants and the Urban Setting: The Sangam Period

reflected in their consumption patterns—silks and coral, sandalwood and eaglewood, perfect pearls, gems, gold and jewels which were available in "immeasurable quantities" in the markets of Puhar.[23]

Foreign merchants were also a major presence on the urban scene—not only in the ports where they had their own segregated colonies along the sea front,[24] but also in inland cities like Madurai, where they came to exchange the goods they had brought in their ships for the commodities available in the local markets.[25] There were settlements of foreign merchants and sailors all along the coast,[26] part of the trade diaspora found all along the coasts of the ancient and medieval trading world.[27]

One last category of merchants that we have not mentioned so far are brokers or intermediaries who were very necessary functionaries in trade down the centuries. Their main role was to act as information channels in an era when transmission of market information was very poorly developed. Even in the ancient period, it would seem that brokers, generally held in low esteem, were evident in trading transactions and earned their livelihood by offering their services to foreign merchants.[28]

Money as a medium of exchange is never mentioned, and it is reasonable to suppose that most transactions were concluded through barter. Both in coastal trade and in the sales of commodities brought in by foreign merchants, transactions were made in exchange for other commodities as the literary sources repeatedly state. However, considering the very wide range of goods and services offered to urban consumers in cities—including the services of courtesans/prostitutes—it can be argued inferentially that these transactions would have needed an independent medium of exchange, either in the form of gold or money.[29]

23. *Silappadikaram*, I, v, lines 18–20.
24. *Ibid.*, I, v, lines 9–13 and I, vi, lines 130–133.
25. *Maduraikkanchi*, lines 537–544.
26. *Ibid.*, lines 322–325; *Perumpanarruppadai*, lines 316–322.
27. Curtin, *Cross-Cultural Trade*, ch. 1.
28. It must be noted that this interpretation of *Silappadikaram* (I, v, lines 38–39), of the mention of inferior persons who offered menial services in the places where the foreign merchants operated, differs substantially from the original commentary.
29. Gurukkal states categorically that all exchange was only through barter and that, "There is no evidence for transactions based on exchange value even in the case of specialist goods." "Forms of Production", p. 171.

In brief, the level of development of mercantile activity and organisation were not uniform or homogeneous. Both relatively primitive and advanced forms—ranging from the itinerant producer peddling his goods as he travelled around, to the big merchants living in the cities, accumulating great wealth—coexisted with one another during this period. It is significant to note that, unlike in ancient Greece, merchants were an esteemed class in society, and commerce a respected occupation,[30] which may partly explain the glorified portrayal of merchants in the literature. For the people at large, merchants, through trade, made possible a higher level of consumption by bringing in goods produced from all over the world. For the rulers, commerce was an important source of revenue for themselves, and of wealth in general for the country as a whole.

The urban setting

Several towns and cities are mentioned in the Sangam literature, and many have survived as settlements down to the present day. It would be unrealistic to interpret this as indicating that the spatial organisation of the region was clearly demarcated and differentiated between rural and urban areas. Nevertheless, it is clear that there were several cities, both along the coast and in the interior, with distinct urban characteristics. The capital cities (Kanchipuram, Madurai and Vanji [Karur]) were major centres because of their administrative functions, while the coastal towns served as ports. The entire Coromandel coast has no natural harbours, and thus any coastal settlement could become a port. Throughout history, the relative prosperity of a port and its trade depended primarily on the local administration. The cities were major centres of cloth weaving, where different kinds of fabrics were produced.[31] Weaving, however, was not only an urban occupation but was, as it continued to be down the centuries, quite widely diffused throughout the country. But cities definitely served as concentrations for trade, consumption and production, where the urban consumers supported a number of artisans, services and tradesmen.

30. Curtin, *Cross-Cultural Trade*, p. 75, and Polanyi, "Economy as Instituted Process", p. 259, point to the low esteem in which merchants were held in Greek culture.
31. For Madurai, *Maduraikkanchi*, lines 519–520; *Silappadikaram*, II, xiv, lines 205–207; for Kanchipuram, *Manimekalai*, xxviii, line 53; for Puhar, *Silappadikaram*, I, v, lines 16–17.

Merchants and the Urban Setting: The Sangam Period

Cities were characterised by a high degree of segregation of space, both for social classes and commercial activity. The topography of Puhar, which was divided into the area along the sea where the foreign merchants lived and the interior, has already been reconstructed by Nilakanta Sastri.[32] All cities were divided into commercial and residential areas, with tall buildings "reaching to the skies", which had grilled windows to catch the breeze. The descriptions of tall buildings and narrow streets convey a picture of cities crowded with people, busy in trade and other activities. Both within commercial and residential areas there was segregation, with streets set aside for different social classes—merchants, brahmins and others—and for specific trades and crafts. The notion of the right of a group to live and work in designated areas became entrenched in social consciousness as the prime constituent of social identity and continued to dominate all social interaction and discourse down to the colonial period.

Most importantly, cities were polyglot and multireligious cosmopolitan centres. Repeatedly they are referred to as places where many different languages were spoken. "Yavanas"—Phoenicians, Arabs or Romans—were found in the cities not only as traders but also as guards employed in the forts and in the palaces, especially in Madurai.[33] They had probably come to the region on the trading ships as sailors or traders and had then stayed on in other capacities. Artisans from many regions—Magadha, Avanti, Gurjara—including Marathas and even Yavanas, all came to the Tamil region to work at their crafts.[34] Perhaps because of this conglomeration of people, temples serving various religions—Vedic and indigenous, Buddhist and Jain—were found in the cities.[35]

The role of state in commerce

Commerce was an important source of revenue to the state, especially in pre-industrial societies, since the overall level of economic activity

---

32. K. A. Nilakanta Sastri, *The Colas* (reprint, Madras: University of Madras, 1984), pp. 81–82.
33. *Silappadikaram*, II, xiv, lines 66–67; *Nedunalvadai*, line 101; *Mullaippattu*, lines 61–66.
34. *Manimekalai*, xix, lines 107–109. The commentary also refers to similar lines from the *Perunkadai*, a post-Sangam Jain poem.
35. *Silappadikaram*, "Introduction", p. xviii; V. Kanakasabhai, *The Tamils Eighteen Hundred Years Ago* (1904; reprint, New Delhi: Asian Education Service, 1989), ch. 15; Champakalakshmi, *Trade, Ideology and Urbanization*, pp. 100–101.

was circumscribed. This was clearly recognized by all early states, including the Tamil kingdoms, and the role of the state with regard to trade thus related to two aspects: first, to organise an efficient administrative apparatus for taxing trade, and secondly, to ensure the smooth flow of trade by protecting the main trade routes. In the Sangam period, a large part of the region was still uncleared and the scattered settlements were separated by thick forests. Further, the main trade routes traversed the Western Ghats which were also heavily forested. Regulating, monitoring and providing security to the travellers, especially traders with their caravans, were functions which devolved upon the state,[36] and bodies of archers guarded the forest tracks through which the merchants travelled. What the bards portray in poetry is also the ideal, and the reality probably fell far short of the ideal, as the reference to armed merchants protecting their own caravans shows.

The collection of revenue from commerce was essential, not merely to finance the other expenditures of the state, but also specifically to cover the cost of protection offered to the merchants. For this purpose, there were customs checkposts *(sungachchavadi)* along the highways, and also in the ports. In the latter, customs were collected on inland goods which came to the ports for export and on goods which had been landed from the ships and meant for the inland markets, which were stamped with the official seal after assessment.[37] The poem *Pattinappalai,* with the usual hyperbole says that the customs officials worked incessantly to stamp the immeasurable volume of goods which were constantly coming in. Even after discounting the exaggeration, it is nonetheless evident that the volume of trade was extensive enough to warrant the employment of a large workforce to monitor and assess the goods.

The state also issued licences for setting up liquor shops which displayed their status as licensed shops by flying flags outside the premises.[38] Flags were used by foreign merchants also, to indicate the

36. *Perumpanarruppadai* (lines 39–41) praised the governance of Ilantiraiyan, King of Kanchipuram, for under his rule, there were no fearsome highway robbers in the countryside.
37. *Pattinappalai* (lines 118–137) describes the customs house in Puhar. The movement of goods inland from the coast, and from the hinterland to the sea is compared to the transference of sea water as rain to the interior which flowed back again to the sea.
38. *Pattinappalai,* lines 179–180; *Maduraikkanchi,* line 366; *Perumpanarruppadai,* line 336.

nature of the goods which they were selling.[39] Flags or banners may have had a dual purpose—while they were used to advertise to the general public the location of a shop and the nature of the wares available, they also indicated that these shops had been officially licensed and the necessary fee had been paid to the authorities. The goods sold by the merchants were also weighed, counted or measured and officially recorded,[40] a further monitoring activity undertaken by the state. Through all these interventions, the state both asserted a right to tax commerce, for raising revenue, and ensured that consumers were protected from fraudulent sales.

The main significance of commerce to the state and polity was that it reinforced the legitimacy of the authority of the ruler. There was a highly sophisticated recognition of the fact that standards of living and consumption were improved through commerce and the greater availability of goods. By ensuring that goods from various parts of the world reached the people of the inland areas through the smooth flow of commerce, the king increased the level of prosperity among his subjects.[41] By an extension of the same line of thought, merchants were also held in esteem because they made it possible for people dispersed across the region to buy and consume commodities from all parts of the country and the rest of the trading world. This consciousness on the part of the rulers thus had two dimensions: first, the need of the ruler to constantly reaffirm his legitimacy by extending his control over other kingdoms through warfare, thus ensuring that the resource areas for commerce would be under his authority; and second, the linking of commerce and merchants (as the agents of commerce) with the ruling classes.

The reconstruction of trade, merchants and urban organisation indicates several underlying interlinkages between the institutions of commerce and the state, which endured through the centuries. The importance of maritime trade—both overseas and coastal, the main directions of and commodities in commerce, the hierarchy of merchants, the coexistence of more primitive forms of trade with more highly developed forms, the distinctive characteristics of urban

---

39. *Silappadikaram*, I, vi, lines 130–133.
40. *Ibid.*, I, v, lines 111–114. In an interesting comment, the text says that "newcomers" to Puhar were likely to indulge in malpractices, and were punished by being made to carry the goods that were short-weight on their backs, which would teach them never to cheat the public again.
41. *Maduraikkanchi*, lines 761–770.

centres and the nature of urban-based trade, and finally, the nature of and the philosophy behind state intervention in trade, all these remained reasonably stable over the centuries, if not continuous at every point of time.

The excessive reliance on literary sources in this chapter also needs to be critically analysed. Some of the basic facts as reconstructed from the literary evidence are also confirmed by archaeological and numismatic evidence. It is also true that the heroic poetry of the Sangam period often described an ideal rather than a real world. Kings were just and fearless, the merchants honest and upright, the men always brave and the women always beautiful. The descriptions of Puhar, Madurai and Kanchipuram in *Silappadikaram* and *Manimekalai* are so similar that they tend to be a little suspect. On the other hand, it is also probable that cities were similar to a substantial extent, while in rural areas in different ecosystems (as classified in Tamil culture), the living conditions and economic activities would have been much more diverse. Both the vividness of the greater part of the poetry—as for instance, in the description of trading activity in the ports, the bustle of urban market streets, the caravans of the travelling merchants and so forth—and the fact that the same information is repeated in different works by several individual poets tend to emphasise the reliability of the information and also the importance of these works as a source for understanding the economy and society of the ancient period.

THREE

Temples, Urbanisation and the Development of Trade in the Medieval Period (900–1300)

The functioning of trade and the development of commercial practices and institutions in the medieval period in the Coromandel have to be understood in the context and as an extension of the wider changes that were taking place in the region—especially the growth of urbanisation and the evolution of the temple as a nodal social and economic institution. The development of trade as a specialised activity presupposes the existence of urban centres. Thus, even in the ancient period (up to the second century C.E.) there were several cities and towns in the Coromandel which acted as ancillaries to internal and overseas trade. This stage of urbanisation, however, did not evolve as an integral part of the process of overall development of agriculture and agrarian society; rather, the urban centres comprised ports, as the necessary concomitant of maritime trade, and inland capital cities, which were administrative centres.[1]

The second urbanisation, Champakalakshmi emphasises, followed on the spread of agriculture and the development of agrarian institutions, especially those which integrated local administrative bodies within a larger polity.[2] As agriculture evolves as the main activity of the economy, social hierarchies and power structures also tend to be tied to land ownership and control over land-based resources. At this stage, two kinds of internally contradictory processes may be envisaged for the development of trade and merchants. The development of settled and prosperous agriculture would automatically involve the growth of populations, market centres and settlements. This would,

1. Champakalakshmi, "Urban Processes", p. 48.
2. Champakalakshmi, "Urbanisation", p. 37.

in turn, generate a higher level of demand for goods and services, stimulating the development of trade. But the primary concerns of such an agrarian society have little to do with merchants. They are, rather, oriented towards the management and control of resources and the apportioning of the surplus between various interests—the king, local administration and the landed elite. Merchants would remain outside this society and alienated from its major focus. The evolution of commerce and merchant institutions, therefore, has also to be seen as a process of the incorporation of merchants and mercantile concerns into mainstream society.[3]

Two new integrative institutions

The actual spread of settled agriculture and the development of agrarian society was a process which gradually evolved over several centuries. In general, the basic unit of the agrarian order in South India was the village economy, based on peasant agriculture, integrated into local, regional units called nadu. There is near unanimity among scholars with vastly different approaches and methodologies that beginning with the Pallava period, from the sixth century onwards, two new integrative institutions were introduced into this agrarian society. The first was the *brahmadeya* or brahman villages established through land grants to the brahmans.[4]

The second important institution was the temple. Inspired by Hindu revivalism and the *bhakti* movement after the seventh century, temple construction was undertaken on a large scale by the ruling classes—especially the royal families, including queens and princesses.[5] The construction of temples and maintaining them through

---

3. Burton Stein presents the obverse of this picture and argues that the actvities of merchant organisations and trade, together constituted the forces which integrated nuclear areas of peasant agriculture into the administrative framework of the Chola state. "Coromandel Trade in Medieval India", in *All the King's Mana: Papers in Medieval South Indian History* (Madras: New Era Publications, 1984), p. 233.
4. For Burton Stein this was more characteristic of the Chola period, though the process of expansion of agriculture had already begun in a major way in the Pallava period, through the spread of tank irrigation outside the river valleys (*Peasant, State and Society*, ch. 2). Champakalakshmi, on the other hand, firmly places it in the pre-Chola period. "Urbanisation", p. 37.
5. George W. Spencer, "When Queens Bore Gifts: Women as Temple Donors in the Chola Period", in *Srinidhih: Perspectives in Indian Archaeology, Art and Culture*, ed. K. V. Raman et al. (Madras: New Era Publications, 1983), pp. 361–373.

endowments of agricultural land *(devadana)* and money, primarily served to legitimise the status and authority of rulers and ruling classes. But most importantly, the temple created an interlocked social value system, a synthesis of religious merit, social control and economic power.

As temple complexes became larger, they also became the nuclei for urban centres. Endowments of land and money created the need for developing organisational structures to manage the resources. Nilakanta Sastri had very early on emphasised the fact that the temple was not just a religious institution. According to him, it was "on the secular side and as a social institution that the temple is seen to have filled in the past a considerable place in the economy of national life."[6] As the number and size of temples increased, their importance in the economy as landowners, employers and consumers also grew.[7]

The temple also became a depository for resources which were endowed for the performance of religious services. Endowments were most commonly made to keep a lamp burning in the temple. When productive assets like livestock were donated, they would be given to shepherds or cowherds who, in turn, would supply a specified amount of ghee to keep the lamps burning.[8] Of greater significance for trade was the practice of giving donations of money or gold, which would then be borrowed by individuals, local bodies or merchant associations. The interest paid to the temple was used to maintain the service for which the endowment was made.

The spread of temples and brahmadeyas resulted in the expansion of urban centres in the heartland of the Chola empire in the eleventh century when Chola power was in the ascendant. After the twelfth century, when the Chola empire faded away, urban centres began to come up further south, in the Pandya country.[9] This pattern of urban growth must also be linked with the growth of trade and commercial organisation, and in medieval Tamil Nadu we see the close correlation

---

6. K. A. Nilakanta Sastri, "The Economy of a South Indian Temple in the Cola Period", in *Malaviya Commemoration Volume*, ed. A. B. Dhruva (Benares: Benares Hindu University, 1932), pp. 305–306.
7. Appadorai, *Economic Conditions*, vol. 1: pp. 274–301. R. Nagaswamy, "South Indian Temple: As an Employer", *Indian Economic and Social History Review* 2, no. 4, 1965, pp. 367–372.
8. George W. Spencer, "Temple Money-lending and Livestock Redistribution in Early Tanjore", *Indian Economic and Social History Review* 5, no. 3, 1968, pp. 277–293.
9. Champakalakshmi, "Urbanisation", pp. 39, 41.

between the increase in the number of temples and towns and the expansion of trade.

Corporate bodies and resource management

Local administration, revenue collection and resource management were in the hands of corporate bodies. The names of the local units of administration in the geographical sense, as well as in the corporate sense, were the same. The basic regional unit of peasant agriculture and its decision-making representative body were known as the nadu. A non-brahman village and its collective assembly were the *ur*. The brahmadeya village assembly was the *sabha*. An urban settlement and its corporate merchant assembly were known as the *nagaram*. The members of these assemblies were referred to as the *nattar, urar, sabhaiyar* and *nagarattar* respectively.[10] The management of temples and temple resources provided a common forum for the interaction of all these corporate bodies and brings into focus the centrality of the temple in linking rural and urban settlements, and agriculture with trade and craft production.

Kenneth Hall explains the interaction between the agrarian and urban settlements through the model of a hierarchy of settlements in Tamil Nadu. According to this model, the nagaram performed the central-place function as the market centre for the villages of a nadu, with a maximum of one nagaram per nadu. The nagaram was, in turn, linked with "higher commercial centres" of three categories—*erivirapattinam, managaram* and coastal ports.[11] The nagaram also performed many other functions. It was responsible for collecting the applicable commercial as well as land taxes, indicating the wide-ranging authority of the nagaram, which extended to "jurisdictional as well as proprietory rights over the neighbouring agricultural land".[12] The autonomy of the nagaram was recognised by the Chola government which initially co-opted the local institutions into its administrative system and allowed them to retain their independence and authority.[13] By the late eleventh century, the potential for

---

10. It is an interesting pointer to the long continuities in Indian social history that down to the eighteenth century, caste leaders were known collectively as the nattar or mahanattar. See ch. 8.
11. Hall, *Trade and Statecraft*, ch. 5. Champakalakshmi points out that there is evidence of more than one nagaram in the densely settled nadus. "Urbanisation", p. 47.
12. Hall, *Trade and Statecraft*, pp. 57, 58, 60.

replenishing the Chola exchequer through conquest lessened as the power of the Cholas also diminished. At this stage, commercial taxes became a very important source of revenue, and to ensure this, the autonomy of merchant organisations had to be protected.[14]

Nagaram

Champakalakshmi notes, further, that three stages can be identified in the expansion of the activities of the nagaram in the Chola period. During the early Chola period, the role of the nagaram became prominent in the first half of the tenth century when there was a noticeable shift in the medium of donations to gold and money, and in the quantum of gifts as well. In the middle Chola period (Rajaraja to Kulottunga II, till 1150), there was a noticeable increase in the number of nagarams which now extended into the newly conquered territories in Karnataka and Andhra, and were used as "agents of political synthesis" together with brahmadeyas. The nagarams were also now linked to interregional and overseas trade in this period. Equally significant was the growing specialisation among merchants who increasingly traded in specific commodities. These included cloth merchants *(saliya-nagarattar)*, oil merchants *(sankarappadi-nagarattar)*, a wider association of oil merchants *(vaniyanagarattar)*, horse merchants and so on. In the late Chola period (1150–1278), nagaram organisation and specialised trading were the major factors in urban growth.[15] Champakalakshmi also observes that the tax-levying authority of the nagarams, in association with the powers of the *chitrameli-periyanadu*, becomes conspicuous during the thirteenth century, when Chola power had become ineffective in most of South India.[16]

Guild

The guild was one of the most significant institutions in South Indian trade, and merchants involved in interregional and overseas trade

---

13. *Ibid.*, pp. 74–75.
14. *Ibid.*, pp. 96–97.
15. Champakalakshmi, "Urbanisation", pp. 47–51.
16. *Ibid.*, pp. 53–54. Champakalakshmi regards the *chitrameli-periyanadu* as a guild of dealers in agricultural commodities, whereas Stein and Hall see the periyanadu as a supralocal association created by the nattar to protect their autonomy which the Chola state sought to dilute through the institutions of the brahmadeya and the nagaram.

organised themselves into guilds. The best known of these were the Manigramam and Ayyavole guilds, though other guilds such as Anjuvannam and Valanjiyar were also in existence. Specialised merchant guilds like the Sankarappadi and Saliya nagarattar also functioned in urban centres. Both the Manigramam and Ayyavole guilds had their bases in Kodumbalur in Pudukkottai, Tiruchi district. The Ayyavole were generally referred to as the Disai-Ayirattu-Ainnurruvar (The Five Hundred of a Thousand Directions), though sometimes, this was prefixed with the term Nanadesi (from several countries). There are a few instances when the Nanadesi are mentioned without including a reference to the Five Hundred, which leads to the inference that the two were different guilds.[17]

The Ayyavole had their home base at Aihole in the Raichur *doab*, in northern Karnataka, as their name suggests. But it is also clear that they had a southern base in Pudukkottai and that the two groups were not part of one centralised decision-making body—though the two groups had a common point of origin, as their *prasastis* (laudatory introductions) indicate. There would seem to have been two phases of migration in the spatial spread of the guild. In the first phase, they migrated from Aihole to Pudukkottai, following the main route for the north-south movement of people, armies and religious bodies. In the second phase, they followed the conquering Chola armies as the empire spread westward into the Coimbatore and South Kanara regions. Pudukkottai was evidently an important commercial region because it was the meeting point for overseas, internal and overland trade routes. The guilds also received the support of the local ruling house of the Irukkuvels who had a close alliance with the Chola royal family, and through the Irukkuvels, the guilds were also patronised by the king.

Champakalakshmi also points out that the guilds, or more correctly, associations of merchants, were a differentiated group. The Manigramam was a localised merchant body, while the Five Hundred was an association of itinerant merchants and was supra-regional in character. The Anjuvannam was an association of foreign merchants first established on the west coast, which subsequently moved to the

---

17. Meera Abraham (*Two Medieval Merchant Guilds*, p. 76) concludes that the Nanadesi and the Ayyavole were distinct groups, since there are references to land sales from one to the other. The following brief outline of the guilds is based on Abraham's study.

east coast ports.[18] This diversity of organisational arrangements of merchant bodies was in keeping with the varying needs and locales of the different merchant groups.

The basic prerequisites for the advancement of merchant capitalism can be seen in the growth of urbanisation, the development of specialised marketing centres (the nagaram) and the evolution of corporate institutions like the guilds. Within this broad outline, several questions—to which we can seek the answers directly from the primary information contained in inscriptions—have to be posed.[19] Among these are: What were the dynamics which governed the interaction between individual merchants and corporate bodies? Was there a transfer of surplus from agriculture and the rural economy to trade and the urban economy, so that in this process we see the genesis of commercial capital? What kind of institutions and commercial practices developed over these centuries which contributed to the development of trade? In trying to answer these questions, I have given references to inscriptions whenever specific points have been made, while the sources of general information have not been specifically mentioned in the footnotes.

Temples and merchants

The growth of urbanisation and the expansion of commerce were interlinked processes which unfolded within the overarching framework of the temple which was evolving into an integrative central institution in medieval Tamil Nadu. Donations to the temple were made by several classes of donors—royalty, landed elite, military officials, merchants, as well as corporate bodies. It was the income from the donation or deposit which would be used to pay for the

18. Champakalakshmi, *Trade, Ideology and Urbanization*, pp. 312–313.
19. Only published Tamil inscriptions have been used.
i. *South Indian Inscriptions*, Archaeological Survey of India, 26 vols. (Madras and Delhi: Archaeological Survey of India, 1891–1990). Hereafter, *SII*, followed by volume and inscription numbers (for publishing details of individual volumes, see bibliography).
ii. *South Indian Temple Inscriptions*, ed. T. M. Subramaniam, 3 vols. (Madras: Government Oriental Manuscripts Library, 1953–57). Hereafter, *SITI*, followed by volume and inscription numbers.
iii. V. Rangacharya, *A Topographical List of the Inscriptions of the Madras Presidency Collected till 1915, with notes and references*, 3 vols. (Madras: Government Press, 1917).

service for which the endowment was made.[20] Occasionally, it was specified that the payment would be in particular commodities equivalent to the value of the interest.[21] If the endowment was in livestock, usually a herd was endowed, which would regenerate itself. If gold or money was endowed, the borrower was expected to derive a sufficient income from this, which would add to his resources as well as enable him to pay interest to the temple to maintain the service for which the endowment was made.

The temple thus became a medium for the circulation of resources. The effective redistribution that resulted would depend on the class composition of the donors and borrowers, as well as on the nature and quantum of the donations. To arrive at a definitive picture of the patterns of resource flows would require a very comprehensive data base recording all the donors, the donations and their utilisation, which is not feasible here. However, certain broad trends are clearly visible. One of the fundamental questions in this context pertains to the direction of the intersectoral resource flows: whether, in South India, there was a skewed flow of resources from agriculture and the rural economy to the urban economy and trade.

Based on his study of the Tanjavur inscriptions, Spencer has concluded that military contributions comprised 79.3 per cent of the donations, and that 95.4 per cent of the borrowers were the village assemblies, while merchants constituted the remaining 4.6 per cent.[22] The treasure from military conquests was thus pumped into the rural economy through the temples. It is not possible to generalise from this finding that this pattern was applicable throughout the Coromandel region and for the entire Chola period. It would, however, seem to be true that most of the gifts were in the form of land, and most of the land was recirculated among the rural power groups.

For the individual merchants such donations could become a source of trading capital, especially when the donations were made by the rural rich or other corporate groups. But the reality was, in

20. The kinds of services mentioned point to the ramifications of the functioning of the temple as a place of worship, as a social welfare institution (which undertook feeding of the poor, especially of brahmans) and as a landowner and employer. Most of the services for which endowments were made were lamps, the ritual bath, turmeric paste, flower garden or supplying flowers and so on.
21. *SII*, II, pt. 2: nos. 24, 37. Both are eleventh-century Tanjavur inscriptions, one for the supply of cardamom and champaka buds, the other for bananas.
22. Spencer, "Temple Money-Lending", pp. 286–287.

fact, quite contrary to this. Out of a sample of 318 published inscriptions, dating from the ninth to the fourteenth century, detailing gifts to temples, 178 (56 per cent) pertained to donations by individual merchants, while only 58 (18.2 per cent) mentioned donations by corporate bodies—nagarattar, guilds, village assemblies and other similar bodies (table 3.1).[23] Interestingly, donations by corporate bodies showed a marked increase from the twelfth century onward (40 of the 58 donations by corporate bodies during the period ninth to fourteenth century took place in the twelfth, thirteenth and fourteenth centuries) and occurred most frequently in Tirunelveli, Coimbatore and Ramanathapuram districts, outside the Chola heartland.

Table 3.1: Donations to Temples by Classes, Ninth to Fourteenth Century

Donor Status	Not mentioned	9th	10th	11th	12th	13th	14th	Total
Not mentioned	5	8	13	10	2	5	2	45
Brahmin			3			1		4
Corporate bodies*	1			1	5	9	1	17
Guild	2		1			3		6
Merchant	10	15	37	58	24	31	3	178
Merchants				1				1
Nagaram	2		6	5	6	8	1	28
Officer (military)				5		1		6
Official		1	2	5	3	3		14
Royalty			3	4				7
Vaniyar						5		5
Village assembly						2		2
Weaver			1			1		2
Woman			1	2				3
Total	20	24	67	91	40	69	7	318

Source: SII and SITI.
* Village assemblies and nagaram acting jointly.

By contrast, very few individual merchants borrowed the endowed resources (only 12 out of 318, i.e., less than 4 per cent). Corporate bodies, including the ur and sabha, the guild and nagaram, outnumbered individual merchants by 68 to 12 among the borrowers, showing

23. Temple inscriptions relate to several activities in addition to the management of temple resources. Out of a sample of 555 inscriptions that I studied, 318 were records of donations, with particular reference to merchants.

almostly exactly the inverse of their relative shares in donations (table 3.2). We can only speculate on the reasons for such trends. Clearly, to the managers of temple funds, giving temple money to corporate bodies, especially to local assemblies, was a minimum risk option and one which enabled an easier monitoring of interest payments. It is more difficult to explain the preponderance of individual merchants among the donors. A plausible answer may be that single merchants, especially in an age when most traders were itinerant merchants, would use their donations to earn recognition and acceptance in local society.[24] While it cannot be said that the resources of the individual merchants went to the corporate bodies, it is quite evident that the former were not able to utilise the temple funds for generating commercial capital. Most of their capital was probably generated from their trading profits. Merchants were also active in the land market and often bought and endowed land. This leads to the inference that trade and landholding were not mutually exclusive categories and that income from land might have been an additional source of capital for the merchants.

Table 3.2: Borrowers of Temple Funds by Classes, Ninth to Fourteenth Century

Borrower status	Not mentioned	9th	10th	11th	12th	13th	14th	Total
Not mentioned	15	13	41	55	31	60	6	221
Brahmin			1	4	4	1		10
Corporate bodies*		4	4	4		1		13
Guild		2		1				3
Merchant				6	2	3	1	12
Merchants						1		1
Nagaram	3	4	11	12	1			31
Officer (military)				1				1
Shepherd	1			1	1	1		4
Temple officials						1		1
Vaniyar				1		1		2
Village assembly	1	1	10	6	1			19
Total	20	24	67	91	40	69	7	318

Source: SII and SITI.
* Village assemblies and nagaram acting jointly.

24. D. N. Jha, "Merchants and Temples in South India", in *Essays in Honour of S. C. Sarkar*, ed. Barun De (Delhi: People's Publishing House, 1975), p. 119.

Several kinds of migration and trading networks are indicated by the inscriptions regarding individual merchant donors. Merchants often migrated to other localities for trade. Since their place of origin is also invariably mentioned in the inscriptions, it would seem that they still had strong links with their own home base and also perhaps that they were regarded as outsiders in their place of trade. Most of the migration took place over very short distances, and merchants moved within a relatively small radius—for instance from Tiruvannamalai to Kanchipuram, or from Tanjavur to Tiruvaiyaru, or Uttaramelur to Tiruvottur (North Arcot).[25]

In some cases, merchants moved over much longer distances, and this trend is evident throughout the medieval period. Merchants from Mylapore had recorded their donations in Tiruvidaimarudur (Tanjavur, tenth century) and in Salem (twelfth century).[26] There are intriguing notices like the incomplete inscription from North Arcot (eleventh century) which refers to the merchant from Bangla-nadu in the north, or to the merchant from Kaiwar-nadu in Hoysala region, who gifted a lamp to the Srirangam temple (eleventh century).[27] By far the most numerous references among migrant merchants are to the merchants from the hill areas of the west *(malai-mandalam)* who specialised in trading of horses *(kudirai-chetti)*. These merchants are again found in the core areas of Tanjavur, Tiruchi (especially Srirangam) and Chinglepet, with a marked increase after the twelfth century.

It is difficult to gauge the degree to which merchants had an individual identity within a corporate identity, or even to assess what percentage of merchants were members of a corporate group—either the nagaram assembly or the guild. There are several instances when a merchant made a donation in his individual capacity, in honour of and under the protection of *(rakshai* or *adaikkalam)* the guild, which perhaps ensured the proper use of the donation.[28] The Manigramam guild, though originating in Kodumbalur, had several local chapters. There are references to the *Tiruneydanattu* (Tillais-thanam, Tanjavur) and *Rajakesaripurattu* Manigramam merchants and to those belonging to the Uraiyur and Tenvaranattunallur

---

25. *SII*, IV: no. 138; V: no. 530; VII: no. 92, respectively.
26. *SII*, V: no. 711; VII: no. 12.
27. *SII*, VIII: no. 7; XXIV: no. 127.
28. *SII*, XIV: nos. 16, 146, 153, Ramanathapuram district. The donations were under the protection of the Nanadesi-Disai-Ayirattu-Ainnurruvar. Also, XXIII: no. 143, Tiruchi district, *disai-ayirattu-nanadesi-adaikkalam.*

Manigramam, who had made endowments to temples.[29] The invocation of guild membership by the merchants would indicate that they functioned within the jurisdiction and under the protective umbrella of the guild.

Powers of corporate bodies

The relationship between the nagaram, the guilds and other corporate assemblies is not clear. In matters relating to the temple, its management and supervision, the local assemblies—the ur, sabha and nagaram—were the corporate decision-making bodies. In no case are the guilds a part of this process. The importance of the local assembly in temple affairs is particularly exemplified by the Tiruvidaimarudur (Tanjavur district) temple. The Tiruvidaimarudur nagaram, in conjunction with the sabha of Tiraimur, the temple officials *(devakarmi)* and occasionally other supervisory officials *(sri-karyam-arayginra)* had both functional and ceremonial duties. They took care of details like arranging a dance, or were present when a royal edict was issued. They also made decisions about the allocation of temple income to provide for oil for lighting lamps, and the management of endowments to the temple.[30] That this continued to be sustained for several centuries is clear since the inscriptions range from the tenth up to the twelfth century.

Another area of corporate decision making was the collection and assignment of taxes for the temple. Though the local assemblies were more prominent in matters relating to the collection and assignment of taxes and duties, there are occasions when the guilds also participated in such decisions. On one occasion, the Nanadesi-Disai-Ayirattu-Ainnurruvar made a pact amongst themselves to collect gold on various social occasions like weddings, and the cess was to be donated to the temple.[31] The most famous inscription is that of

---

29. *SII,* IV: no. 147; XIV: no. 235 (Kodumbalur); V: no. 590 (Tillaisthanam); XIII: no. 26 (Rajakesaripuram); XIII: no. 28 (Uraiyur); XIX: no. 417 (Tenvaranattunallur). The names in parentheses are places where the inscriptions were located.
30. Evidently the accountability of the assemblies could occasionally be very nominal. In the tenth century, the three hundred members of the sabha and the four hundred members of the Tiruvidaimarudur nagaram converted an endowment for digging a tank into a golden necklace, which they named, with self-congratulation, "the seven hundred" in honour of themselves. *SII,* XXIII: no. 212.
31. *SII,* XVII: no. 389 (Pudukkottai, Tiruchi).

Piranmalai (Ramanathapuram) of the thirteenth century, when the Ayyavole, the Manigramam of Kodumbalur and several other nagarattar from areas as far away as Kerala and Sri Lanka (*Kerala-Singala-nattu*) came together to assign a long list of taxes and duties on goods to the Tirukkodukuram temple in Tirumalainadu.[32] Since there is no context to the inscription, it is difficult to comprehend what unusual circumstance prompted such a massive display of solidarity among the various merchant groups. This deliberate expansion of the authority of the nagarams and guilds in the later years of Chola rule was probably also intended to enhance their social status, and create a larger political and social space for them. The merchant groups retained and continued to exercise such authority well into the eighteenth century (see ch. 8).

The same inscription also has a long list of trade goods which were taxed, which is a good index of the volume of trade and the nature of commodities traded. Paddy and rice were both important commodities in internal trade, indicating that rice was an important commercial crop. Salt, lentils, castor, arecanut, pepper, turmeric, ginger, onion, mustard, cumin, cotton, yarn, cotton cloth, wax, honey, sesamum, silk, sandalwood, eaglewood, rosewater, hair for *chauris* (ceremonial fans), camphor, musk, civet, horses and elephants are all included. There was a brisk trade in agricultural and manufactured commodities, as well as several luxury imports for which the temple and elite groups provided a ready market.

In the arena of trade, Hall argues that the nagarams were the regulatory market bodies through which all merchandise, including commodities brought in by itinerant merchants and guilds, were channelled to the local markets.[33] This inference would seem to receive corroboration from the fact that the nagaram fixed the duties payable on all commodities imported and exported, many of which were obviously imported from overseas markets. Abraham, on the other hand, is of the opinion that while there were many instances of cooperation between the nagaram and the Ayyavole guild, there is no direct evidence that the guild dealt only with the nagaram and not directly with local markets.[34]

---

32. *SII*, VIII: no. 442.
33. Hall, *Trade and Statecraft*, p. 109.
34. Abraham, *Two Medieval Merchant Guilds*, p. 122.

Commercial practices

Several institutionalised commercial practices which were necessary for the functioning of more specialised forms of trade were already well established. The first of these was the principle of lending at prescribed interest rates. The returns on the endowments to the temple were calculated as interest *(palisai)* at rates ranging from 12½ to 15 per cent, though much higher (2½ per cent per month or 30 per cent per year) or lower rates are also mentioned. A very early inscription dating to the ninth century refers to the donation as capital *(mudal)* and also refers to the interest on it *(idan palisai)*.[35] There is even a reference to a permanent interest-bearing deposit *(nilaip-poliyuttu)*.[36]

The degree of monetisation is evident from the frequency with which money *(kalanju, kasu, ilakkasu, tulaippon)* as well as gold were endowed to the temple.[37] Specialised commercial services like moneylending were also known by the eleventh century, besides the refinancing through the temple. An inscription of Melsevur, South Arcot, refers to merchants whose business was to lend money on interest. They comprised merchants who had come from other places to the town to set up business, as well as the local moneylenders.[38] There is also a mention of brokers *(taragar)* in some fourteenth-century inscriptions, indicating that another intermediary function of trade had also developed in the intervening period. The taragar of Madurai district joined with the local merchants and the eighteen *vishayattar* (regional officials) to assign taxes for the temple.[39]

The development of designated market areas in urban centres was another feature associated with expanding city-based trade. The Tanjavur inscriptions and the Madras Museum Copperplates[40] give vivid descriptions of the layout of Tanjavur and Kanchipuram, which were both known as *mahanagaram*.[41] The segregation of urban space

---

35. *SII*, VIII: no. 308.
36. *SII*, XII: nos. 90, 91.
37. Hall notes that most prices were listed in paddy equivalents in Tanjavur, and that paddy was perhaps the more commonly used medium of exchange, especially in the local markets. *Trade and Statecraft*, p. 119.
38. *SII*, XVII: no. 235.
39. *SII*, XXIII: nos. 431, 433, 434.
40. *SII*, II, pt. 2: nos. 24, 25, 37; II, pt. 3: nos. 89, 94, 95 for Tanjavur; III, pt. 3: no. 125, for Kanchipuram.
41. See Hall, *Trade and Statecraft*, pp. 90–96, for a detailed description of urban land use and spatial patterns.

by allocating special streets to different occupational groups was very evident in both cities. More interesting are the references to various kinds of commercial areas—like *angadi* (market), *perangadi* (the main market), *perunteru* (the commercial main street usually named after the Chola emperor, Rajaraja)—which were developed both within the towns and in the suburbs.

Expansion of maritime trade

The inscriptional evidence also shows that maritime trade had revived to a considerable extent after the tenth century. Both Nilakanta Sastri and Meera Abraham link this to an aggressive policy of conquest and commercial expansion followed by the Chola state.[42] An important instance of the latter were the trade missions sent to China by Rajaraja and Rajendra to reopen the trade links which had been disrupted due to internal political problems in China.[43] Even Rajendra's expedition against Kadaram and Srivijaya would seem explicable, given the other circumstances, only if Kadaram and Srivijaya were trying to obstruct this renewed trade.[44] This analysis is in contrast to Spencer's argument that the military campaigns of Rajaraja and Rajendra were undertaken more for reasons of expediency—to replenish the resources of their treasury and as an integrative strategy designed to compensate for a lack of effective political centralisation—than dictated by long-term policy.[45] The Sri Lankan expeditions yielded an impressive amount of plundered treasure. Even if this had been the primary motive of the invasions, one of the long-term effects was the higher visibility of the Ayyavole guild members in northern Sri Lanka after the campaigns ended.

The presence of the guilds in several Southeast Asian trade centres is recorded in inscriptions—among which are the fragments found in Takuapa in Thailand, referring to the Manigramam,[46] and two inscriptions which refer to the Ayirattu-Ainnurruvar (but the first word Disai is probably missing). One is from Sumatra, dated 1088,

---

42. Abraham, *Two Medieval Merchant Guilds*, p. 130.
43. Nilakanta Sastri, *The Colas*, pp. 604–606.
44. *Ibid.*, pp. 218–220.
45. George W. Spencer, *The Politics of Expansion* (Madras: New Era Publications, 1983), ch. 4.
46. Abraham, *Two Medieval Merchant Guilds*, pp. 29–33. Nilakanta Sastri dates this to the Pallava period. *The Colas*, p. 459.

and the other, of the thirteenth century, from Pagan in Burma which refers to a locally resident merchant and a temple built by the Nanadesi, called Nanadesi-Vinnagar-Alvan.[47] All this scattered evidence collectively establishes the wide-ranging activities of the guilds, and the links between merchants, temples, trade and urbanisation both within and outside the Coromandel. The expansion of maritime trade is also confirmed by the inclusion in inscriptions, dating from the mid-twelfth century onward, of commodities imported from Southeast Asia, West Asia and China in sizeable quantities.[48]

By the thirteenth century, the patterns of Asian sea-borne trade were becoming well established with a regular pattern of commodities traded as well as of shipping routes. That the Coromandel had also been incorporated into this pattern is confirmed by the accounts of Chau Ju Kua and Marco Polo. The information in the *Chu-fan-chi* about South India is so sketchy that except for the reference to the embassies to China, it adds very little to what we already know of the region.[49] The importance of the Chinese work lies more in the fact that it establishes the trade links which operated in the Indian Ocean and the position of the Coromandel in this larger trading world. Marco Polo, writing at the end of the thirteenth century, clearly states that Kayal at the southern extreme of the Coromandel was a favourite centre for foreign merchants, who were well received and well treated by the king. All the ships coming from the west—Ormuz, Chisti, Aden and various parts of Arabia—laden with merchandise and horses, came to Kayal,[50] which was obviously a major entrepôt on the Asian sea routes.

Marco Polo's observations about how young boys were apprenticed into trade are very interesting, because the parallel with the commercial practices of the Nattukkottai Chettiars is quite remarkable. Marco Polo observed that as soon as a son attained the age of thirteen, he was given a small amount of money with which he was encouraged to trade. The boys would move around the whole day,

---

47. Nilakanta Sastri, "A Tamil Merchant Guild in Sumatra", in *South India and South East Asia* (Mysore: Geetha Book House, 1978), pp. 236–245.
48. Abraham, *Two Medieval Merchant Guilds*, pp. 143 ff.
49. Chau Ju Kua, *His work on the Chinese and Arab Trade in the Twelfth and Thirteenth Centuries, entitled Chu-fan-chi*, trans. and annot. F. Hirth and W. W. Rockhill (St. Petersburg: Imperial Academy of Sciences, 1911), pp. 93–96, 100–101.
50. Marco Polo, *The Travels of Marco Polo*, ed. by M. Komroff, rev. from Marsden's trans. (New York: Modern Library, 1953) pp. 295–296.

buying and selling commodities, earning profits on their transactions. During the pearl fishery season, they would buy small pearls and sell them to merchants, and in this manner they became the most acute and excellent traders.[51] For generations, this was the custom among the Nattukkottai Chettiars or the Nagarattar, as they still refer to themselves. Boys were inducted into business at the age of ten and a half, and trained in business for about ten and a half years. When these boys *(podiyan)* became twenty-one, they became assistants *(aduttavan)* in the business. At thirty-one, they became partners *(pangali)* and at forty-one, independent businessmen *(mudalali)*.[52]

This is only one of the many threads of continuity which marks the social history of South India. If we look at medieval Tamil Nadu (900 to 1300) as a stage in the evolution of trade and commerce rather than as a self-contained age, sufficient unto itself, we see continuities as well as the gradual evolution of corporate and commercial institutions, and the changing structure of trade and mercantile activities. The most important feature of the economic history of this period was that well-defined commercial organisational forms and institutional practices were current, testifying to the functioning of trade as a specialised economic activity.

---

51. *Ibid.*, pp. 287–88.
52. Personal communication from the late Mr M. V. Arunachalam, chairman, Parry and Company.

FOUR

Trade and Merchants: The Vijayanagar Period (1400–1600)

The recorded history of mercantile activity in the Coromandel is punctuated by discontinuities and gaps in the sources of information. The two hundred years from 1400 to 1600 mark one such interregnum, for which the information is generally scattered and scanty. We also find that the nature of the information sources changes in this period. There is a near total shift from indigenous sources—comprising almost exclusively inscriptions—to European sources, consisting primarily of contemporary travel accounts and the records of the various European nations trading in the Indian Ocean.

The Tamil region did not ever regain the degree of political stability and continuity that it had enjoyed for nearly three centuries under the Cholas, after the final dissolution of the Chola empire in the early decades of the thirteenth century. Even as kingdoms were established and then disintegrated, the predominant feature of the political history of the region was the fragmentation of political authority under local chiefs like the Sambuvarayar and Kadavarayar. The Muslim invasion of South India and their capture of Madurai, which was finally recaptured by King Kumara Kampana of the Sangama dynasty (c. 1370), added to the generally chaotic political scenario.[1]

Vijayanagar rule: Political and economic changes

By 1500 all of South India till the Cape had been consolidated under the Vijayanagar empire. But within this consolidated and unitary

---

1. For a more detailed outline of the confused history of this period, see Nilakanta Sastri, *South India*, chs. 10 and 11. For a brief analysis and discussion of the political history of the period, see Stein, *Vijayanagara*, ch. 2.

Trade and Merchants: The Vijayanagar Period

framework, several local centres of power had also come up under various nayakas, though with varying degrees of autonomy. Karashima sees in this process the gradual evolution of a feudal political system, which was particularly evident in the major resource areas of the Tamil country—North Arcot, South Arcot and the Kaveri valley.[2] Stein integrates the changing political alignments into an intricate and composite analysis of the Vijayanagar state, polity and economy. The extension of the Vijayanagar kingdom into the Tamil region was motivated, among other factors, by a need to gain control over the surplus-generating agricultural resource areas,[3] and also over the human resources of the agriculturally less developed hinterland.[4] Perhaps in order to extend more centralised control over the major resource regions, between 1500 and 1550, the Tamil country was reorganised into three major principalities, at Tanjavur, Madurai and Gingee (Senji), with Telugu nayakas as viceroys appointed by the emperor. At this time, however, they had no autonomous status other than as feudatories under the sovereignty of Vijayanagar, with some ceremonial roles in the court hierarchy.[5]

While there are different opinions about the extent to which resources were actually transferred to Vijayanagar—Stein holding it to be negligible and Baker arguing that it was considerable—there is a great degree of consensus about the several changes which took place in Tamil society and economy after the region came under Vijayanagar rule. The first was the extensive migration of peoples from the north *(vadugar)*, mostly Telugu speaking, and their gradual assimilation into local society. The impact of this process on the rural economy and the political power structure in rural society has attracted considerable attention. What needs to be noted further is that the very visible presence of Telugu-speaking merchant

---

2. Karashima, "Nayaka Rule in North and South Arcot Districts", "Changes in Vijayanagar Rule in the Lower Kaveri Valley", and "Nayakas in Chingleput Inscriptions", in *Towards a New Formation*.
3. Stein, *Vijayanagara*, pp. 40-60.
4. C. J. Baker analyses the impact of Vijayanagar on the two main ecosystems of the Tamil regions: the older "valleys"—the river-fed irrigated zones—and the "plains"—the agriculturally less developed regions of western Tamil Nadu. The demand for resources and men to maintain the military might of Vijayanagar was met from these regions, with a concomitant phenomenon of the diminishing importance of autonomous village and local bodies. *An Indian Rural Economy, 1880-1955* (Delhi: Oxford University Press, 1984), pp. 34-48.
5. The Tanjavur nayaka was the ceremonial betel bearer *(adappam* or *tambulakarandavahin)* to the emperor.

groups—Balijas, Komatis and Beri Chettis—in the Tamil country and local trade was also, arguably, the result of this migration. Another change was the legitimisation of the authority of non-Tamil military nayaka rulers during this process of assimilation. This was achieved by the nayaka rulers taking control over the management and resources of local temples, which were the dominant integrative institutions in South Indian society.[6]

The third change relates to the expansion of trade under the nayakas. They promoted the overall growth of commerce through the remission of taxes and granting social privileges to artisans and weavers *(kanmalar* and *kaikkolar)*, tax concessions on commodities sold in local markets and fairs *(pettais* and *sandais)*, and on articles brought in for use in temples.[7] Quite often, such concessions had to be given because overtaxed weavers and artisans had left a settlement en masse, and had to be wooed back with promises of lowered or fair taxation.[8] Temples, or to be more precise, temple towns, were also major market centres, and the remission of taxes by the local ruler on perfumery and other commodities used for temple services[9] would offer a further incentive for the expansion of overall trade in the urban centres. Encouragement was also given to commerce through incentives offered to artisans and weavers by way of gifts of land and establishment of new villages, where land for house sites was provided free of tax *(sarvamanniyam)* for a certain period of time.[10]

For merchants, especially those belonging to the itinerant merchant guilds (Nanadesi), specific inducements were offered by declaring a town or port as a sanctuary. Interestingly, the term 'sanctuary' is used in the medieval European sense of a place where people would be free from persecution *(anjinan-pugalidam)*. Annapottu Reddi, the local ruler of the Bapatla region, declared in 1358 that Motupalli, a major port of the northern Coromandel coast, was such a sanctuary.

---

6. David Ludden, *Peasant History in South India* (Delhi: Oxford University Press, 1989), p. 45; Karashima, "Nayakas and Merchants as Lease-holders of Temple Lands", in *Towards a New Formation*, pp. 131–139, and "Nayaka Rule", *ibid.,* pp. 30 ff.
7. Karashima, "Growth of Power in Kaikkola and Kanmala Communities" and "Development of Overseas Trade", *ibid.*
8. *SII*, XXVI: no. 375 (no. 354 of *Annual Report of Epigraphy* [hereafter *ARE*] 1909), dated 1388–89, records such an instance at Olakkur in South Arcot.
9. *SITI*, I: no. 446, dated 1508 at Kanchipuram. Customs duties on camphor, civet, musk, rosewater, saffron, incense, muslins and silk were waived.
10. *SII*, XXVI: no. 336 (no. 318 of *ARE* 1909), dated 1489 at Kanchipuram (Tirukachchur).

Trade and Merchants: The Vijayanagar Period

Merchants from overseas and itinerant merchants belonging to the Nanadesi guild who had come to Motupalli were assured that their requirements would be fulfilled, and that they were free to go anywhere while residing at Motupalli. They would not have to pay the penalty cess levied on the childless.[11] Taxes on gold and silver were waived in full, while on sandalwood, 75 per cent was waived. Merchants were assured that they could sell their goods and buy goods for export as they pleased.[12] The fact that it was found necessary to make such an unambiguous statement on the rights of merchants indicates that merchants had boycotted Motupalli because they had been subjected to precisely such restrictions and extortion, and that the local economy and revenues had suffered in consequence. Similarly in 1507, the six leading Chettis *(adichetti)* of Pattanam in Coimbatore had it declared as *nanadesipattanam* (the town of the Nanadesi) and a sanctuary in order to recolonise the town.[13]

A major institutional change that evolved in this period was the redefinition of the role of the temple. Association with a local temple did not merely provide to the rulers the means for validation of their political authority. For merchants who might not have been regarded as belonging to the local community—because of their ethnic origins and because of the fact that they were transients—association with a local temple was also the medium for achieving a social identity. The economic function of the temple as a depository and conduit for redistribution of resources to the commercial groups receded in this period, though the practice of depositing money with (or for) a temple so that the interest could be utilised to provide continuous services was still in evidence.[14]

However, there are many more instances of merchants voluntarily raising money for a temple, by imposing a duty themselves on imports and exports—either ad valorem or specific, as well as an annual per head or per household cess, a special cess collected at weddings and other similar cesses. While two such agreements, one recorded at

---

11. This levy is called *aputrika dandam,* and this is the only instance that I have come across of such a tax.
12. *SII,* XXVI: no. 635 (601 of *ARE* 1939). Interestingly, this long inscription is in Tamil, and is evidently intended to reassure and appease Tamil merchants who used to trade in the port.
13. *Ibid.:* no. 222 (210 of *ARE* 1939).
14. For example, there are three such inscriptions from Kanchipuram, dated 1509, 1541 and 1542. *SITI,* I: nos. 411, 361, 353.

Tirukkalukunram by the merchant communities of Sadras (Sadiravachakanpattinam) in 1374 and the other at Nagalapuram in 1521 (both in Chinglepet district),[15] are often cited, there are records of such a practice from other parts of the Tamil country also.[16] The argument that merchants used this channel to achieve social acceptance gains strength when we see that among the merchant groups, communities like *kavarai*[17] (the Tamil word for Balija merchants) are specified in the inscriptions after the fifteenth century, whereas previously they were referred to generically as chettis or as nagarattar, or were identified as merchants belonging to the major guilds.

Ports and trade

It is evident that Vijayanagar itself was more oriented to the ports of the west coast for its trade networks, which was perhaps partly due to the great demand for horses for its military. The eastern ports were thus not of primary importance as far as the imperial centre was concerned and came under the autonomous control of the local nayakas and rulers. In the early days of European traders and trading companies in the region, this became a crucial factor which influenced the future growth of trade, commerce and mercantile institutions in the area. Nayakas with very small areas under their control, and thus with a narrow power base, sought to extend both their economic and political power through their control over trade and ports.

It is well known that the entire coast of Tamil Nadu lacks any natural harbours. Several ports further south like Korkai, Kayal and others had been well known for centuries, while contemporary inscriptions of the fifteenth century also name Sadras and Pulicat (Palaverkadu) as the major ports further to the north. Otherwise, since no port offered any particular locational advantage, any seaside settlement could become a port if some merchants started trading from there. Seaborne trade—either coastal or overseas—was carried on from several ports up and down the coast. At Tirumanikuli in

---

15. *Ibid.*: no. 466 and *SII*, XVII: no. 679 (623 of *ARE* 1904), respectively.
16. *SII*, VII: no. 21, dated 1541 at Taramangalam, Salem district; and Rangachari, *Topographical List*, I: (North Arcot) no. 4, dated 1455 at Kaveripakkam; (Coimbatore) no. 260, c. 1340s.
17. For instance, *SITI*, I: no. 475, dated 1406 at Tirukkalukkunram.

South Arcot, merchants setting out on an ocean voyage made a gift of land to the temple to ensure a safe and successful voyage,[18] indicating the hazards involved in ocean travel. In addition to the local merchants, merchants of the Nanadesi and Paradesi guilds engaged in overseas trade were found in towns all along the coast. But other overseas (foreign?) merchants also came to trade and stay in the port towns all along the coast, all evidence of an extensive trade diaspora on the Coromandel coast in the fourteenth century.[19]

The staple commodities of trade were cloth, areca, pepper, cotton wool and yarn, pearls, coral, rosewater, copper, musk, sandalwood, camphor, silk yarn and other such products. These are commodities routinely mentioned in most inscriptions, while several varieties of foodgrains, cattle and spices are also mentioned as commodities transported to local markets. The former list clearly contains goods involved in long-distance overland trade —such as pepper, pearls and areca which were region-specific products—as well as imported commodities like camphor, silk yarn, coral and copper. The fact that this is an exhaustive list of commodities traded in a smaller internal market like Taramangalam in Salem district[20] is indicative of the nature of internal cross-country trade and its links with external, overseas trade. Another interesting development is that the term *chetti* or *chettiyar* is from now on used as an appellation along with traders' names with the connotation of a specific endogamous trading caste, and not as a generic term for a merchant.[21]

European accounts: Coromandel merchants and Asian trade

The earliest European observations about the region date back to the first two decades of the sixteenth century and are contemporaneous

---

18. *SII*, VII; nos. 777 and 778, dated 1435.
19. The merchants at Sadras included the locals *(uravar)* and merchants of the Nanadesi and Paradesi guilds *(SITI*, I: no. 466, dated 1375), while at Motupalli there were Nanadesis and other overseas merchants *(dipantirattil viyaparigal)*. *SII*, XXVI: no. 635, dated 1358.
20. *SII*, VII: no. 21, dated 1541.
21. *SII*, XVII: no. 679, dated 1521 at Nagalapur (no. 623 of *ARE* 1904) refers to the heads of the merchant communities *(pattanasvamigal)* of Vaisyur and Pulicat as Chittam Chettiar, Lakshmipati Chettiar, Pengandai Chettiar, Pattapillai Chettiar, Ulagu Chettiar, Narayana Chettiar and Tiruvattipillai Chettiar.

with the later inscriptions which, in fact, become progressively infrequent after this period. The accounts of three major travellers, Varthema (1502–1507), Barbosa (1518) and Pires (1512–1515), add to the general picture of mercantile activity and organisation outlined above. Pulicat and Kayal were identified as the major ports on the Coromandel coast by all three. While Kayal and the ports further to the south like Kilakkarai were under the King of Kollam, Pulicat was in the Vijayanagar kingdom and was its major port. Both Varthema and Pires mention a third major port which they call "Choromandel", which was to the north of Kayal, according to Varthema. Pires mentions several ports all along the coast from Kayal to Pulicat, identified as Kilakkarai, Adriramapattinam, Nagore, Tirumalairayanpattinam, Karikal, Tarangampadi, Tirumullaivasal and Kunimedu (near Cuddalore).[22]

The most detailed and authentic account of the period is that of Barbosa.[23] His account highlights, among other details, the extensive trading network of the Coromandel merchants, the "Chatis", who were to be seen in Malabar and in the major ports all over Southeast Asia. They were not the only foreign ("outlandish") merchants in Malabar, for many other merchant communities from other parts of India also came to trade and live there, "where they possess houses and estates, living like the natives yet with customs of their own".[24]

Pegu, Ava, Tennassery, Kedah and Malacca were major trade centres among the ports of the Bay of Bengal where merchants from the east and west coasts of India, as well as other regions, came to buy and sell their wares. Barbosa's graphic account of trade in these "emporia" has been utilised by Chaudhuri to develop an analytical framework of the nature of Asian trade with some well-defined characteristics, of which the segmentation of trade was an important feature.[25] Southern Coromandel was one of the intermediate points

---

22. Ludovico di Varthema, *The Travels of Ludovico di Varthema*, trans. John Winter and ed. George Percy Badger (London: Hakluyt Society, 1863), pp. 186–195; Tome Pires, *The Suma Oriental of Tome Pires,* trans. and ed. Armando Cortesao (London: Hakluyt Society, 1944), vol. 2: pp. 271–272. The editor tentatively identifies Varthema's Choromandel as Nagapattinam.
23. Duarte Barbosa, *The Book of Duarte Barbosa*, trans. and ed. M. L. Dames (London: Hakluyt Society, 1918). Volume 2 covers the Coromandel coast and its trade.
24. *Ibid.,* pp. 70–71. There is a striking resemblance between Barbosa's description and the characteristics of trade diaspora as analysed by Curtin, *Cross-Cultural Trade,* ch.1.
25. K. N. Chaudhuri, *Trade and Civilisation in the Indian Ocean* (New Delhi: Munshiram Manoharlal, 1985), pp. 102–103.

in this segmented trade, where ships from Malabar brought rice, "abundance of goods from Cambaya [Gujarat]", pepper, and commodities like copper, quicksilver and vermilion which normally were imported from Europe. From the east, "Moorish" ships came with spices and drugs, from Malacca, China and Bengal, but did not venture to sail further west because they feared the Portuguese fleets.[26] The return cargoes from southern Coromandel comprised printed cotton cloth which fetched high prices in Malacca, Pegu, Sumatra, Gujarat and Malabar.[27]

Merchants from the Coromandel and the other parts of India also sailed in their own ships to Ava, Tennassery, Pegu and other ports, and Barbosa's account indicates the centrality of Indian merchants and commodities in intra-Asian trade. At Ava, for instance, "many Moorish ships" brought in both "Cambaya" and "Paliacat" cloth, as well as a variety of other goods like copper, opium, vermilion and quicksilver[28]—commodities which came from diverse parts of Asia and Europe, mostly bought in exchange for Indian cloth.

The Coromandel merchants primarily invested in gems and precious stones to bring back to India. Trading in precious stones, pearls, coral, silver and gold was an important part of their business, both in the Coromandel and in Malabar. Barbosa observed that in several port towns the Chetti merchants dealt in gemstones, pearls and precious metals. In Malabar, he commented, "This is their principal trade, and they follow it because they can raise or lower the prices of such things many times",[29] testifiying to the shrewdness of the Chetti merchants who were able to both manipulate and exploit the elastic demand in the market for high value-added commodities.

Malacca was the major trade centre or emporium on the east-west axis of Asian trade, with extensive links with both the west and east coast of India. The trade between the Coromandel region and Malacca has been studied extensively,[30] and it may be worthwhile, here, to touch on some of the salient features of mercantile

26. Barbosa, *Duarte Barbosa*, vol. 2: p. 125.
27. *Ibid.*, p 132. Barbosa mentions only Pulicat as the centre for textiles, but cloth was certainly the major export for the entire region.
28. *Ibid.*, pp. 153–154.
29. *Ibid.*, p. 28.
30. M. A. P. Meilink–Roelofsz, *Asian Trade and European Influence in the Indonesian Archipelago between 1500 and 1630* (The Hague: Martinus Nijhoff, 1962), chs. 3 and 4; Sanjay Subrahmanyam, "The Coromandel-Melaka Trade in the Sixteenth Century", in *Improvising Empire* (Delhi: Oxford University Press, 1990), pp. 16–46.

organisation that these studies highlight. There was a substantial settlement of Tamil merchants—Hindus and Muslims—in Malacca, locally known as "klings". They were "men of great estates and owning many great ships. . . . They trade[d] everywhere in goods of all kinds." In addition, Barbosa specifically mentions the Chettis of the Coromandel, "very corpulent with big bellies", who owned houses in the city and in the country and lived in Malacca with their families.[31] Such merchants were quite distinct from itinerant merchants who spent only a part of the year in ports, perhaps waiting for the proper sailing season while collecting a suitable cargo for re-export. The former had emigrated with families to settle down in a foreign land,[32] indicating a process of cross-cultural assimilation.

Because of the large numbers of foreign merchants in Malacca, each nation was represented by a *shahbandar* or port officer from amongst themselves, who looked after their interests. Pires noted that ten merchants were called together—five "klings" and five from some other nations—for customs valuation of the goods which had arrived at Malacca on large ships.[33] The immigrant Tamil merchants had risen to positions of power and authority in local society, and one of them, Tuñ Mutahir, had even become the prime minister *(bendahara)* of Malacca.[34]

Merchants of the Coromandel had also settled in other Southeast Asian ports. In Bantam, as in Malacca, the powerful posts of shahbandar and admiral were held by "kling" merchants.[35] The greater part of the shipping from Molucca which came to Malacca was owned by a Hindu merchant from the Coromandel.[36] In Ava, Ralph Fitch (c. 1580) noted that the eight town brokers who sold all the goods brought into Pegu for a 2 per cent commission were known as "taragar".[37] Since this is a Tamil word for a broker, it is reasonable

---

31. Barbosa, *Duarte Barbosa*, vol. 2: pp. 171–172, 177 ff.
32. F. R. J. Verhoeven, "Notes on the Tamil Community in Dutch Malacca", in *Proceedings of the First International Seminar of Tamil Studies* (Kuala Lampur: International Association of Tamil Research, 1966) vol. 1: pp. 156–163.
33. Meilink-Roelofsz, *Asian Trade,* p. 42; Pires, *Suma Oriental,* vol. 2: p. 273.
34. Meilink-Roelofsz, *Asian Trade,* p. 53–54; Orient Lee, "Mutahir, a Tamil Prime Minister of Malacca" in *Proceedings of the Second International Conference of Tamil Studies* (Madras: International Association of Tamil Research, 1968), vol. 2: pp. 328–332.
35. Meilink-Roelofsz, *Asian Trade,* p. 246.
36. *Ibid.,* p. 57.
37. Ralph Fitch's account in *Purchas, His Pilgrimes* (Glasgow: University of Glasgow, 1905), vol. 10: p. 191.

Trade and Merchants: The Vijayanagar Period

to infer that these merchant functionaries came from Coromandel. Thus, while the Tamil sources indicate the presence of foreign merchants in urban centres and ports along the Coromandel coast, the European sources point to the extensive settlement of Tamil merchants in ports in Malabar and the countries around the Bay of Bengal.

It is difficult to determine how this widespread trade network was organised, largely because the sources remain quite silent on this question. The recurrent references in the inscriptions to merchant guilds, especially of merchants involved in overseas trade, would lead us to infer that merchants organised themselves as a group to venture on voyages to other ports in the South Asian region. Pires says cryptically that the "Malabares" formed their "company" in Coromandel and Pulicat, and that they came to Malacca "in companies".[38] On the assumption that by "Malabares" he meant the Tamil merchants, Pires's references to "companies" can be explained in two different ways. The first would be that this was a reference to members of merchant guilds trading as a group at Malacca and other Asian ports. This explanation gains strength when taken in conjunction with the frequent references to guild organisation in local Tamil inscriptions.

An alternative explanation would be that merchants organised their trade on the "commenda" or respondentia system, which is also well documented for the period. The *nakhuda* or captain of a ship represented many merchants, and his ship could be carrying either cargo or money belonging to several merchants, who would receive a return on their investment from the profits made on the voyage by the nakhuda.[39]

The major exogenous factor which intruded into traditional intra-Asian trade after the sixteenth century was the arrival of the Europeans. The impact of European trade and shipping and the attempts by Europeans to monopolise Asian trade routes and trade continues to raise considerable debate even till today. Traditional historiography had concluded that while Portuguese control had seriously diminished the trade and shipping of the Gujarat and other west coast merchants, their impact on the economy and trade of the east coast

---

38. *Suma Oriental*, vol. 2: pp. 271–272.
39. Meilink-Roelofsz, *Asian Trade*, pp. 49–51, for an account of the commenda system and the profits made in several ports.

of India was negligible. Pearson has convincingly challenged the first proposition and argued that the impact of the Portuguese on Gujarat merchants and trade was quite marginal.[40] More recently, Sanjay Subrahmanyam has questioned the validity of the latter assumption. He has pointed out that in the latter half of the sixteenth century, Portuguese intervention affected the pattern of shipping from Coromandel ports. The Portuguese introduced the system of granting monopoly rights or concessions to individuals to trade to Malacca and other ports, in return for services rendered to the Crown. As Malacca was under Portuguese control, this monopoly could be enforced. This resulted in the decline of Pulicat as a port, since a great part of the shipping, especially to Malacca, was diverted from Pulicat to San Thome, the Portuguese enclave.[41]

---

40. M. N. Pearson, *Merchants and Rulers in Gujarat* (Berkeley: University of California Press, 1976).
41. Subrahmanyam, "Coromandel-Melaka Trade", pp. 36–42.

FIVE

Merchant Capitalists in the Early Decades of the East India Companies (1600–1670)

There can be little doubt that the advent of Europeans into the Coromandel and their increasing participation in the local textile trade after 1600 was the major exogenous factor in the history of commerce of the region, and its impact was sustained throughout the seventeenth and eighteenth centuries. The trading activities of the Dutch, the English and the French—the most prominent among the Europeans on the Coromandel—did not result in any significant structural change in commercial organisation or mercantile institutions in this period. What the European presence did was to offer new channels to local merchants to enlarge their economic and non-economic spheres of action and power. How the merchant classes responded to this impetus and exploited the openings offered by the European companies is the theme of this and the following chapters.

The available sources of data comprise almost exclusively the records of the European companies.[1] In addition, there are a few contemporary travel accounts. These sources provide a one-sided view of the local merchants—essentially refracted through the prism of European priorities, prejudices and interests—and thus have

1. I have relied extensively on the following printed records and sources:
a. William Foster, ed., *English Factories in India*, (1618–1669), 13 vols. (Oxford: Clarendon Press, 1906–1927). Hereafter *EFI*, followed by year.
b. Henry Davidson Love, *Vestiges of Old Madras, 1640–1800*, 3 vols. (London: John Murray, 1913).
c. *Dagh Register gehouden in't Casteel Batavia*, (1624–1682), 31 vols. (The Hague: Nijhoff, 1888–1919). Hereafter *DR*, followed by vol. no. and date. The dates mentioned refer to the entries made at Batavia in the *Dagh Register*, pertaining to those dates.

· 53 ·

obvious limitations. At the same time, these sources give very detailed accounts of the organisation of trade and mercantile practices which cannot be discerned from the indigenous sources.

Nayaka rule

By the beginning of the seventeenth century, most of the Tamil region was consolidated under the three nayaka kingdoms of Madurai, Tanjavur and Gingee (Senji). They were virtually autonomous, though still acknowledging the sovereignty of the Vijayanagar emperor and superseding the many smaller nayaka chiefs who had come up in the earlier stages of Vijayanagar rule. The Kannada areas of the west were divided between the nayakas of Ikkeri and Mysore, and these five nayakas ruled most of the erstwhile Vijayanagar empire.[2] This territorial division remained a stable feature of the political map of South India throughout the seventeenth century. Even after the nayaka kingdoms of Gingee and Tanjavur fell (in 1648 and 1675 respectively), Gingee and Tanjavur continued, with Madurai, as the major capitals and centres of authority.

Several localised power centres under military chieftains with some degree of autonomy also continued to exist, and they were accommodated within the framework of the nayaka kingdoms. For instance, in the 1530s Visvanatha Nayaka of Madurai, with his second-in-command, Ariyanatha Mudaliar, organised the Pandya country into *palayam*s (small principalities) ruled by *palayakkarar* (poligars or chiefs). The Portuguese had already established themselves in several settlements along the Coromandel coast in the sixteenth century, and it seems evident that neither the more land-

---

2. The following brief account of the political developments in southern Coromandel is drawn from the following sources:
a. K. A. Nilakanta Sastri and N. Venkataramanayya, *Further Sources of Vijayanagar History*, vol. 1 (Madras: University of Madras, 1946).
b. R. Sathianathier, *Tamilaham in the Seventeenth Century* (Madras: University of Madras, 1956).
c. R. Sathyanatha Aiyar, *History of the Nayaks of Madura* (Madras: Oxford University Press, 1921).
d. C. S. Srinivasachari, *A History of Gingee and its Rulers* (Annamalainagar: Annamalai University, 1943).
e. *Vijayanagara Sexcentenary Commemoration Volume* (Dharwar: Vijayanagara Empire Sexcentenary Association, 1936).
f. V. Vriddhagirisan, *The Nayaks of Tanjore* (Annamalainagar: Annamalai University, 1942).

bound nayaka kings nor the many local chiefs regarded their arrival, or later that of the Dutch and the English, as a matter of concern. However, the assumption of independent judicial and revenue-collecting authority in the coastal settlements by the Portuguese, who considered the pearl divers and fishermen converted to Christianity as Portuguese subjects finally aroused the Nayaka of Madurai to action. In 1605, the Marava (as the local region was known) country was organised under the Setupati (title of the raja) of Ramanathapuram to counteract Portuguese power and protect and keep safe the pilgrimage routes to Ramesvaram.

This loose confederation of nayaka kingdoms owing allegiance to a rapidly weakening Vijayanagar emperor was fraught with inherent fissiparous tendencies. There ensued in the seventeenth century, after the death of Venkata II in 1614, an almost continuous state of political instability.[3] This was the result of both the recurring wars of succession to the Vijayanagar throne and the attempts of the nayakas to rid themselves of their allegiance to the emperor,[4] while simultaneously striving to expand their power base and dominions at the expense of each other. The expansionist policies of Bijapur and Golkonda added new players to the political game. New configurations and alliances evolved from time to time, when the Vijayanagar king (or aspirant to the throne) would ally himself with the Bijapur or Golkonda forces to defeat the external aggressor or counter the internal threat of rebellious feudatory nayakas. More usually, the external threat of invasion by the Muslim states united the nayaka kingdoms in a common cause of Hindu survival.

The setting up of newer, smaller power centres like Ramanathapuram under the Setupati also encouraged such centres to declare their autonomy and independence. Within three decades, in 1635, the

---

3. Velcheru Narayana Rao, David Shulman and Sanjay Subrahmanyam remind us that the continuous state of warfare in the nayaka period should not mislead us into subscribing to a view of *pax Vijayanagarica* which collapsed only after the defeat at Talikota, for even the golden age of Krishnadeva Raya was marked by frequent conflicts, both internal and external. *Symbols of Substance: Court and State in Nayaka Period Tamil Nadu* (Delhi: Oxford University Press, 1992), p. 220.

4. In a telling comment on the biases of historians, Stein points out that the histories of the Tamil kingdoms published forty to sixty years ago "all sought to soften the charge that these regimes contributed to the ignominious demise of the Vijayanagara kingdom. Generally the attempt is to date the independent rule of each as late as possible and to claim that its nayaka rulers before that time were loyal 'governors' or 'feudatories' of the Vijayanagar kings. But the facts are obstinately otherwise for the most part." *Vijayanagara*, p. 132.

Madurai armies under Ramappayyan (celebrated in the folk song *Ramappayyan Ammanai*) went to war against the Setupati. The faction-ridden political scenario also encouraged the rise to power of several highly capable individuals like the Velugoti or Damarla families who exercised considerable political influence and power.[5] In short, the Coromandel region witnessed a series of military encounters decade after decade in the seventeenth century.[6]

This constant climate of political instability was the major endogenous factor which influenced the economy and trade of the region. This is not to deny the importance of understanding the character of the state which is usually analysed within the feudal/segmentary/patrimonial framework, nor of administrative structures—especially revenue systems of the states—which are discussed in several works. But frequent warfare brought with it its own imperative—the necessity of raising resources for the mass mobilisation of men and arms. Losers had to pay an annual tribute—to signify their tributary status—to the victors, as well as large indemnities to them to pay for their war efforts. This meant that all productive activities and sectors were taxed to pay for the power struggles of the ruling classes. Armies on the march also disrupted agriculture, manufacture and trade, and the affected populace—especially cultivators and artisans—tended to

---

5. See Rao, Shulman and Subrahmanyam, *Symbols*, pp. 242–264, for an account of the Velugoti family.
6. A brief chronological list of the various battles and wars in the region between c. 1590 and 1650 is given below to illustrate this statement:
1595 Madurai vs. Tanjavur.
1607–8 Revolt of Krishnappa Nayaka of Gingee against Venkata II.
1611 Tanjavur vs. Madurai.
1614 Civil war to decide the succession after the death of Venkata II.
1616 Tanjavur against Solaga, a local chief, and Gingee.
1620 Invasion of Madurai by the Nayaka of Mysore.
1625 Invasion of Madurai again by the Nayaka of Mysore.
1630 Civil war after the death of Rama Deva II.
1635 War against the Setupati of Ramanathapuram, by Madurai.
1635 Nayakas of Tanjavur and Madurai against Venkata III.
1638–9 Invasion of the Karnatak by Bijapur.
1641 Invasion of the Vijayanagar kingdom by Bijapur, stopped by the combined forces of the three nayakas.
1642 Invasion of the Vijayanagar kingdom by Golkonda.
1644 March by Sri Ranga III against Golkonda, with the help of the Bijapur army.
1645 Joint invasion of the Vijayanagar kingdom by Bijapur and Golkonda. Sri Ranga III under attack from the Nayakas of Tanjavur, Madurai and Gingee.
1648 Fall of Gingee to Bijapur.
1649 Invasion of Tanjavur by Bijapur.

migrate en masse from the locales of war to avoid the looting and robbing. This left large areas depopulated for several years.[7]

The growing presence of Europeans

The Europeans also involved themselves in the local wars to advance their trading interests.[8] Furthermore, they tried to use their political influence with the rulers, local chiefs and other ruling elite to obstruct the expansion of the establishments of other Europeans. The initial efforts of the Dutch to establish a trade settlement at Pulicat in 1610 met with stiff resistance from the Portuguese. The latter tried their best to manipulate the local authorities to deny the Dutch any trade privileges and even attacked Pulicat harbour several times.[9] The Dutch were equally busy trying to keep the Portuguese out of Tevanampattinam (Tegnepatnam), Tiruppapuliyur and Pulicat, which was a condition built into their agreements with the local rulers.[10] The English, in their turn, faced similar obstructions from the Dutch both at Batavia and in the Coromandel, when a peace treaty signed in Europe allowed them trading privileges in Pulicat. Ultimately this unsuccessful experiment had to be abandoned in 1623.[11] Further south, the Portuguese and the Danes thwarted the

---

7. For a discussion of the overall ramifications of war in the nayaka period, see Rao, Shulman and Subrahmanyam, *Symbols*, pp. 220–241.
8. The Portuguese sided with Chief Solaga of Kottaitivu when Achyutappa Nayaka marched against him in 1616 (Vriddhagirisan, *Nayaks of Tanjore*, pp. 75–76). In 1635, when the Nayaka of Madurai went to war with the Setupati, the Portuguese supported the Nayaka, and the Dutch the Setupati. Sathyanatha Aiyer, *Nayaks of Madura*, pp. 122 ff.
9. Raychaudhuri, *Jan Company*, pp. 15–38. The English also recorded that the Portuguese attacked Pulicat harbour in 1623 and burnt two ships there. Letter from Masulipatnam to Surat, 8 September 1623, *EFI 1622–23*, pp. 259–260.
10. Agreements between the Raja of Gingee and Captain de Bitter, 30 November 1608; Captain Maarts and "Tier Wingelaya, Governor of the Islands of Tindamandalam" [Tiruvengalaya, the chief minister of Gingee] 29 March 1610; Captain Maartsen with the King of the Carnatic, 24 April 1610; Director van Berchem with the Raja of the Carnatic, 12 December 1612. Abstracts of all the contracts ... made ... or obtained from various native sovereigns in the name of Governors General and Council for India, representing the General Dutch East India Company (Translated from Corpus Diplomaticum Neerlando Indicum), Dutch Records of the Tamil Nadu State Archives, Madras. Hereafter, Abstracts.
11. The complaints of Thomas Mills and John Milward, the English factors at Pulicat, reached a peak in September 1622 (*EFI 1622–23*, pp. 126–127). Finally, the President and Council at Batavia decided to close the factory in April 1623. 11 April 1623, *ibid.*, p. 220.

English when they tried to get a foothold in Karikal on the Tanjavur coast, with the Danes claiming that they had the sole right to set up establishments all along the coast from Nagapattinam to Pulicat.[12] The Danes also "intercepted a factory" at Puducheri (Pondicherry) which the English tried to establish,[13] while the Dutch worked with great fervour to have the English thrown out of Armagon.[14] The English were unable to enter this power game in the first decades of the seventeenth century due to their relative powerlessness.

At the beginning of the seventeenth century, the general picture of the trade of the Coromandel region was not very different from the trends in the previous century. Trade was carried on extensively from ports all along the coast, though there could be little doubt that Masulipatnam had emerged as the major port on the coast, while Pulicat had declined towards the end of the sixteenth century. The Portuguese introduced the system of monopolistic concessional trading privileges to individuals in return for services rendered to the Crown. It has been argued that this resulted in a great part of the shipping, especially to Malacca which was under Portuguese control, being diverted from Pulicat to San Thome.[15] Contemporary observers also attributed the decline of Pulicat to the depopulation following civil wars, and wondered what encouragement there could be for productive activities "in these troublesome times, when on all sides there is burning and spoiling".[16]

For the Europeans the attraction of Coromandel lay in its continuing centrality in Southeast Asian trade. It remained the primary supplier of a variety of textiles, the major commodity of consumption and exchange in the region. Their trading ventures received a positive response from local merchants and governments[17] almost everywhere in the Coromandel region, which was completely at variance with the antagonism they faced in Surat. The inescapable explanation for

---

12. Captain John Buckley's account, 8 June 1624, *EFI 1624–29*, p. 15.
13. Letter from the President and Council at Batavia to the Company, 6 February 1626, *ibid.*, p. 119.
14. Thomas Mills and Thomas Johnson at Armagon, 1 March 1626; Letter from Armagon to Masulipatnam, 13 May 1626, *ibid.*, pp. 120, 130–131.
15. Subrahmanyam, "Coromandel-Melaka Trade", pp. 40–41.
16. Letter from Masulipatnam to the Company, 15 November 1620, *EFI 1618–21*, pp. 209–210; Letter from Pulicat to Batavia, 6 November 1622, *EFI 1622–23*, pp. 138–140.
17. The Dutch were able to procure favourable trade and customs concessions from various rulers: from Golkonda (for Masulipatnam) in 1606; from Gingee (for Tevanampattinam) in 1608; from Vijayanagar (for Pulicat) in 1612. Abstracts.

this would be that in the Coromandel, the Europeans were never thought of as potential competitors, and their trade was seen as providing opportunities for expanding the local economy, commerce and revenues. Within this broader response, we must also accommodate the behaviour of local governors (revenue farmers) or, occasionally, even of rulers, who tended to see in the Europeans enhanced opportunities for extracting additional revenue through legitimate or non-legitimate demands.[18]

The frequency of political conflicts in the region increased the requirement for resources at a time when the disruption of production would have reduced the revenue-yielding potential of the economy. Consequently, offices tended to be farmed out at much higher rates than could be recovered from local taxes. Moreover, given the uncertainty of their tenure in the current political climate, local officials also wished to recoup maximum revenues from their offices as fast as they could. The targeting of Europeans for additional demands probably seemed feasible in view of the fact that they had no standing or ties in local society. This problem of the rapacity of local officials did not ever get fully resolved throughout the seventeenth century, though the fact that the Europeans were willing and able to use their undoubted naval superiority to back their trading rights did act as an effective countervailing force in restraining local officials.[19]

Traditionally, merchants all over Southeast Asia dealt with attempts by port officials to squeeze extra revenue by quickly shifting to better administered ports. This neutralised the extortionate powers of local officials, and trade in the Asian region remained an open system of free markets. A new dimension was added to this system when the Europeans began to use their naval power to monopolise trade. Every European nation tried to enlarge its trading rights both by controlling local shipping and overseas trade and by attacking the ships of its European rivals. This policy, first used by the Portuguese, was adopted enthusiastically by all the Europeans who followed, and it

18. The first English attempts to settle a factory at Tanjavur were not successful, primarily because the merchants found the nayaka "very covetous" and he expected a large present each year, besides 7000 *reals* for the use of the port of Karikal. Captain John Buckley's account, 20 November 1624, *EFI* 1624–29, p. 19.

19. Raychaudhuri, *Jan Company*, pp. 15–37, for a detailed account of the Dutch experiences in this regard. The English observed that if they could also stop the native junks and gain some trade advantages, as had happened in Surat, it would be good. Letter from Masulipatnam to Surat, 27 August 1621, *EFI* 1618–21, pp. 264–265.

introduced the totally alien element of organised violence into intra-Asian trade and shipping. This was the larger world within which the Coromandel merchant functioned in the seventeenth century.

The emergence of merchant capitalists

After the Europeans began to participate in local trade, the merchants also acted as the interface between them and the local economy and state authorities. From this time onward, well until the end of the eighteenth century, we repeatedly come across the phenomenon of a few prominent merchants who dominated commerce, both on account of their individual trading ventures and their functional capacity as chief merchants to the Europeans.

These merchant capitalists were distinguished by some common, shared characteristics which are worth enumerating. They were large-scale export merchants, often possessing their own ships, who traded extensively with the Southeast Asian ports. They functioned from many ports along the Coromandel coast, usually through an extended network of kinsfolk related by birth or marriage. The trade links of these merchants radiated from the ports to the hinterland, giving them a very large sphere of influence. This pre-eminence, though primarily earned through their business acumen and wealth, was reinforced through their contacts with the local rulers. They were the recognised leaders of society, especially in urban centres. After the Europeans started trading on the Coromandel coast, these merchants provided them access to the local economy for purchasing textiles and other export commodities and for vending their imports. These merchants were the all-important intermediaries in the Europeans' discourses with the local authorities, which greatly enhanced their undoubted primacy in the local economy and society.

Was this class of dominant merchants only an incidental by-product of the exogenous agency of European trade, when occasionally more enterprising individuals exploited the opportunities offered by the requirements of the Europeans? If each of these great merchants, beginning with Malaya Chetti (Astappa Chetti) is studied only individually, as an extraordinary case,[20] this would seem to be the implicit

20. This is the orientation of both S. Arasaratnam and Sanjay Subrahmanyam. Arasaratnam studies merchants across various social categories like caste, religion and

interpretation. In that case, the death (or eclipse) of any one merchant would leave an irreplaceable vacuum in the system. But this pattern is replicated so often that this seems untenable. I would posit that while the personal qualities of leadership and business abilities of these merchants cannot be denied, as a class they transcended the political and economic ambience at any particular point of time and were part of a larger historical process. Further, that this dominant merchant group constituted a specific class of merchant capitalists who exercised great power over the economy and society in the Coromandel for the next two centuries.

There is no recorded evidence to show that these merchant capitalists antedated the Europeans. However, even in the descriptions of trade in Malacca in the sixteenth century, there are references to very rich individual merchants. It does not seem logically sustainable to argue that what was a characteristic feature of the commercial world of the Coromandel after the seventeenth century did not develop to some extent out of previously existing structures. The rapidly deteriorating state of centralised political authority and the enhanced need for resources and revenues at all levels of authority facilitated the politicisation of these merchant capitalists. Their entry into revenue farming—and concomitant enhancement of social status and control—enabled these merchants to augment their already considerable economic power.

The first mention that the merchant class was functionally and hierarchically differentiated came early in the seventeenth century. It should come as no surprise that trading functions should have become specialised in an economy which had diversified beyond subsistence production into distinct agricultural and non-agricultural production, with a surplus which was traded internally and which served international trade as well.

---

others to support his proposition that merchants did not come only from occupational trading castes. But he treats these exceptional merchants only as individuals, and not as a class (*Merchants, Companies and Commerce*, pp. 213–273). Subrahmanyam, following Perlin's critique of the "functionalist method", argues that commerce and politics were not exclusive spheres as usually assumed. Further, that these merchants were "portfolio capitalists" who occupied, in the early seventeenth century, a "middle ground between the worlds of mercantile capitalism and political capitalism" (*Political Economy of Commerce*, pp. 298–300). By locating these merchants only in the early seventeenth century, Subrahmanyam also typifies them as the products of the specific political and economic milieu which prevailed in that period.

William Methwold, the English factor at Masulipatnam, noted (c. 1620) at least four classes of merchants.[21] At the top were merchants (whom Methwold calls generically 'Committys' or Komatis) who were the bulk sellers of cloth and other export commodities in the port towns—either selling for money or bartering their goods. They usually employed agents, subordinate merchants, to travel into the country to collect the cloth from the weavers. Some merchants were money changers, which was an absolutely essential service to sustain a complex commercial network—both because the multiplicity of coinage in circulation had to be tested and valued with respect to the local currency, and because of the common practice of devaluing old coinage. The poorest merchants were the plain shopkeepers or retailers who sold groceries and other everyday necessities. Although Methwold does not mention this, there must have also been a class of exporters who bought from the wholesale merchants of the port cities. Thus a hierarchy of merchants existed, with the shopkeepers forming probably the most numerous class at the lowest rung, while at the apex of the pyramid were the merchant capitalists who dominated both export and internal trade. Almost all the surplus required for commerce and the profits generated from trade were controlled by these capitalists, and this is the class that we shall concentrate on, to understand the nature of merchant capitalism in the Coromandel region.

Malaya Chetti

The career of Malaya Chetti, the foremost merchant capitalist of his time, has fascinated many a historian, and is thus already well documented.[22] What is presented here is a brief review touching on the salient features of such prominent merchants outlined earlier. Malaya Chetti[23] began to interact with the Dutch in 1608 and was involved in their trade

---

21. W. H. Moreland, ed., *Relations of Golkonda* (London: Hakluyt Society, 1931), p.16.
22. J. J. Brennig was the first scholar to give a detailed account of Malaya Chetti, his family and genealogy, and also identified him as a Balija ("Textile Trade", pp. 55–64 and fn. 22). More recently, Subrahmanyam has examined the career of Malaya Chetti and especially that of his brother and successor, Chinnanna, most comprehensively. *Political Economy of Commerce*, pp. 300–314.
23. The Dutch records refer to him as Malaya or Asty Pachitty/ Astyappa/Astappa, which Subrahmanyam transliterates as the more Sanskritised Achyutappa. I retain the more widely used Malaya. The Europeans had a common habit of referring to all family members, especially the heirs who succeeded the chief merchants, by the same name, so that Malaya's brother Chinnanna is often referred to as Malaya, especially in the English records.

for twenty-six years until his death in 1634. Though a resident of Pulicat,[24] he also had establishments all along the coast, managed by his brothers or nephews. When the English were planning to settle a factory on the Tanjavur coast in 1624, perhaps at Karikal, instructions were sent from Batavia to the emissaries that "there is a great Committee [Komati] in the Nayak's country named Malaya, which will be your chief merchant and undertake great matters."[25] His white house in Tevanampattinam was a landmark, which could be seen from several miles out at sea[26] and was almost as prominent as the temple towers of Chidambaram. Malaya Chetti is referred to as the governor of the town,[27] and the English there expected to deal with the brother of Malaya, who was earlier referred to as "their principal merchant".[28] Lakshamma Nayak, the son of another brother, was the governor of Puducheri (Pondicherry), whom the English hoped to use as the intermediary for their trade. They also hoped to establish a fort with his help in the region.[29]

That Malaya Chetti owned several ships and traded primarily to Tennassery, Pegu and Arakan is also well recorded.[30] He was first associated with the Dutch in 1608 when he served as an interpreter in their negotiations with the Nayaka of Gingee,[31] and when he must have already been a merchant of considerable influence.[32]

There was a fundamental difference between the way the Coromandel merchants saw the Europeans and the Europeans saw each other. Whereas to the latter, every other European nation was a rival who threatened their share of Asian trade, for the local merchants all Europeans offered a welcome opportunity to increase their volume of business. Initially, therefore, Malaya Chetti was also happy to trade with the English and lend them money,[33] so much so that the English

24. 14 August 1634, *DR*, vol. 2, 1631–34, pp. 364–365.
25. Instructions from Batavia, 27 March 1624, *EFI*, 1624–29, p. 9.
26. John Buckley's account, 21 May 1624, *ibid.*, pp. 13–14.
27. *Ibid*, 17 July 1624, *ibid.*, p.16.
28. Letter from Pulicat to Batavia, 6 November 1622, *EFI* 1622–23, p. 141.
29. 14 March 1637, *DR*, vol. 4, 1637, p. 94.
30. Subrahmanyam, *Political Economy of Commerce*, pp. 305–306.
31. *Ibid.*, p. 301.
32. It is difficult to agree with Subrahmanyam (*ibid.*, p. 302) that Malaya, at this time, was no more than an interpreter, which would mean that his commercial empire was built up within just one decade or so. It also seems doubtful that the Gingee rulers would have been accessible to any individual who did not exercise considerable social and economic power.
33. Letter from Pulicat to Masulipatnam, June 1623, *EFI* 1622–23, p. 288.

referred to him as their "principal merchant". The Dutch soon made clear their opposition to this, and within a couple of years, the English began complaining about the obstructions which Malaya Chetti and the Dutch were putting in their way when they attempted to settle a factory in 1626 at Armagon (Durgarajapatnam), on the northern tip of Lake Pulicat.[34] The Indian merchants learnt the rules of the game quite early. They usually stuck to dealing with only one European company, though they were also able to manipulate this rivalry to their own advantage, whenever possible.

In an effort to monopolise the local trade more effectively, the Dutch also got Malaya to farm the revenues of commercially strategic areas, which again became a standard practice followed by the English and the French during the next century and a half. In 1620, Malaya, with his associates Gurua and Raghava Chetti, farmed some of the taxes of Pulicat from Etiraja, the chief of Pulicat.[35] This contract was renewed again in 1629, directly with the King.[36] The same year, Malaya Chetti's brother Chinnanna farmed from the King, on his brother's behalf, the revenues of San Thome for three years—at 7,000, 7,500 and 8,000 *pardao*s for the first, second and third years respectively,[37] which meant that the Dutch had gained some measure of control over a major Portuguese port. In 1630, the Dutch masterminded an agreement between the Danish officers at Tarangampadi (Tranquebar) and Malaya Chetti, by which Malaya would take over the security of Fort Dansborg in return for the revenues of Tarangampadi.[38] The English complained that the Dutch also sent Malaya Chetti "to farm the government of Armagon at treble its usual rent" from the local nayaka in order to disturb their trade at Armagon.[39] The benefits of these manoeuvres did not go to the Dutch alone, for by controlling the port towns in his own name, Malaya also felt more secure from extortions by the local officials.[40]

---

34. Letter from Armagon to Masulipatnam, 20 May 1626; from the President at Bantam to the Company, 28 October 1629, *EFI* 1624–29, pp. 131, 358.
35. Agreement between "Itterage chief of Paliacat . . . and Asty Pachitty, Groah and Ragua Chitty", 28 August 1620, Abstracts.
36. Contract between the King and "Malayo", 4 December 1629, *ibid.*
37. Contract between the King of Carnatic and Chinnanna, 24 December 1629, *ibid.*
38. Agreement relative to Fort Dansborg, 23 January 1630, *ibid.*
39. Letter from the President at Bantam to the Company, 28 October 1629, *EFI* 1624–29, p. 358.
40. Malaya had a great trade on the coast "and was afraid of being plucked by one or other of the Nayaks", the English noted, predicting that if the Dutch did not acquire Tarangampadi, Malaya would. *Ibid.*, p. 359 n.

In 1632 Malaya Chetti again made overtures to the English to resume their trade on the coast, which the Dutch complained was only intended to spoil their trade. He offered the English, cloth at much cheaper rates than were paid by the Dutch.[41] Nevertheless, after Malaya Chetti's death in 1634, the Dutch mourned their great loss, since their affairs were no longer as carefully looked after as in Malaya's time.[42]

Chinnanna

From the 1630s till the end of the 1640s, Dutch trade was dominated by Chinnanna, Malaya Chetti's brother. Other surviving heirs were Seshadri Nayak (Malaya Chetti's nephew and son-in-law), Lakshamma Nayak (the nephew at Puducheri) and Koneri Chetti, another nephew, who was Chinnanna's partner. Chinnanna had high political ambitions and was involved with the Nayaka of Gingee, who seized a large fortune in 1640 from Chinnanna when the latter fell from grace. Chinnanna then decided to shift to Tanjavur and to take on lease Tirumullaivasal and another port to advance Dutch trade. In 1642 he ran into problems with the Nayaka of Tanjavur as well. With active support from the Dutch, Chinnanna then gained the favour of the Vijayanagar king in 1643. During all these political adventures, he was carrying on an extended trade from Pulicat and other ports, both on his own account and as an intermediary of the Dutch. As a shipowner and an exporter, his trade was probably of greater magnitude than that of his late brother Malaya.[43]

By 1644, Chinnanna's overextended activities had left him almost bankrupt, and he owed 15,000 pagodas to the Dutch.[44] He was also at odds with them, a fact which was noted with great satisfaction by the English. There was a short-lived reconciliation between him and the Dutch in 1645,[45] before hostilities resumed. The Dutch noted that he was also out of power with the king, while the English, more accurately, said that Chinnanna was "in such favour with the King

---

41. 25 November 1632, *DR*, vol. 2, 1631–34, p. 120. The English records also indicate a resumption of negotiations with Malaya Chetti. Letter from Armagon to Petapoli, 16 November 1632, *EFI* 1630–33, p. 243.
42. 23 May 1637, *DR*, vol. 4, 1637, p. 243.
43. The details of Chinnanna's career have been put together from the information in the *Dagh Registers* from 1634 onward. See also fn. 22.
44. 1 June 1644, *DR*, vol. 7, 1643–44, p. 288.
45. 6 May 1645, *DR*, vol. 8, 1644–45, p. 337–339.

that he ruleth both King and country", and was also harassing the Dutch—even threatening to seize Pulicat.[46] Chinnanna's differences with the Dutch continued till 1647, during which time he was also making friendly overtures to the English.[47] There was a final reconciliation with the Dutch in 1647, when he handed over the fort at Tevanampattinam and lived from then on under Dutch custody.[48] Chinnanna's last service for the Dutch came nearly a decade later when he interceded for them with Vijayaraghava Nayaka of Tanjavur, and negotiated the cession of Nagapattinam to the Dutch in 1658.[49]

Chinnanna's relations with his family members were also far from harmonious. Seshadri Nayak, the nephew and son-in-law of both Malaya and Chinnanna, claimed that he was Malaya Chetti's heir, and in 1641, he appealed to the king that the property taken over by Chinnanna should be restored to him. According to Gardenis, the Dutch governor at Pulicat, Chinnanna had left Seshadri as his representative in Pulicat because he himself was busy at Gingee, but Seshadri had mismanaged affairs, which included the Dutch trade, to such an extent that Chinnanna had been compelled to return and expel Seshadri.[50] This resulted in a protracted family feud. Soon Seshadri began to trade with the English, confirming the long-held suspicions of the Dutch.[51] Finally, because of the animosity of the Nayaka of Gingee towards Chinnanna and his family members, Seshadri fled to Madras,[52] where he became the English "broker".[53]

The year 1646–47 is noteworthy for two events. The first was a devastating famine which was the result of the failure of the monsoon in October 1646. By January 1647, 3,000 people had died in the

---

46. 9 November 1645, *ibid.*, p. 356. Letter from Fort St George to Surat, 8 September 1645, *EFI 1642–45*, pp. 279–282.
47. Letter from Fort St George to the Company, 9 October 1647, *EFI 1646–50*, p. 165.
48. Contract between A. Heussen, Governor on the Coromandel coast, and Chinnanna Chitty, 19 September 1647, *Abstracts*.
49. The Dutch version is ambiguous about Chinnanna's role and refers to him as "Ambassadors of the Naik of Chanjore" (Articles agreed upon between Chinnanna . . . and Admiral Ryklof van Goens at Negapatam, 15 September 1658, *Abstracts*). But the original *kaul* (agreement) in Telugu clearly states that Chinnanna had "most earnestly petitioned" Vijayaraghava Nayaka for this grant on behalf of the Dutch. K. A. Nilakanta Sastri, "Two Negapatam Grants from the Batavia Museum", in *Indian Historical Records Commission, Proceedings and Meetings* (1937), vol. 14: pp. 39–50.
50. 26 December 1641, *DR*, vol. 6, 1641–42, p. 262.
51. 24 April 1642, *ibid.*, p. 275.
52. 15 February 1643, *DR*, vol. 7, 1643–44, p. 249.
53. Love, *Vestiges*, vol. 1: p. 54.

"little town" of Madras. In the larger towns of Pulicat and San Thome, the number of dead was put at 15,000. This was a widespread famine which affected the region from Pulicat down to Tevanampattinam, and by October 1647, the toll in Madras was estimated at 4,000. The mortality was so high that the corpses could not be disposed of, and only one-third of the weavers, painters and washers were left. Cloth prices had increased by 15 per cent, and little was available even at that price.[54] The other event, with much wider long-term ramifications, was the conquest of the region from Pulicat to San Thome by Mir Jumla, the commander of the Golkonda forces,[55] at the end of 1646. This meant continuous confrontations of the Dutch and the English at a personal level with Mir Jumla, who maintained a remarkably contentious relationship with them—even after he went over to the Mughals in 1656—until his death in 1663. It also meant that the region was brought under the centralised administration of Golkonda, in place of the relatively lax and decentralised rule under the local nayakas of the Vijayanagar kingdom.

Madras: The vertical division of society

By 1650, Fort St George, along with the town of Madras (Chennapattinam) which had grown up around the Fort, had become stabilised and properous. Seshadri Nayak and Koneri Chetti were the chief merchants through whom the English conducted their trade. However, when both merchants got into financial difficulties and were unable to meet their commitments, a brahmin merchant named Venkata was appointed the chief merchant. Venkata's brother was the local magistrate ("*choultry* justice"), a position of great influence in local government. Both sets of merchants wanted to retain their monopoly trading rights, and to gain the upper hand, they resorted to orchestrating and inciting a large-scale caste conflict which demonstrated in ample measure the social moorings of the merchant class.

54. Letters from Fort St George: 4 and 21 January 1647, 4 July 1647, and 9 October 1647, *EFI 1646–50*, pp. 70, 74, 135, 163–164.
55. Mir Jumla's extraordinary career has been recounted in Jagdish Narayan Sarkar, *The Life of Mir Jumla* (Calcutta: Thacker, Spink & Co, 1951). For details of the problems faced by the Dutch with him, see Raychaudhuri, *Jan Company*. Subrahmanyam (*Political Economy of Commerce*, pp. 322–327) looks at his career within his framework of portfolio capitalists.

The local merchants were mostly Balijas and Beri Chettis,[56] belonging respectively to the right-hand and left-hand castes. This vertical division of society into a left and right side, each comprising a range of castes, was unique to South Indian society. Each group of castes, irrespective of the ranking of each component caste in the horizontal hierarchy, regarded itself as an integrated holistic social unit. Each group had a deep-seated antagonism towards the other and was very jealous of preserving a normative social space which defined its social status. The two trading communities of Balijas and Beri Chettis were business competitors, and the riot of 1652 was the first of many occasions when the leading merchants found it expedient to exploit the social tensions between the right- and left-hand castes to advance their economic interests.[57] The right side was incited by Seshadri Nayak and his adherents, while the brahmins, who normally were outside this division and were a "neutral" caste, instigated the left side.

There were several undercurrents, besides the overt caste antagonism between the two groups, which underlay the caste conflict of 1652. Seshadri Nayak and several other right-hand merchants were associated with Henry Greenhill, president of Fort St George during 1648–52 and 1655–59, while the brahmins were associated with Aaron Baker, president from 1652 to 1655. Greenhill was convinced that the brahmins had started the disturbance as a smokescreen to cover up the large sums they still owed the English East India Company and various other irregularities. What is quite evident is that the conflict was equally an expression of the animosity and power struggle between Greenhill and Baker.

This caste conflict posed a major law and order problem and the Fort St George president and council wrote in bewilderment, "We know not what spirit of factious madness hath of late possessed our

---

56. The Fort St George Council noted in a letter to Surat that "the country roundabout, as well as this and all other towns in this kingdom are divided into two general castes, namely the Belgewarras and the Bereewarras, who for many hundred years together have ever had a quarrel one with the other". 5 February 1653, *EFI* 1651–54, pp. 155–156.
57. Arjun Appadurai was the first of the present-day social scientists to analyse this form of social organisation in a theoretical framework ("Right and Left Hand Castes in South India", *Indian Economic and Social History Review* 11, nos. 2–3, 1974, pp. 216–259). For an economic interpretation of the conflict, see Kanakalatha Mukund, "Caste Conflict in South India in Early Colonial Port Cities, 1650–1800", *Studies in History* 11, no. 1, 1995, pp. 1–27.

townspeople in general, but the like, we assure you, in all our lives we never knew".[58] One repercussion of this conflict was that it caused the English to intervene into local social customs and practices to resolve the conflict. The streets of Madras—as was the traditional practice in most towns in the region—were segregated into right- and left-hand streets. The marriage and funeral processions of each group could pass only through their respective areas, as demarcated by the Fort St George Council.[59] This intervention also had more far-reaching consequences. Until then, the primary concern of the English had been in protecting Fort St George which was regarded as a trading post, but this intervention created in the English the consciousness that they were rulers. With increasing frequency, in subsequent years their norms of governance and an orderly society were applied to the people of Madras, essentially creating an embryonic colonial state.

This conflict also makes clear the different facets of the relationship between the English and the local merchants. At one level, the merchants dealt with the Company, and the equations in this relationship were quite distinct from the personal relationships the merchants had with the president and other members of the Council of the Fort. The personal relationships often spilled over into the public one, and, frequently, the business and fortunes of the Indian merchants grew or declined in consonance with the personal biases of the presidents of Fort St George towards them.

Beri Timmanna

The personal association of the Indian merchants with the English was as agents, or *dubashes*, in the private trade of the latter. Beri Timmanna and "Rudriga" were both dubashes to Greenhill, and were also embroiled in the disputes. Venkata and his brother had them arrested on the charge that they were using their position to extort commissions from people who dealt with the Company. Though the brahmins had also done the same thing, they were not arrested, while Timmanna and his associate were fined, which Greenhill again saw as an expression of Baker's personal antagonism towards himself.[60]

---

58. Letter from Fort St George to Surat, 5 February 1653, *EFI* 1651–54, p. 155.
59. President Baker's Award, 5 November 1652, *ibid.*, pp. 135–136.
60. Greenhill's remonstrance to President Baker, 1 March 1654, *ibid.*, p. 235.

This is the first mention we have of Timmanna, another remarkable merchant capitalist of his time. Even in 1646, he was referred to as the native head in the affairs of the English Agent, that is, Greenhill. He had built two temples, dedicated to Chennakesava Perumal and Chenna Mallikesvarar, known as the town pagodas.[61] One of the many accusations levied against Timmanna was that in order to maintain these temples—as well as the Triplicane temple of which he was a trustee—he was levying a cess on the townspeople, besides rallying the right-hand weavers and artisans in support of Seshadri Nayak.[62]

This entire episode serves to emphasise the fact that merchant capitalists derived their status, influence and authority from their social relations as much as from commerce. This social leadership had to be validated in a number of ways. One was by making endowments to construct temples, and controlling their administration and finances. By becoming patrons of the pivotal institution of local society, the social status of the merchants was consolidated and reaffirmed. These powers of patronage also entitled them to be the acknowledged leaders of their castes, as well as of the collective affiliated castes of the right and the left sides. It was their social position that gave the merchant capitalists legitimacy, while their economic activity was the instrument which enabled them to achieve this social position.

We next hear of Timmanna in 1661, when it was alleged that Agent Winter and "Timana (a black servant)" made all the decisions, while the Fort St George Council was completely ignored. Timmanna was accused of monopolising all the rice in Madras, which increased the price so much that all the artisans were discouraged from moving to the town.[63] Beri Timmanna and his partner Kasi Viranna (another great merchant capitalist) were the chief merchants to the Company, in charge of their cloth trade. Timmanna, "the Company's ancient broker", was considered to be the "only [person] experienced and to

---

61. Love, *Vestiges*, vol. 1: pp. 93–95. Love mentions that one "Nagapattan", a gunpowder maker, is also credited with the construction of the temple. This seems very far-fetched. The Beri family continued to manage the temple for several generations.
62. The Brahmans' declaration, 4 April 1654, *EFI* 1651–54, pp. 258–262; Love, *Vestiges*, vol. 1: pp. 126–129, 140–141.
63. Rev. William Isaacson to the Company, *EFI* 1661–64, p. 58; Love, *Vestiges*, vol. 1: pp. 179–180.

be trusted" at a time when cloth supplies were very poor,[64] and who also financed the Company's trade by lending them money. By 1664, Timmanna got into trouble with the irascible Winter. Being regarded as Winter's man did not prevent the latter from erecting gallows in the town and threatening to hang Timmanna on it, by which Winter extorted 15,000 pounds from Timmanna.[65] Timmanna was clearly too powerful to be popular with the English, as the snide remark about the all-powerful "black servant" indicates.

In 1665 Agent Foxcroft, convinced that Winter, Timmanna and Kasi Viranna, all three were defrauding the Company in many ways, arrested Timmanna and Viranna.[66] Here, once again, the unstated, real reason for this action was the enmity between Foxcroft and Winter (who gained fame by overthrowing Foxcroft in 1666 in a coup, the only one in the history of Fort St George), and the merchants were caught in the crossfire. Winter—his differences with Timmanna now forgotten—wrote that Timmanna's influence was very great, and that his friendship with the Golkonda governors had been of much use to the Company. If he made a profit on the cloth trade by buying cloth at prices lower than the contracted price at which he supplied the Company, this was quite legitimate. Winter also pointed out that without Timmanna, no other merchant would come forward to contract with the English and that when he had been removed as the choultry justice, customs revenue had also fallen.[67]

The dependence of the English on Beri Timmanna and Kasi Viranna was acknowledged by Foxcroft himself after he was reinstated as the governor of Fort St George. He wrote that "we have thought it a point of wisdom in respect of the main business of investment, for the present to waive any former matters and to encourage them to come in". The results fully justified this step, and the trade of the city picked up considerably as weavers and washers began to return to Madras.[68] In spite of the obvious uncer

---

64. Fort St George Consultation, 4 August 1662, EFI 1661–64, pp. 165–66, 167 fn.
65. Letter from Court of Committees, 16 December 1663, ibid., p. 365. Winter himself claimed that he had imprisoned Timmanna and threatened to hang him because he had learnt that Timmanna had employed people to "bewitch" Winter to death. Ibid., p. 388.
66. A private letter, 1 July 1665, EFI 1665–67, p. 117.
67. Winter to the Company, 9 January 1666, ibid., p. 132.
68. Letter from Foxcroft to Masulipatnam, 19 October, 1668; Letter to the Company, 12 November 1668, EFI 1668–69, pp. 141, 145.

tainties and hazards of being too closely identified with the English, and the entirely capricious treatment which they received, the Coromandel merchants emerge as the ultimate survivors in this process.

Chief merchants and joint-stock companies

All these episodes in fact highlight the inherent contradictions which the Europeans had to come to terms with in a system which employed chief merchants to be in charge of all their trade. While the Europeans were aware that they could not carry on their trade without the help of the merchants, they were also wary of trusting to just a few merchants.[69] The posthumous tribute paid by the Dutch to Malaya Chetti in fact encapsulates the symbiotic relationship between the European companies and the merchant capitalists who became their chief merchants. For the local merchants, one of the main attractions of dealing with the Europeans was that their demand for cloth and other export goods was very large, and there were obvious advantages in dealing with a single big buyer. For instance, the total annual value of Dutch exports from the Coromandel rose from about 200,000 guilders in the 1620s to 500,000 guilders in the 1630s, to well over 1,300,000 guilders in the 1640s and to almost 2,000,000 guilders in the late 1660s.[70]

Why the Europeans needed a chief merchant, in spite of all their suspicions, is explained in a somewhat woeful letter from Fort St George in 1642. They explained that they were aware that by dealing directly with poor weavers and painters they had incurred several losses due to bad debts, but that this could not be avoided unless they had "one pri[me] merchant as have the Dutch who secures all." They themselves had had one chief merchant for some time, but he had left Madras "when he saw we had more occasion to borrow of him

---

69. The English factors were told that while the Komatis had always been reliable and that Malaya was the biggest merchant, they would do well if they also dealt with some smaller Komatis, which would help corroborate the information from Malaya. Instructions from Batavia, 27 March 1624, *EFI* 1624–29, p. 9.
70. Kanakalatha Mukund, "Coromandel Trade and Economy in the Seventeenth Century: Some Insights from Dutch Records" (paper presented at the seminar on Non-English European Sources of Indian History, Nehru Institute of Social Sciences, Pune, March 1994), table 1.
1 pagoda = 84 to 90 stuivers = 4.2 to 4.5 guilders. 14 March and 27 May 1637, *DR*, vol. 4, pp. 88, 265.

to feed ourselves than any way to drive a trade".[71] The merchant capitalist followed the remorseless logic of all trade, and would supply only to a large buyer. He would put up with other hazards, including threats to his person, provided the stakes were high enough, but indigent foreigners struggling to survive were not an attractive prospect.

The Dutch did not have a chief merchant to succeed Chinnanna. Over a period of time, and especially as their textile exports to Asia and Europe grew, they also discovered the problems of dealing with smaller merchants. The total resources of these merchants could not match the resources of the merchant capitalist, and therefore they ended up quite hopelessly behind on their contracts and in debt to the Dutch. The Dutch wrote off the desperate debts, and tried to recover 15 to 20 per cent of the money against new contracts each year.

Faced with the problem of erratic supplies on the one hand, and the rising demand for fine textiles from Holland, on the other, Governor Laurens Pit decided in the 1650s to form in Pulicat a "head company" of suppliers who were jointly to provide just the fine cotton fabric which the Dutch called "ternatanes". This improved deliveries to such an extent that such companies were formed for other fabrics as well. The merchants "shared" the capital, and by thus pooling their resources, they were able to trade on credit up to 70,000 to 80,000 guilders for a few months at a time, whereas individually their credit worth was negligible.[72] Pit's successor Cornelis Speelman extended this arrangement to several other varieties of textiles like painted cloth, cloth with gold thread and other types of cloth.[73] These contracts were also extended to other towns. In 1665 such companies were formed both among the textile producers—the dyers of Nagapattinam and Nagore, the weavers of Porvacheri, the weavers of Tirumalairayanpattinam—and the merchants of Nagapattinam and Tevanampattinam. The latter companies had a capital stock of 3,600 pagodas and 7,600 pagodas respectively.[74]

This innovation was also adopted by the English a few years later, with some modifications. They insisted that their contract merchants

---

71. Letter to the Company, 20 September 1642, *EFI* 1642–45, p. 46.
72. The Memorie of Laurens Pit, 1663, pp. 4 ff. Dutch Coromandel Records, Tamil Nadu State Archives.
73. The Memorie of Cornelis Speelman, 1665, pp. 35–39. Dutch Coromandel Records.
74. Agreements with weavers and merchants, 17, 24, 27 and 30 April 1665; 4 and 18 May 1665. Abstracts.

should come together in a joint-stock company, all holding shares in it and subscribing to its capital stock, which would be used in cloth procurement. This would release the Company of the necessity of making advances to the merchants and also increase the accountability of the chief merchants to the other merchants involved in the textile trade, while simultaneously diluting their control.

These experimental reincarnations of "European" organisational forms had excited much academic attention earlier, and both Raychaudhuri and Arasaratnam were convinced that if this experiment had succeeded, it would have had the potential to modernise the Indian economy.[75] Arasaratnam subsequently reconsidered his earlier stand and came to the conclusion that partnership trading was a common practice among the Coromandel merchants. What was innovative was that the initiative came from the buyers.[76] Brennig's analysis indicates the irrelevance of the earlier views of Raychaudhuri and Arasaratnam, ignoring as they do the fact that there was a basic difference in the approach of the Dutch and the English in the way they organised the joint stocks, which was due to their differing requirements from Coromandel trade. The modernisation argument also overlooks the fact that most Indian merchants responded favourably to this new form of organisation because of the monopoly it gave them over the trade of the Europeans.[77]

It is worthwhile to enlarge on Brennig's observation in a slightly modified form. The Dutch introduced the system mainly because of the problems they faced in the absence of a chief merchant who would have had the necessary resources to manage a large contract. The English introduced the system in order to control their chief merchants, because the English were suspicious of the few merchants who dominated trade as well as the other smaller merchants. However, unlike the Dutch, the English were not willing to dispense with the institution of the chief merchant altogether. As we shall see later, this

---

75. Raychaudhuri, *Jan Company*, pp. 147–148. Arasaratnam, "Indian Merchants and their Trading Methods (circa 1700)", *Indian Economic and Social History Review* 3, no. 1. 1966, pp. 86–90, and "Aspects of the Role and Activities of South Indian Merchants, c. 1650–1750, in *Proceedings of the First International Conference of Tamil Studies* (Kuala Lampur: International Association of Tamil Research, 1966), vol. 1: pp. 588–591.
76. Arasaratnam, *Merchants, Companies and Commerce*, p. 240.
77. J. J. Brennig, "Joint-Stock Companies of Coromandel", in *Age of Partnership*, ed. Blair B. Kling and M. N. Pearson (Honolulu: The University Press of Hawaii, 1979), pp. 71–96.

did not really change the power equations among the merchant classes, and the dominant merchants continued to control the other merchants even within the restrictions of the joint-stock companies.

The advent of the Europeans into the trading world of the Coromandel merchant certainly widened its horizons. By providing the Europeans the necessary access to not only the local economy but also the ruling classes and centres of power, the dominant class of merchant capitalists was able to enlarge its own sphere of influence—both as an economic and as a social class. The contemporary political scene, with all its attendant chaos, also contributed to the process in two ways. The rapidly weakening central authority of Vijayanagar contributed to the rise of smaller local centres of power where the rich merchants could play a larger role. Conversely, the visibility of these merchants made them easier targets for extortion at a time when feuding chiefs with very small resource areas needed more money. This in turn drove the merchants towards the Europeans to seek an outlet for their commercial and social ambitions.

SIX

Textile Trade (1670–1750): Structurally Fragmented Markets and Prices

After the first quarter of the seventeenth century, in our analysis, the trade of the merchant capitalists in the Coromandel becomes virtually synonymous with the merchants' participation in textile trade, mainly because this was the focal point of their interaction with the Europeans. Textile trade primarily functioned as two different markets—one, where the Europeans and the local merchants were the negotiating parties and the other, where the primary producers negotiated with the merchants. The European market was essentially an "artificial" market, where prices were determined by many considerations other than the natural interaction of demand and supply. In contrast, the other market may be considered to be a more "natural" market where competitive buying and selling took place. The coexistence of the two markets governed by widely varying factors, can be described as "structural fragmentation".

Merchants were the essential link and common factor between these two markets, and it is necessary to explore the functioning of both markets to understand textile trade and all its ramifications. The availability of time-series data of the textile prices paid by the English and of total quantities demanded by them enable us to study the movement of prices and their relationship to the "natural" variables—demand on the one hand, and input prices on the supply side, on the other.

Price revolution in India: A review

Prices and price movements are generally explained in terms of the various factors which contribute to an upward or downward movement of prices. Among the most persuasive and pervasive theories of prices are those which link price movements with money supply and the volume of money in circulation, which for the period under study would mean the quantity of silver or gold in circulation. These theories, generally referred to as the quantity theory of money, were in vogue even during the sixteenth and seventeenth centuries.[1] Based on Irving Fisher's theory of money, these theories have been rearticulated and redefined in the present century, with the proposition of a general, destabilising inflation or 'price revolution' in Europe after the sixteenth century caused by the influx of silver from America.

Though some historians have expressed reservations about the validity of the hypothesis of a general price rise in seventeenth-century Europe,[2] a similar theory has been posited by historians of Mughal India. According to them, there was a general price rise in the Mughal empire after 1600 fuelled by the inflow of American silver in the seventeenth century.[3] In a further refinement of this basic proposition, Habib has more recently argued that the general price rise was the result of a two-stage transition—first, the gradual replacement of copper by silver as the medium of exchange in post-Akbar Mughal India, and second, a general fall in the value of silver as the capacity of the monetary system to absorb the silver was exhausted.[4] While this theory has been questioned almost from the beginning,[5]

---

1. Joseph A. Schumpeter, *History of Economic Analysis* (London: George Allen & Unwin, 1954), pp. 311–317.
2. Carlo M. Cipolla says of the label "Price Revolution" that the "'average general level of prices' is an extremely ambiguous statistical abstraction" which does not explain how in the same market prices of different commodities moved in different ways. *Before the Industrial Revolution* (New York: W. W. Norton & Co, 1976), p. 211.

  For a brief review of the historical application of Fisher's theory of money and the ongoing discussions of the 'price revolution' outside Europe, see Sanjay Subrahmanyam, ed., introduction to *Money and the Market in India, 1100–1700*, Oxford in India Readings: Themes in Indian History (Delhi: Oxford University Press, 1994), pp. 43–49, especially footnotes 72 and 73.

3. Irfan Habib, *The Agrarian System of Mughal India* (Bombay: Allied Publishers, 1963), pp. 81–89 and Aziza Hasan, "The Silver Currency Output of the Mughal Empire and Prices in India during the 16th and 17th Centuries", reprint, in Subrahmanyam, *Money and the Market*, pp. 156–185.
4. Irfan Habib, "A System of Trimetallism in the Age of the 'Price Revolution': Effects of the Silver Influx on the Mughal Monetary System", in *The Imperial Monetary System of India*, ed. J. F. Richards (Delhi: Oxford University Press, 1987), pp. 137–159.
5. Subrahmanyam, introduction to *Money and the Market*, pp. 50–52; "Precious Metal Flows and Prices in Western and Southern Asia, 1500–1750: Some Comparative

the alternative framework suggested by Om Prakash has not received sufficient attention. His argument is that imports of bullion into India were, after all, in exchange for commodities produced in the country, and, as such, would stimulate the economy to further expansion and higher levels of production.[6]

If money supply is taken to be an exogenous variable, prices and price movements can also be explained in terms of endogenous factors. On the supply side, the most important would be the cost of production. In pre-industrial economic and social organisation, this was primarily accounted for by labour and material costs. Since wages were kept close to subsistence, foodgrain prices are used as a proxy for wages and a major determinant of production costs. The selling price of a commodity in any market would in turn be determined by the basic cost of production, transit costs (cost of transportation and internal customs), brokerage fees paid to intermediaries at the buying/selling markets, and the percentage appropriated by merchants. Of these, the basic input costs are taken to be the important determinants of long-term price trends. Transit costs, especially internal customs, would be a secondary factor which explained year to year, short-term fluctuations, since these costs reflected the existing political conditions of stability or instability.

Chaudhuri notes that there were two divergent views in contemporary (seventeenth-century) Europe on price movements in India. While theorists in Europe were often alarmed that the sustained export of precious metals to Asia would eventually lead to higher prices, paradoxically, the East India Company officials in India, with local experience, always related price movements to the prices of cotton and foodgrains, which in turn were determined by the harvests and political conditions.[7] The limitation of linking prices only to production costs is that it does not take into account demand-side factors in determining prices, nor does it distinguish between factors contributing to short-term fluctuations and long-term trends. The effects of demand and changes in the volume of demand (given the

---

and Conjunctural Aspects" in *ibid.*, pp. 203–204. The criticisms relate both to the assumption that the silver which came in was only American silver, and to the extremely scanty and scattered price data which have been used to support this hypothesis.
6. Prakash, *Dutch East India Company*, pp. 248–256.
7. K. N. Chaudhuri, *The Trading World of Asia and the English East India Company, 1660–1760* (Cambridge: Cambridge University Press, 1978), p. 99.

Textile Trade: Structurally Fragmented Markets and Prices

limits to productivity and levels of output under the slowly changing technology of the time and the consequent pressure on resources like raw materials and labour availability) have to be incorporated into a general understanding of long-term price movements.

When we come to the disaggregated level of prices in different regions within India, there is no uniform pattern to be seen, nor can a hypothesis of an overall price rise be sustained.[8] There is no extensive study of prices for the southern Coromandel (i.e., the region extending south from Pulicat, corresponding to the present-day state of Tamil Nadu). Chaudhuri presents a composite graph of the weighted moving average price of 'Madras' textiles from 1670 to 1760. He finds that there was a gradual price rise in the period which was similar to the movements of the prices of cotton textiles in Gujarat and Bengal, and of raw silk and saltpetre.[9]

Arasaratnam also supports the proposition of a general price rise in the Coromandel from 1650–1740. He divides this period into two sub-periods, the first up to 1690 which experienced a stable price level with a gradual upward movement, and the second after 1690 which witnessed both violent fluctuations in prices and a continuing rising trend in the prices of basic commodities—rice and cotton.[10] Arasaratnam bases his conclusions on the very scattered evidence of the price of rice at different places and at different points of time, but makes no allowance for the possibility of either interregional variations or intertemporal fluctuations of prices in premodern markets which were spatially fragmented. It is also not clear how he has converted the then current volumetric units for foodgrains into weight equivalents.[11]

Movement of prices in the Coromandel region

To test the validity of the hypothesis of a sustained upward movement of prices with reference to the Coromandel region, the prices of three

8. For a capsule review of works on different regions—Bengal, Surat, Masulipatnam and Agra—see Subrahmanyam, "Precious Metal Flows", pp. 205–209.
9. Chaudhuri, *Trading World of Asia*, p. 100 ff.
10. Arasaratnam, *Merchants, Companies and Commerce*, pp. 335–339.
11. In the Tamil country, foodgrain was commonly measured in volumetric units of *padi, marakkal,* and *karisai* (measure, mercall and garce in the English records). 8 padi = 1 marakkal and 400 marakkal = 1 karisai. Further, these units were not standardised in all areas. These measures, in fact, continued to be in use until the 1950s when India switched over to the metric system.

commodities—cotton textiles, raw cotton and foodgrains (paddy) —and the relative prices of gold and silver between 1670 and 1750 are taken up for analysis. Since the only time-series of prices available are the prices listed in the English East India Company records, it would be useful to begin with a brief sketch of the method followed by the Company while drawing up contracts with the Indian merchants for the supply of cloth.

The standard practice of the English in their textile contracts with the local merchants was to give lists of the varieties and quantities of the textiles they needed and arrive at the prices at which the textiles would be supplied. Several varieties, especially longcloth and salempores, which for the major part of the period accounted for the bulk of the exports, came in different qualities of fineness, and different prices were specified for the ordinary, medium and fine varieties. These variations in fineness were not haphazard, but were specifically manufactured to ensure a high degree of product differentiation. The fineness depended on the yarn count *(punjam)* as well as the fineness of the yarn used in weaving.

Since all the cloth that came in would not be of uniform quality, a further gradation was made when the cloth was sorted and numbered according to variations in quality. Prices were then adjusted accordingly, with a standard reduction for each grade or number. For ordinary longcloth, this reduction was usually 1 pagoda per score[12] for each lower 'number' of cloth, and for ordinary salempores, it was half a pagoda per score. Thus, the total and/or average value of any cargo of cloth would depend on the varying quantities of different grades and varieties of textiles, and this information is not available from the general records of Fort St George.[13]

---

12. South India was on a gold-based currency system, and in the southern region the coins in circulation were *varahan, panam* (both gold) and *kasu* (copper). In the European records these coins are referred to as pagoda, fanam and cash, and the same terms are used throughout the text for the sake of simplicity. The English had standardised the currency equivalencies as 80 cash = 1 fanam, 36 fanam = 1 pagoda, which prevailed upto the 1750s, and these have been followed here, though there were many local variations in these exchange values.

During the seventeenth century the pagoda was valued at 9 shillings, which was depreciated to 8 shillings sometime after 1720. 1 pagoda was the equivalent of about 3.5 rupees, though the exchange value fluctuated between 3.05 and 3.75 (table 6.7).

The score of 20 pieces ("corge") was a normally used unit in the textile trade, though the origins of this term are not clear.

13. It is therefore a puzzle as to how Chaudhuri has arrived at the weighted moving average of textile prices.

Textile Trade: Structurally Fragmented Markets and Prices

Table 6.1 gives the prices of cotton textiles at Madras. Since longcloth and salempores (ordinary) together constituted the bulk of the textile exports of the English, the price series for these two fabrics have been taken as being indicative of general textile prices.[14]

Table 6.1: English Textile Trade in Southern Coromandel

	Prices at Madras (Pagodas per score)				Total quantity contracted				
	Longcloth		Salempore		Pagodas			Number of pieces		
Year	Con-tract	Actual	Con-tract	Actual	Madras	Fort St David	Total	Madras	Fort St David	Total
1674	27.50	27.50	12.00	12.00	80,000		80,000			
1676	27.50	27.50	12.00	12.00				99,300		99,300
1677	27.50	26.12	12.00	11.40	74,000		74,000			
1678	27.50	25.70	12.00	11.22				119,000		119,000
1679	27.50	25.85	12.00	11.28						
1680	27.50	25.85	12.00	11.28				118,000		118,000
1681	27.50	25.85	12.00	11.28				134,000		134,000
1684								72,400		72,400
1685					60,000		60,000	47,400		47,400
1686					12,000	80,000	92,000			
1688	25.55	25.55	11.14	11.14	40,000		40,000			
1692	25.55	27.59	11.14	12.03	40,000	10,000	50,000			
1693	27.50	27.50	12.00	12.00	27,000	20,000	47,000			
1694	25.55	28.10	11.14	12.25	20,000		20,000			
1695	25.55	28.10	11.14	12.25	15,000		15,000			
1696	27.50	30.80	12.00	13.44	20,000	20,000	40,000			
1697	27.50	30.80	12.00	13.44	52,560		52,560			
1698	27.50	34.37	12.00	15.00	60,000	27,000	87,000			
1699	34.00	34.00	16.50	16.50	151,125		151,125	87,500		87,500
1700	34.00	34.00	16.50	16.50	150,000	30,000	180,000	85,500		
1701	34.00	36.04	15.90	16.84	196,278			105,500	32,000	137,500
1702	34.00	36.04	15.90	16.84					62,600	62,600
1704	34.00	31.96	16.00	15.04		170,000		48,000		
1705	31.00	31.00	15.00	15.00				51,800	60,500	112,300
1706	31.50	31.50	14.50	14.50		50,000		49,000	37,000	86,000
1707	31.50	31.50	14.50	14.50	121,000			77,600	104,000	181,600
1708	31.50	31.50	14.50	14.50		40,000		10,720	31,250	41,970

Contd...

14. These data have been taken from the Public Consultations, Fort St George Records, (hereafter PC) and Fort St David Consultations, Records of South Arcot District, (hereafter FSDC), Tamil Nadu State Archives.

Table 6.1 contd...

Year	Prices at Madras (Pagodas per score)				Total quantity contracted					
	Longcloth		Salempore		Pagodas			Number of pieces		
	Contract	Actual	Contract	Actual	Madras	Fort St David	Total	Madras	Fort St David	Total
1709	31.50	29.92	14.50	13.77		85,000	85,000		62,500	62,500
1710	31.50	29.92	14.50	13.77		50,000		95,540	38,940	134,480
1711	31.50	29.92	14.50	13.77	54,439			41,465	61,500	102,965
1712	31.50	29.92	14.50	14.50				57,000	54,510	111,510
1713	31.50	28.35	14.50	13.05						
1714	31.50	33.07	14.50	15.22				98,000	52,680	150,680
1715	31.50	33.07	14.50	15.22				58,000	64,600	122,600
1716	31.50	33.07	14.50	15.22						
1717	31.50	33.07	14.50	15.22				76,350		76,350
1718	31.50	33.07	14.50	15.22				96,000		96,000
1719	31.50	33.07	14.50	15.22				142,400		142,400
1720	31.50	31.50	14.50	14.50	117,119			98,680	115,900	214,580
1721	31.50	31.50	14.50	14.50	254,539		254,539	210,600		210,600
1723	31.50	31.50	14.50	14.50				138,928	186,700	325,628
1724	31.50	31.50	14.50	14.50				160,405	182,700	343,105
1725	31.50	31.50	14.50	14.50	109,381	146,785	256,166	82,230	127,480	209,710
1727	31.50	31.50			135,773		135,773	76,385		76,385
1728	31.50	31.50	14.50	14.50						
1729	31.50	31.50	14.50	14.50						
1730	33.50	33.50								
1732	39.50	39.50	16.80	16.80						
1733	39.50	39.50	19.00	19.00						
1734	39.50	39.50	19.50	19.50						
1735	39.50	39.50	16.87	16.87				72,580		72,580
1736	39.50	39.50	16.87	16.87				54,220		54,220
1737	39.50	39.50	16.87	16.87						
1738	39.50	39.50	19.00	19.00				67,380		67,380
1739	39.50	39.50								
1740	40.00	40.00			86,920		86,920	36,477		36,477
1749	42.00	42.00	19.00	19.00						
1750	43.00	43.00	19.00	19.00						

Source: PC and FSDC. In some cases the prices at Fort St David are taken as the price at Madras also, since the prices rarely varied.

One peculiar feature of the cloth trade in the region was the use of a stated reference price and an actual price negotiated with respect to the reference price. While the former held steady for several years at a stretch, the actual prices would show greater year to year fluctuations, and therefore the actual prices arrived at each year are also given for both varieties.

The total *contracted* quantities of cloth at Madras and at Fort St David (Tevanampattinam, near Cuddalore) are given both in value and by the number of pieces.[15] In spite of the obvious limitation of gaps in the data, the broad trends of expansion or contraction of demand for cloth, by the English East India Company, as well as the general price movement are quite clear. These can be used to establish the causal relationship, if any, between demand and prices. It must also be remembered that these are prices which were arrived at on the basis of negotiations between a monopsonistic buyer (the English) and monopolistic sellers (the merchants). They may not always reflect the prices which would prevail in an open market where there is free play of supply and demand.

Grain and cotton prices

Whether any significant correlation exists between the price of textiles and the prices of inputs—labour and raw material—would depend, as Chaudhuri has pointed out, upon the relative weights of raw-material prices and wages in the production cost.[16] The prices of paddy and cotton are given in tables 6.2 and 6.3.

While the data do not indicate the relative shares, it can be deduced that labour cost was a significant element in production cost, and that wages were closely linked to foodgrain prices. Even when the Fort St George Council urged the merchants to reduce the prices of textiles because cotton had become cheaper, the latter would refuse on the grounds that grain was still expensive. This meant that the "price of labour" had to be increased, for otherwise the "manufacturers" would not be able to support their families.[17] This was not so much

---

15. Details on prices and quantities are not available for each year, and there are some unavoidable gaps in table 6.1. For some years, only the total number of bales is given. Though this indicates the trends in exports, it is not possible to convert this into an estimated number of pieces, since the number of pieces per bale would depend on the dimensions as well as the texture (fine, medium or ordinary) of the piecegood. (For instance, 100 pieces of fine salempores constituted 1 bale. For ordinary salempores this was 80 pieces; for fine longcloth 40 pieces and for ordinary longcloth 30 pieces.) Textiles like neckcloths, which were of very small dimensions, have not been included in table 6.1, since the very large number of pieces would distort the quantity/value ratio.
16. Chaudhuri, *Trading World of Asia*, p. 266.
17. Reply of Sunku Rama Chetti and other merchants to the President and Council, Fort St George, PC, 3 February 1718.

Table 6.2: Prices of Paddy in Madras and Fort St David, 1693–1750 (marakkals per pagoda)

Year	Madras	Fort St David
1693	24–26	
1694	14–13	
1695	10.5	
1696 (Feb)	10	
1696 (May)	20–21	
1702	45	26.66
1703 (Feb)	35	
1703 (Aug)	38–40	
1709	14–15	22.5
1711	17	
1712	14	
1720	20–22	
1729	13–12	
1735		20.25
1736		24.75
1738		16.66
1741	15.9	
1742	17.4	
1743	13.8	
1747		10
1750	10	7–10

Source: PC and FSDC.
Note: The prices have been standardised in terms of marakkals per pagoda, which is the most commonly used unit of reference. Rice prices generally were double paddy prices. The marakkal was standardised at 800 cubic inches in 1846. Henry Yule and A. C. Burnell, *Hobson-Jobson: The Anglo-Indian Dictionary,* new ed., ed. W. Crooke (1903; reprint, Delhi: Munshiram Manoharlal, 1968), p. 567.

Table 6.3: Cotton Prices, 1670–1742

Year	(Pagoda/candy)
Pre-1672	9
1672	14–15*
1710 July	23
1710 August	25
1711	26
1712	24*
1716	30
1733	24
1737	More than 30
1740	24
1742	23–26**

Source: PC and FSDC.
* Prices in Visakhapatnam.
** Rs 80 to 90 per candy, at Rs 3.5 per pagoda.

a question of wages immediately adjusting to the cost of living, or of the producer passing on these increases smoothly to the consumer, but that of wages being maintained so close to subsistence that any increase in the foodgrain price automatically increased wages. More importantly, foodgrain shortages disrupted production severely since artisans and other labourers tended to migrate en masse in order to survive the famine, which left many areas depopulated.

In order to have a better idea of the movement of grain prices, the years of foodgrain shortage and famine in the period 1678 to 1750 are indicated in table 6.4. This supplements the data on grain prices in table 6.2. The prices of paddy show no statistically significant trend over this period. If the prices of paddy are compared to the textile prices for the corresponding years, a positive correlation is seen, but this also is not statistically significant.

Table 6.4: Years of Grain Shortage in Madras

1678
1685–87*
1694–96
1709*
1711–12*
1718–19*
1727–30*
1733–38*
1743
1750

Source: PC and FSDC.
*denotes widespread famine in the region.

Two characteristics stand out: first, the frequent recurrence of droughts, famines and grain shortages not only in Madras but in the entire southern region (table 6.4), and second, the tendency for prices to fluctuate widely between years of plenty and shortage, and from place to place at any given point of time. This is evidenced by the fall in prices by half in Madras within a period of three months (between February and May 1696) and the difference between the prices at Madras and Fort St David in 1702 and 1709 (table 6.2). Such fluctuations were very typical of price behaviour in the entire region.[18] A similar pattern without any definitive long-term rising

---

18. Sarada Raju notes the same characteristic in her study of Madras Presidency in the first half of the nineteenth century. *Economic Conditions in the Madras Presidency, 1800–1850* (Madras: University of Madras, 1942), pp. 225–226.

trend in rice prices has also been noted for Tanjavur in the latter half of the eighteenth century.[19]

The trends in grain price movements in Madras becomes clearer from graph 1. Two patterns can be seen in two sub-periods: first, from the 1690s till the 1720s when there were violent price changes, but with an overall lower average price; and second, after 1729 when the range of prices was narrower, but with a general upward shift in prices which varied around an average at a higher plateau. This rising price trend in Madras continued till the 1800s[20] after which there was a secular decline in the price of rice.[21]

The very scanty evidence on cotton prices (table 6.3) suggests a definite increase between 1672 and 1710 over the pre-1672 price level. Between 1711 and 1750, cotton prices, when high, averaged 24 to 26 pagodas per candy (500 lb), and occasionally even went as high as 30 pagodas or more. A comparison of the periods of high and low prices of cotton (table 6.3) and conditions of cotton supply (table 6.5), with the fluctuations in the volume of textiles supplied to the English East India Company (table 6.6) show almost no correspondence between expansion and contraction of the latter and the availability of cotton.

Table 6.5: Conditions of Cotton Supply, 1672–1746

1672–81	Cotton shortage
1697	Cotton shortage
1700–01	Cotton prices high
1705–06	Cotton prices higher by 30–40%
1710	Cotton prices high
1716	Cotton prices cheaper
1717–19	Cotton prices cheaper
1729–30	Cotton prices higher
1733	No cotton in the market
1742	Cotton crops destroyed
1746	Cotton prices cheaper

Source: PC and FSDC.

19. Lalitha Iyer, "Trade and Finance on the Coromandel Coast, 1757–1853" (Ph.D. diss., University of Hyderabad, 1993), p. 23.
20. *Ibid.*, p. 122 ff. Iyer ascribes the high prices at Madras in the second half of the eighteenth century to the monopoly of the English merchants who supplied rice to Madras on fixed contracts.
21. Raju, *Madras Presidency,* pp. 228–229. In 1813, the price of rice in Madras was 5 marakkals per pagoda, or 10 marakkals for paddy, which was the same as in 1750. *Ibid.*, p. 277.

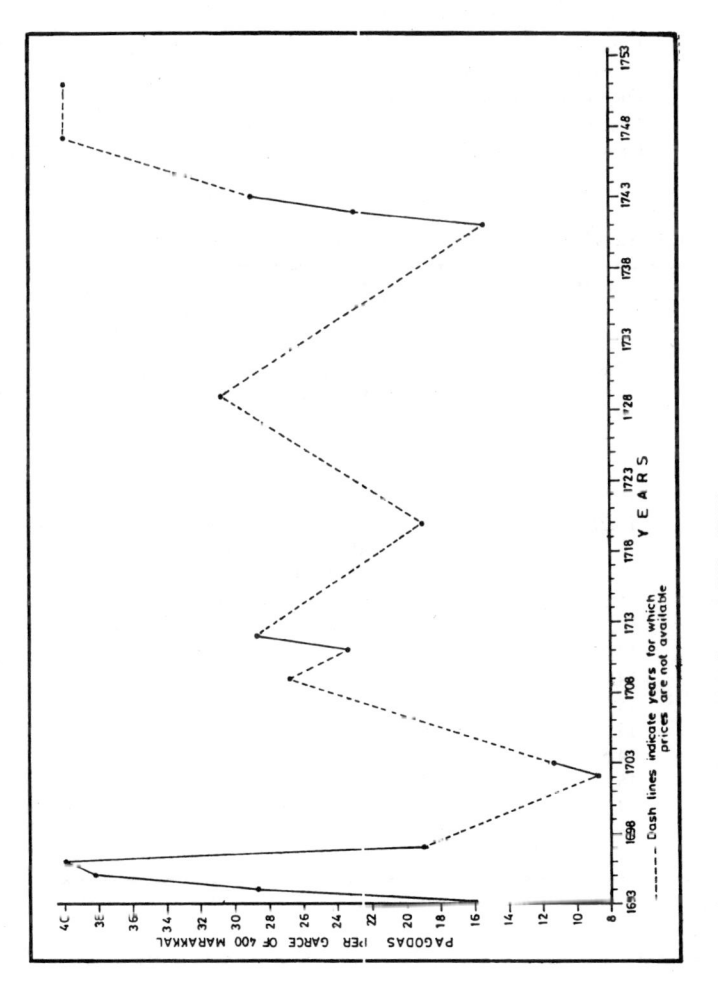

Textile Trade: Structurally Fragmented Markets and Prices

Graph 1. Grain Prices at Madras, 1693–1750
Prices are given per garce which was equal to 400 marakkals. Wherever there are two prices for the same year, the second price is given for the following year.

Table 6.6: Pattern of English Textile Trade, 1672–1750

1672–81	Expansion
1684–95	Contraction
1696–98	Moderate recovery and expansion
1699–1701	Expansion
1702–03	Contraction
1704–07	Expansion
1708–09	Sudden contraction
1710–15	Expansion
1716–18	Contraction
1719–25	High volume, peaking in 1723 and 1724
1726–39	Gradual decline
1740–50	Generally low volume

Source: Table 6.1.

Table 6.7: Silver Prices in Madras, 1680–1750

Year	Dollars/10 pagoda	Year	Rupees/100 pagoda
1680	15.5	1695	348.5
1681 (Nov)	16.75	1697	354
1681 (Dec)	16.825	1699 (Sep)	360
1685 (Jan)	16.5	1699 (Nov)	372
1685 (Aug)	17.31	1699 (Dec)	375
1689	17.25	1703	330
1704	17.125	1704	360
1706	16.5	1743	305–310
1711	16.25	1744	336.5–338
1717	15	1748	450**
1718 (May)	15.375	1750 (Feb)	375
1718 (Jun)	15.25	1750 (Mar)	360
1719	15.25		
1722	14.375		
1723 (Jul)	14.75		
1723 (Sep)	15		
1724	15		
1728	14.5		
1733	15		
1744 (Feb)	14.25		
1744 (May)	14.375		
1747	15.125*		

Source: PC and FSDC.
*At Fort St David.
**At Visakhapatnam.

Silver and gold prices

Since South India was on a gold currency system, the value of silver is given in terms of gold (table 6.7) to see if there was a significant fall in the value of silver or gold in the period, and to relate this to the price of textiles or foodgrains. As far as the silver value is concerned, it fell after 1680 and remained at a lower level till about 1711. After 1717, it fluctuated around the older exchange level of 1680. This rise in the silver value can be attributed to the greater demand for silver from the Mughal court, especially with the appointment of a Nawab at Arcot[22] and the wider use of the silver rupee. There was a significant fall in the value of pagodas after 1739, which was due to the debasement of the pagodas minted in the country mints.[23] This caused a serious disruption of trade since payment by pagodas was accepted only after discounting. Finally the English decided to introduce the "star" pagoda in 1741[24] which, after some time, became the standard currency throughout the South.

Silver and gold prices fluctuated, even in the short term, because of the relative shortage of one metal or the other. But it does not seem valid to talk in terms of a general "price rise" because of the fall in the value of the medium of currency. As we have seen, foodgrain prices do not show a statistically significant rising trend over the period, and while textile prices did rise, no contemporary English official of the East India Company ever related this rise to the supply or value of silver or gold.[25]

Textile prices and textile trade: By sub-periods

The regression result of the time-series of the actual prices of textiles shows a significant rising trend between 1670 and 1750. The graph of cotton textile prices at Madras (graph 2) shows two distinct periods of rising prices—one from 1696 to 1702, with a decline thereafter, and another from 1732 to 1750, with a pattern of peaks and troughs very similar to Chaudhuri's graph.[26] But this price rise cannot be explained generally in terms of an increase in either foodgrain prices or cotton prices—though of the two, foodgrain prices did have a greater impact on textile prices—nor in terms of the values of

22. PC, 23 January 1722/3 noted that the Nawab had returned to Arcot and his presence had raised the price of silver.
23. PC, 2 April 1739.
24. PC, 7 and 9 April, 14 June 1741.
25. Chaudhuri (*Trading World of Asia*, pp. 102, 108) also points out that the monetary explanation for the price rise needs much more evidence.
26. *Ibid.*, pp. 106–107, figs. 17, 18.

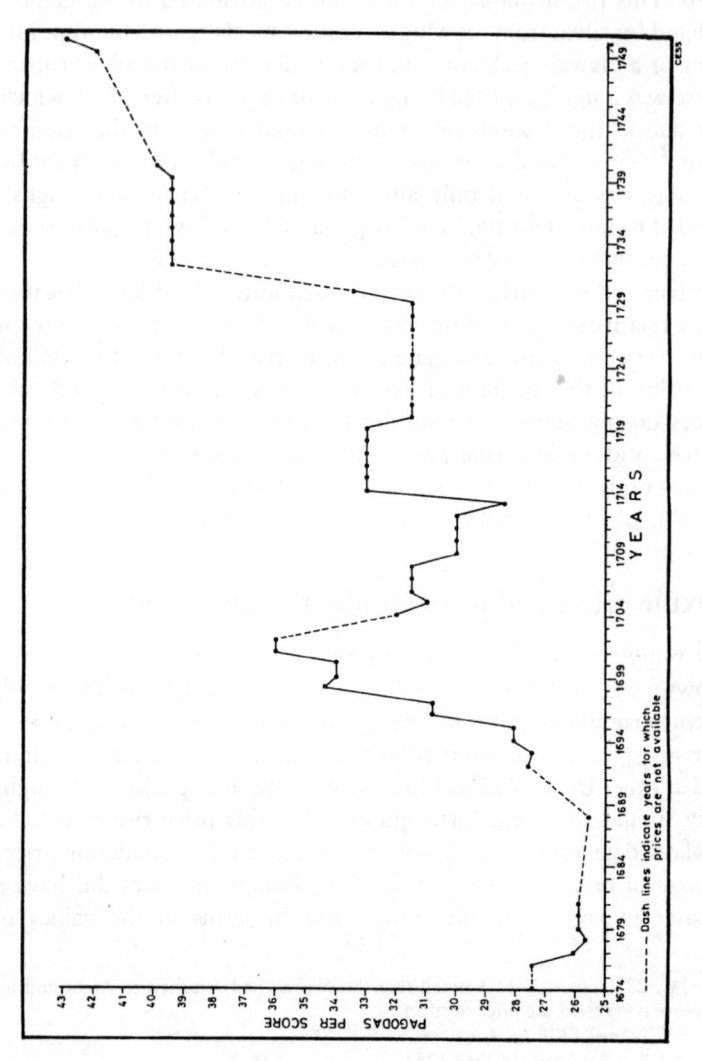

Graph 2. Prices of Longcloth at Madras, 1674–1750

precious metals. On the assumption that cloth prices were determined by a much more complex interaction of several exogenous factors, which also explained the expansion or contraction of the textile trade of the English East India Company, the trading conditions are examined in greater detail by dividing the period covered into sub-periods (table 6.6).

Textiles from southern Coromandel, as from all regions of India, were exported to several markets in East and West Asia, and from the middle of the seventeenth century, in increasing quantities to Europe. It is not possible to estimate the relative shares of the European and Asian markets at any given time, or over a period of time. However, if we assume the exports to Asia as given, the main variable which has to be taken into account is the additional European demand which rose very sharply after 1710. This strained production at all levels—at the level of availability of cotton and yarn, weavers' output, and the finishing processes. At a macro level this created a shortage of supply and pushed prices up.

1672–1683: The year 1683 was the last of a cycle of boom in the textile exports from the Coromandel to Europe, which was true for both the English and Dutch East India Companies. The average annual value of Dutch exports from the Coromandel (including north and south Coromandel), of which textiles constituted the major part, rose steadily from 1.5 million guilders in 1663–66 to 1.86 million in 1667–69, to a peak of 1.92 million in 1670–72. Exports remained high at 1.7 million guilders from 1675 to 1682 and reached a record high of 3.78 million guilders in 1686.[27]

Paradoxically, this expansion took place during a period of high prices and shortage of cotton. The weaving areas near Madras and Pulicat got their cotton from Bijapur. Before 1672, the price of cotton from Bijapur and Srikakulam used to be 9 pagodas per candy, but in 1671–72 the crop failed and the price rose by 55 per cent to 14 pagodas.[28] Throughout the rest of the decade there are frequent references to the high price and short supply of cotton and yarn. The Dutch investments were also very large in this period, because they were buying a wider range of grades of cloth, sending the first quality to Europe and the second and third to Macassar, the Spice Islands, Japan

---

27. All except the last figure are computed from the *Dagh Registers*. See Mukund, "Coromandel Trade", p. 14, table 2. For 1686, Arasaratnam, *Merchants, Companies and Commerce*, p. 150.
28. PC, 18 April and 14 June 1672.

and other Asian markets.[29] In spite of these factors which would normally be expected to raise the price, the English were able to negotiate lower prices of cotton textiles during 1677–81 and insist on a rebate which was normally 5 or 6 per cent of the reference price (see table 6.1).[30] The value of the rebate was taken to be the implicit interest on the money advanced by the Fort St George Council to the merchants for procuring cloth.

In addition to the high price of cotton, there were several other factors in this period which normally would have been expected to depress the cloth trade. One was the attack by the soldiers of Madanna, the powerful minister of Golkonda, on the English company's merchants in Karedu (to the north of Nellore) and other cloth-producing villages where the Madras merchants had paid advances to the weavers. The advances had to be written off because the weavers had all run away in panic.[31] This episode was symptomatic of the generally poor state of law and order in the peripheral areas of the Golkonda kingdom in its twilight days, and it was also one of the many factors which could have caused short-term disruptions in supply. Another was the sudden death in 1680 of Kasi Viranna, the chief merchant and the acknowledged leader of the local merchant community. After his death, a disruptive dispute broke out among the Company merchants regarding their internal accounts, and it was more than one year before the entire tangle could be sorted out and the former chief merchants reinstated.[32]

In spite of the trend of growth of English exports which the numbers indicate, the cotton shortage and, perhaps more important, the prices kept low by hard bargaining were factors which limited the supply of cloth to the English Company. Quite often, the quantity that the merchants agreed to supply was less than half of what the Company wanted to purchase.[33] The shortage and high price of

---

29. Merchants' representation to the President and Council, Fort St George, PC, 29 September 1674.
30. In 1678, Streynsham Master, the then President, Fort St George, was able to negotiate a reduction of 6.5 per cent, which he felt was a personal triumph he had scored over the local merchants, and especially the chief merchant, Kasi Viranna. *The Diaries of Streynsham Master, 1675–1680*, ed. R. C. Temple (London: John Murray, 1911), vol. 1: p. 71.
31. PC, 28 September 1675.
32. PC, 12 and 14 July 1681.
33. In 1676, the Company had ordered an investment of 202,400 pieces, while the merchants agreed to supply only 99,300 at Madras. In 1681, against 298,000 pieces, they contracted for 134,000. PC, 21 July 1676; 20 July 1681.

cotton continued till 1681, but 1682 and 1683 were both boom years with the merchants bringing in cloth faster than what Fort St George was able to pay for.[34]

To what extent the merchants were able to squeeze the producers by passing on to them the burden of lower cloth prices and higher demand for cloth in a period of high prices and shortage of cotton is difficult to ascertain. The Dutch were able to keep up their investments because they were offering 10 per cent higher prices than the English,[35] while the Fort St George Council was constantly pressing for lower prices. It can be inferred that the merchants did not offer higher prices to the weavers as it would have meant that they would operate at a loss (for the price did not allow them a very substantial margin). The weavers' response ultimately was to make thinner cloth by using thinner yarn and thereby economising on the amount of cotton. This occasioned endless complaints from the Company in London to the Fort St George Council, to which the merchants had a stock reply that unless prices were raised, the problem could not be solved.[36]

The evidence on the different prices paid by the Dutch and the English highlights the fact that there was no single uniform textile price for the entire region. Markets were highly segmented and non-transparent, and a multiplicity of prices could prevail simultaneously for the same product in a very restricted geographic area.

1684–1695: The downturn in cloth procurement in Madras clearly began in 1684 when the contracted quantity was only 54 per cent of that in 1683.[37] This was partly due to the decision of the Fort St George Council not to trade in the Poonamallee/Chinglepet area which was under the local governor Podala Lingappa, as a protest against his interference in the English trade. The Council's efforts since 1681–82 to explore alternative sources of supply further south at Cuddalore, Kunimedu (Conimere) and Porto Novo had not been

---

34. The figures are not available for 1682 and 1683, but the boom conditions and the high volume of trade are evident from the Consultations. PC, 18 November 1682; 6 December 1683.
35. PC, 29 September 1674; 24 July 1679.
36. PC, 14 September 1676.
37. Arasaratnam (*Merchants, Companies and Commerce*, p. 140) gives 1684 as another boom year, but the contract at Madras definitely shows that the recession in cloth trade had already begun. It can be therefore inferred that the cloth exports for 1684 came mainly from Masulipatnam, where the contract was negotiated independently with local merchants.

successful. The major event which disrupted textile production and trade was undoubtedly the Mughal invasion of Golkonda in 1687 and the subsequent years of unstable political conditions. This meant the virtual stoppage of cloth supply from the cloth-producing regions near Masulipatnam. Secondary factors which contributed to the general reduction in cloth supply were intermittent famines and continual squabbles among the merchants of Madras.

By 1689 the combination of all these factors—scarcity and high prices of foodgrains, troubles and wars, the shortage of cotton and weavers (who had fled to safer areas), and the high risk involved in sending money into the hinterland for cloth—had resulted in the Company's merchants claiming a loss on their trade with the English.[38] They were unable to bring in even the relatively small volume of the contract for 1689. Faced with competition from the Dutch and the French who had raised their prices by 10 per cent, as well as the knowledge that the merchants could always sell even rejected cloth at much higher prices in the open market, the Fort St George Council was finally forced to offer a higher price to their merchants.[39]

In 1692 prices were raised by 8 per cent over the reference prices and in 1694 by 10 per cent[40] (see table 6.1), but this did not result in any increase in the volume of contracts at Madras, partly because the English were very short of cash and mainly because the merchants were "so engaged in lawsuits and controversies amongst themselves" that their trade had suffered. To add to this, 1694 was a famine year in Madras (table 6.4). With the expectation that the shortage of grain would worsen in the coming season, weavers were migrating out.[41] The year 1695 marked an all-time low, and while the English wanted a contract of 100,000 pagodas, the merchants would only accept for 15,000.[42]

1696–98: The main reason for the gradual recovery in this period was the emergence of Chikka Serappa as the chief merchant (with an entirely new company of merchants) supplying cloth to Fort St George. He was able to organise the procurement of cloth with an efficiency which the earlier company of merchants had not achieved for several years. The Fort St George Council had also finally come

38. PC, 21 and 24 June 1689.
39. PC, 14 November 1689; 11 February 1689/90.
40. PC, 25 July 1692; 18 October 1694.
41. PC, 26 November 1694.
42. PC, 7 March 1694/5.

Textile Trade: Structurally Fragmented Markets and Prices

to terms with the local realities and both the reference price and the actual price were revised upwards steadily, which also reinvigorated their investment. In 1698 the very high price margin of 25 per cent over the reference price (table 6.1) for goods brought in on time[43] was perhaps partially in response to the cotton shortage of 1697.

It is not really possible to ascertain whether the famine and high foodgrain prices of 1694–96 and the cotton shortage of 1697 were contributory factors of any significance in the general increase of textile prices, though they would undoubtedly have helped in keeping the prices from regressing to a lower level as happened in 1674–81. But the fact that the price increase began in 1692, before the shortages, leads one to conclude that other exogenous factors were more decisive. Of these, the continued pressure from the European competitors (the Dutch and the French), who had raised cloth prices by 20 per cent, was undoubtedly the immediate reason for the price increases.[44]

One fact which emerges from the foregoing is that the interplay of prices and supply did not follow the normal behaviour of a market. Prices were determined through a process of negotiation in which the relative strengths of the bargaining parties were important. Input prices on the supply side were undoubtedly one component of the level of prices, but exogenous factors, especially other competition, were of greater critical importance in determining prices in the contracts between the English and the local merchants. Given that supply responded positively to prices in this period, we can also infer that the supply or production of cloth at a macro level had not yet become a constraining factor and that textile production was still able to meet the entire demand. Another important factor on the supply side was entrepreneurial skills. As was the case with Beri Timmanna and Kasi Viranna in the earlier decades, Chikka Serappa was a chief merchant with undoubted leadership qualities. His dominance in the textile trade of the English also contributed to the revival of that trade in Madras.

1699–1701: These three years were a period of smooth and continuing expansion of the textile trade of the English. With the establishment of Fort St David at Tevanampattinam near Cuddalore, the southern centre had also become important as an additional

43. PC, 1 August 1698.
44. PC, 25 July 1692.

source for tapping the textile-producing hinterland to supply cloth to the English. It perhaps compensated for the downturn in the northern Coromandel. Though grain prices had fallen slightly, the merchants refused to reduce the price of cloth, since they said that cotton was still very expensive.[45] More persuasive was perhaps the aggressive expansion of textile investments by the Dutch all over the southern coast to the tune of 400,000 pagodas, said to be their highest in fifty years, which helped the Fort St David merchants bargain for a 6 per cent increase (table 6.1) over the contract price of 1701.[46] In 1701 there was a boom in the European demand for cotton textiles with Dutch and English investments amounting to 650,000 pagodas, and production in the region had to increase correspondingly.[47]

1702–1703: There were no contracts in Madras in 1702 and 1703 because of the embargo by the Mughal authorities as a retaliatory measure. The seizure of the ship of the Surat merchant, Abdul Ghafur, by European pirates in the Red Sea provoked a very strong reaction from the Mughal authorities in Surat and in the Coromandel.[48] By this time the company of merchants led by Chikka Serappa had also become entangled in endless wrangles over their accounts, and their trade transactions had consequently suffered.[49] No contract is mentioned at Madras or Fort St David in 1703.

1704–1708: Another powerful merchant personality, Kelavi ("Colloway") Chetti,[50] emerged as the supplier to the company in this period. He was soon joined by Sunku Rama Chetti, whose family network covered most of the ports and trading regions in the south.

To some extent the English, as did all the Europeans, used their imports to finance a part of their exports. The Dutch were in a more advantageous position because their imports—spices, Japanese gold and copper—had a ready demand in the Coromandel. The English, on the other hand, always had an uphill task in convincing their merchants to accept silver and broadcloth and give equivalent values

---

45. PC, 13 and 15 August 1700.
46. PC, 28 June 1701 and FSDC, 2 August 1701.
47. The English investment is calculated to be 250,000 pagodas by a rough estimation of the total values for the different textiles listed in the Fort St David contract.
48. PC, 6–10 February, 1701/2. For a detailed account of the entire episode, see Das Gupta, *Decline of Surat,* pp. 101 ff.
49. PC, 14 May, 12 and 16 August, 9, 15 and 20 September, 11 October 1703.
50. PC, 3 and 4 July 1704. "Colloway" or Kalavai Chetti always signed his name as Kelavi Chetti in the contracts, which is the name used throughout this work. There is still a Kalavai Chetti Street in Chintadripet in Madras.

in cloth. In the 1670s the merchants had grudgingly accepted broadcloth at invoice value.[51] However, with the Mughal forces in the region, there was a more ready demand for English broadcloth, and the English were able to negotiate for the broadcloth at a considerable percentage—ranging from 20 to 50—over the invoice value. They were also able to treat the profits earned by the merchants on the broadcloth, notionally, as an addition to the cloth prices paid to them and thereby keep the prices down.[52]

The merchants at Madras and Fort St David wanted an increase in the price of cloth in 1705 and 1706 because cotton prices were higher (table 6.5). However, the English were able to insist on keeping the prices at the old rates,[53] which again demonstrates the lack of correspondence between cloth prices and cotton availability or price. The merchants could only restrict the quantities that they contracted for. In Fort St David, the English could negotiate with a much wider circle of merchants, since many ports in the vicinity—Tevanampattinam, Cuddalore, Porto Novo and Pondicherry—were established trade centres. This also helped them counter the monopoly of the Madras merchants in price negotiations, and the latter had to accept the Fort St David prices if they wanted to remain competitive.

1707–1709: The sharp contraction of trade in 1708 was very simply due to the non-arrival of English ships.[54] In 1709 cotton prices were high and rising, but the Fort St David merchants had actually agreed to a price reduction of 5 per cent on the contract price.[55] The Madras merchants were persuaded to effect a similar reduction. However, they ultimately refused to sign a contract, though they promised to bring in as much cloth as possible.[56]

1710–1715: From 1710 to 1713, once again the downward trend in prices and upward trend in contracted quantities coexisted with

---

51. See, for instance, PC, 21 August 1677.
52. In 1704, broadcloth was sold to Kelavi Chetti and his partner Venkata Chetti at 20 per cent over the invoice value. PC, 5 October 1704.
53. PC, 10 July 1705, 14 September 1706. FSDC, 6 and 9 September 1706. Cloth prices would be expected to react to higher prices of inputs with a lag, but it must be noted that the prices for each year's contract were in fact the prices which would prevail for the following year, while the prices of cotton (or foodgrain) which are mentioned were already current.
54. PC, 16 October 1708.
55. FSDC, 30 April 1709.
56. PC, 3 and 18 October 1709.

shortages of cotton and widespread foodgrain scarcity. A further development which is seen with increasing frequency after this period is the discrepancy between a contracted quantity and the quantity actually supplied, though instances of failures of contract were not unknown even in earlier periods. Both in 1710 and 1711, the Madras merchants had been virtually forced into signing the contracts,[57] and in neither year was the contract fulfilled. It was finally agreed that if they brought in 300 bales (instead of the contracted 800), this would be in settlement of all previous contracts.[58]

The Fort St George Council pressed for a 10 per cent reduction on the contract price in 1712, though they admitted the truth of the protests of the merchants about their losses on these contracts when grain and cotton prices were high. Further, the unsettled conditions under the "weak government" of the then Mughal emperor greatly increased the risks (for the merchants) of sending up their money into the country. The Council finally settled for the existing rebate of 5 per cent and reduced the total quantity to be supplied, but held the merchants to an additional 5 per cent rebate in 1713 (table 6.1).[59]

The expansionary trend in cloth investment by the English in this period, which the figures (table 6.1) indicate, is thus more of an illusion, and the real increase began only from 1714 when the Fort St George Council agreed to a 5 per cent increase over the contract price. This was again forced on them by the 200,000 pagoda investment in cloth by the French in Pondicherry.[60] In 1715 the merchants refused to reduce cloth prices though cotton and rice prices had fallen, because of the unusually large demands of the French and the Dutch.[61]

1716–1718: There was a contraction in cloth supply in 1716 because of the high price of cotton, and the Madras merchants would agree to supply only 400 bales.[62] The following year was the beginning of a gradual expansion which even the conflicts among the right- and left-hand castes and the exodus of the left-hand merchants could not affect to any degree.

57. PC, 27 September 1710; 19 June 1711.
58. PC, 25 October 1711.
59. PC, 18 and 21 January 1711/2; 23 March 1712/3.
60. PC, 13 and 23 March 1713/4.
61. PC, 28 March 1715.
62. PC, 23 April 1716. The Fort St David Consultations are not available for some years (1713–1715 and 1717–1723) and so only the Madras contracts are discussed.

1719–1725: There was a quantum increase in the demand for cloth from England as well as the other European countries from 1719 onward. This was the beginning of the "Indian craze" in European markets. In 1719 the East India Company wanted the Fort St George Council to make a contract for 7,700 bales, which was twice as large as the contract of the previous year.[63] Such a large demand posed problems other than that of procurement of cloth, since it strained the post-production cloth-finishing processes. The washers were unable to wash and cure (which involved washing, beating, bleaching and starching) such large quantities of cloth in time for these to be packed for shipping.

Tambu Chetti, another merchant who dominated the trading arena at Madras, came on to the scene in the 1720s. By 1723 the great increase in external demand was beginning to outrun the productive resources of the economy of the region. The English could keep cloth prices at the reduced price of 1720 just by the size of their demand and the opportunities for greater trade that this presented. However, when the English tried to reduce prices further on the grounds that cotton and grain prices were lower, the merchants resisted, applying the economic logic that prices would not be lowered when demand was increasing fast. The English demand alone had quadrupled from 1,000 to 4,000 bales, and the general high level of demand of all the Europeans had raised the wages of the weavers. Even cloth meant for export to Manila—normally cheaper than the cloth supplied to the English because it was slightly coarser—was fetching a price in the market that was higher than the contract price.[64]

The quality of the cloth also deteriorated since the weavers had to produce more cloth than they normally could in a given period of time. The knowledge that the cloth, even if rejected, would find a market also made for poor cloth.[65] The major disadvantage of the English vis-à-vis the local merchants was that they could not afford to send back their ships without cloth, that is, with dead freight. So ultimately, even cloth which was not up to the sample or "muster" would be accepted as a preferable alternative.

By 1724 and 1725 the merchants began to suffer from the repercussions of overextending themselves in the previous years. They

63. PC, 22 June 1719.
64. PC, 29 August 1723.
65. PC, 2 January 1723/4; 4 May 1724.

were almost hopelessly in debt to the Company. In 1725 a contract for 4,000 bales was forced on Sunku Rama Chetti and Tambu Chetti, which they were unwilling to accept even though this was in fact less than the contract of 1724 (table 6.1). The Fort St George Council insisted that this was to make up for the shortfall on the 1724 contract,[66] but this contract also remained unfulfilled.[67]

1726–1740: These fifteen years witnessed a steady decline of the Madras merchants, in particular, and of the cloth trade of the English, in general. The merchants gradually cleared their outstanding debts in 1726 and stabilised their financial position in 1727 when they contracted for about 3,000 bales, which they were able to supply.[68] But they again fell short of the contract of 1728 and could supply only 1,300 bales against the contracted amount of 3,000. The Fort St David merchants also had not been able to supply the entire contracted quantity.[69] After 1727 the region went through a prolonged famine and grain shortage which lasted for more than a decade.[70] At Madras and Fort St David, the cycle of unfulfilled contracts and stopgap measures to procure more cloth (without penalising the merchants for non-fulfilment of contracts) was repeated several times.

The Fort St George Council was finally forced to raise prices by a substantial margin in 1732 (table 6.1). As a further concession to the realities of the times, the Fort St David merchants were allowed an additional 5 pagoda per score on longcloth. They had pointed out that the French, Dutch, Danes and even the Portuguese were all in the market buying large quantities of cloth. Further, the merchants were paying 5 pagodas more per score for cloth supplied to the English.[71]

In 1734, the Fort St George Council again conceded that if the merchants were paying more than the contract price for the cloth, the difference would be paid to them. This was because the Company had also given instructions that they wanted their merchants to get a reasonable profit on their investment.[72] But these concessions

66. PC, 11 and 15 February 1724/5.
67. PC, 7 June 1725.
68. PC, 11 February 1726/7 and 31 July 1727.
69. PC, 24 February 1728/9; 11 April 1729.
70. A contemporary poet described such famines as times when rice was sold for its weight in gold.
71. FSDC, 11 July 1733. Agreed to by Fort St George on 5 September 1733.
72. PC, 2 February 1733/4; FSDC, 17 February 1733/4.

came a little too late for leading Madras merchants like Tambu Chetti and Sunku Rama Chetti, who receded into the background during this decade.

The English increasingly began to look to the Fort St David merchants for their cloth supplies after this. The composition of their exports also changed, and they were beginning to export more "fine" varieties of cloth. Salem, Udaiyarpalayam and other cloth-producing centres of the interior began to be tapped for keeping up cloth supplies to the English. By 1736-37, the Fort St David merchants complained again about their losses on the contracts and that they were paying more for the cloth than the contract prices.[73] Though the cloth prices were revised subsequently to allow for the higher prices of foodgrain, the primary motivation was to not lose the merchants—especially the Fort St David merchants—to the French. The latter were also making very large investments, occasionally as large as 300,000 pagodas in one year.[74] But the prevailing high level of prices also affected other costs for the merchants. It directly raised the cost of starching since rice was more expensive, and the washers and other workers also wanted higher wages for their labour. Indigo prices went up and so did dyeing costs, and the increase in the contract price of cloth did not compensate for such an overall price and cost increase.

1740-1750: This was a decade of war and turmoil in the region, following the invasion of the Marathas. At Arcot there was feuding about the succession to the Nawab's office. Though the French continued to have large investments, the English suffered. This was partly because the governor at Fort St George was not as forceful as Dupleix at Pondicherry in seizing the political opportunities, and also because the English had not backed the winning horse in the race, at least for the time being. The invasion and the battles which ensued devastated the countryside, with standing crops of cotton and rice destroyed and plundered. All the inhabitants, including artisans and poor labourers, fled for safety, leaving entire villages depopulated.

In the final analysis, what does stand out indisputably is that it was the absolute constraint on the supply of cloth which resulted in a noticeable and sustained increase in the prices offered by the English, especially after 1730. It was a general feature of the economy of the

---

73. FSDC, 20 January 1736/7.
74. PC, 25 March 1733/4.

region that prices were characterised by wide fluctuations within relatively short periods of time and over relatively small distances at a point of time. While there is no statistically significant pattern to the price of paddy, cotton prices rose between 1672 and 1710 and stabilised thereafter. The prices of textiles as negotiated in the contracts with the English show a weak association with foodgrain prices and no correspondence at all with cotton availability or prices.

Several factors had an impact on textile prices. In the contracts, it was a question of the relative bargaining strengths of the English and the Indian merchants which ultimately decided the price. Though the merchants were influential and wealthy, they were constrained by the fact that they wanted to live in Madras under the English to have a more stable and protected trade. Their advantage lay in the fact that they provided the English the necessary conduit to the local economy, both for the procurement of their exports and for selling their imports. The importance of merchants, and especially the merchant capitalists, in the textile trade becomes quite clear. The rapidly rising demand of the English for cloth—which they wanted with as little price increases as possible—could be met with continuity and efficiency only because of the economic power of these merchants.

In a market characterised by structural fragmentation, between the base market where the merchants bought the cloth and the secondary market of contract with the English (and the other Europeans) lay a complex interaction of motivations and exogenous influences which determined prices. The experience of the Coromandel shows that there was an absolute limit to the growth of the economy that could result from foreign trade and demand, imposed by technological limits to productivity. Supply was constrained both because the total demand was too high, given the productive resources of the region, and also because local wars disrupted production for considerable periods. This combination of economic and non-economic factors created the ultimate crisis which the merchant capitalists could not tide over even with all their resources.

SEVEN

Textile Trade (1670–1750): Merchant Capitalism at its Zenith

The merchants, especially the merchant capitalists who were involved in the textile exports of the Europeans, straddled two market structures, as already noted in the previous chapter. Consequently, any changes in the environment and general conditions in one would, in a chain reaction, be transmitted to the other. To fully understand the impact of such changes, we cannot merely focus on what happened to the merchant capitalists, to the exclusion of the artisan producers and other institutions in the economy.

Political scenario

The political environment in which the merchants functioned remained neither static nor stable between 1670 and 1750. Gingee had fallen to Bijapur as early as 1648. By the 1660s the remnants of the Vijayanagar empire had faded away, and the region directly under the king had been divided between Bijapur and Golkonda. In 1675, nayaka rule ended in Tanjavur and was replaced by Maratha rule. In 1677 Shivaji invaded the Karnatak and captured Gingee. In 1686 Bijapur was conquered by the Mughals, and Golkonda fell in 1687. In 1698, after an eight-year siege, Gingee was also captured by the Mughals.

In spite of all the disruptions caused by the invasions and widespread wars, after the consolidation of Mughal power in the Coromandel, *pax Mughalica*, however diluted, was in evidence. For two decades the region enjoyed some sort of peace and stability. By the 1740s, this fragile equilibrium was shattered, and the region was subjected to renewed attacks by the Marathas. There were also internal struggles for succession to the offices of the Nizam and the Nawab of Arcot. The English and the French, by then the two major

European powers in the Coromandel, now began to intervene in internal politics—a feature which was to become a routine part of their policy and functioning in the subsequent decades.

Both the Mughal emperor, Muhammad Shah, and the Nizam-ul-mulk died in 1748. In Hyderabad, both Nasir Jung and Muzaffar Jung laid a claim to the succession. Similarly, in the Karnatak, there were two claimants for the office of the Nawab of Arcot. The English supported Nasir Jung for the Nizam's post, and Anwaruddin—and later his son Muhammad Ali—to be the Nawab of Arcot. The French supported Muzaffar Jung to succeed as the Nizam, and the family of Dost Ali—of whom the last representative was Chanda Sahib—for the position of the Nawab of Arcot. The hostilities between the English and the French in the Coromandel were a spillover from the enmity between the two countries in Europe, though in the 1740s the two were nominally at peace.[1]

There can be little doubt that by the 1740s the English at Madras and the French at Pondicherry had become major forces on the local political scene, and this also reinforced their economic power. The fact that Madras and Pondicherry were regarded as inviolate and secure strongholds certainly changed the power equations between the English and the French, on the one hand, and the local merchants, on the other.

The general political instability also affected the viability of the other local ports, which further reinforced the perception of the English and French enclaves as stable and secure. San Thome, for instance, was destroyed in 1674 when it was retaken from the French by Golkonda with the help of the Dutch. However, by the end of the century, it had revived to become a major port, frequented by Pathans, Armenians and other Europeans (especially the Portuguese). But the average annual value of imports of Bengal goods (piecegoods, silk and opium) at San Thome fell from 233,550 pagodas (in the period 1711–12 to 1713–14) to 168,276 pagodas (in the triennium 1719–20 to 1721–22), 144,215 pagodas (in 1722–23 to 1724–25) and 71,000 pagodas (in 1725–26 to 1727–28). There was a moderate recovery in the subsequent triennium but much short of the high volume of trade in the period 1711 to 1715.[2] Such a deterioration had implications for the local merchants in terms of the choices

1. Love, *Vestiges*, vol. 2: pp. 388-389.
2. Memorandum of an Account of Imports at San Thome, PC, 27 November 1733.

Organisation of cloth trade: From weaver to exporter

The 1670s began with a steep rise in cotton prices because of the failure of the cotton crop. In Bijapur and Srikakulam, the price per candy of cotton went up from 9 pagodas to 14–15 pagodas in 1672.[3] In spite of this, Dutch exports did not suffer much. In 1672 their total exports from the Coromandel amounted to 1.9 million guilders (430,000 pagodas) and 6,723 bales of cloth, as compared to the peak of 2.2 million guilders (490,000 pagodas) and 6,877 bales in 1670.[4] The relative position of the English vis-à-vis the Dutch can be assessed from the fact that the textile investment of the English in Fort St George in 1672 totalled only 75,000 pagodas, whereas the Dutch were procuring cloth for 300,000 pagodas which they had given out in advance.[5]

The English at this time were dealing with a group of twenty-six chief merchants, led by Kasi Viranna and the three heirs and successors of Beri Timmanna—his son Venkatanarayana, and his brothers Pedda Venkatadri and Chinna Venkatadri. Under them were many lesser merchants, evidently employed by the chief merchants, to organise the procurement of cloth from the weaving villages.

The Dutch had given up the practice of employing one or a few chief merchants. They had organised their cloth-supplying merchants into a joint-stock company in the 1660s in order to avoid bad debts. But, in spite of the fact that under this form of organisation the merchants had created a common stock of capital, the Dutch were still giving advances to the merchants.

For the English, the medium of chief merchants who were individually wealthy and powerful was a great necessity. In the 1670s, the financial resources of the English at Fort St George were still very meagre. Most of the investment was financed by the merchants out

---

3. PC, 18 April and 14 June 1672. Brennig notes that Srikakulam used to grow a coarser variety of cotton which could not be used for finer fabrics, and a red-tinged cotton in the deltas, known as Cocanada (*Textile Trade*, p. 230.). Though few people are aware of it, red-tinged cotton is still grown in Srikakulam and is used by the local weavers.
4. Export totals calculated from *Dagh Registers*. 1 pagoda = 4.2 to 4.5 guilders = 84 to 90 stuivers (14 March and 27 May 1637, DR, vol. 4, 1637, pp. 88, 265). Cloth normally constituted about 70 to 75 per cent of the total value of Dutch exports.
5. PC, 14 June 1672.

of their own resources and by borrowing money on interest.[6] The Fort St George Council repeatedly assured the English East India Company that they needed a person like Kasi Viranna or Beri Timmanna for the smooth functioning of the textile trade. Further, according to them, from the time that this trade had been entrusted to these merchants, there had been virtually no defaulting on advances or bad debts.[7] The Council also asserted that giving money to merchants in advance was the normal practice all over India. Interest on the money was not the prime consideration, and the timely dispatch of goods was much more important.[8]

Dutch exports continued to be high throughout the 1670s. Even in 1674, which was a relatively poor year for the Dutch because of their war with the French in Europe and the siege of San Thome, their exports stood at 1.25 million guilders (278,000 pagodas). In contrast, the value of English exports from Madras was only 80,000 pagodas.[9] Apart from their resources, the reasons for the better performance of the Dutch are quite clear. While the East India Company, in London, was pressing for a reduction of 20 per cent in the price of cloth (stubbornly unmindful of the local realities—the unsettled political conditions and higher yarn prices), the Dutch were paying prices that were higher than those that the English sought to reduce further. As compared to the 1.36 pagodas which the English paid, the Dutch were paying 1.5 pagodas per piece for ordinary longcloth. The Dutch were also giving ready money in advance to their merchants, and they did not insist that the merchants should take European goods as part payment. Finally, they were buying both finer and coarser varieties of cloth—the first sortings for export to Europe, and the second and third for export to the eastern markets in the Spice Islands, Macassar and Japan.[10]

The chief merchants of the English felt that they were at a disadvantage. While they had to buy in a competitive market where other buyers could outbid them, when it came to selling, they were committed to supplying a given quantity of cloth at a contracted price.

6. PC, 18 April 1672; 20 October 1674.
7. PC, 30 June and 28 September 1675; 29 February 1676.
8. PC, 28 September 1675.
9. This was only the value of exports from Madras. The total textile exports of the English from the Coromandel, that is, including Masulipatnam, was probably double this figure.
10. PC, 29 September 1674.

The chief merchants insisted that the Fort St George Council should ensure that private merchants from Madras did not hinder them or spoil their procurement by buying the same sorts of cloth (perhaps by imposing a total prohibition on their purchase of such cloth).[11] However, the only way they could really continue to get more cloth was to increase the price paid to the weavers.

The importance of the organisational aspects of cloth procurement has not received much attention from historians. Initially the chief merchants used to employ factors to manage the procurement of cloth, but these merchants had not been able to function efficiently during "the great troubles in the country" in 1674. At the request of the Governor (Agent) of Fort St George, Langhorn, the chief merchants themselves went up-country. However, they had had to pay such a high price for cloth that their profits were wiped out.[12]

The following year, in 1675, the English placed two chief merchants, with many other merchants under them, in each weaving centre. The chief merchants were instructed that they had to coordinate their purchases in such a way that they did not compete with each other, but instead maximised their procurement of cloth. In spite of this, the chief merchants reported that their losses were high. Kasi Viranna said that the other chief merchants did not take care to organise their cloth procurement as carefully as he did, nor did they look after the weavers properly. Consequently, they ended up making a loss. There were eighteen main areas producing cloth, which Viranna had divided and further subdivided into many circuits. Five of his employees were sent to each main centre and thoroughly covered all the weaving areas.[13] According to Viranna, without such careful management, the cloth trade could not prosper.

Weavers were usually paid money in advance by the merchants, which financed their purchases of yarn besides ensuring the delivery of a given quantum of cloth. The interest lost on the money was compensated by the reduced risk of not getting cloth in time. In any case, the weaver would probably never have undertaken the large-scale production of cloth without advances.

11. PC, 18 April 1672. The merchants often imposed this condition to protect their monopoly of buying cloth from the weavers to supply to the English, which might otherwise be bought up by competing merchants from Madras.
12. PC, 29 September 1674.
13. PC, 28 September 1675.

Throughout the 1670s there are several references to an increase in the prices paid by the merchants to the weavers. In 1675 prices were increased so that the weavers would weave cloth to specified lengths and widths (since the English demand was for greater width than was produced for the local market) and they would also increase the thread count from 16 to 17, 17½ and 18—as thicker and more closely woven cloth was required. However, because of the high prices of yarn, the weavers resorted to using thinner thread and, consequently, the cloth was still not as thick as required.[14]

Weavers could not be held to advances, mainly because they could always leave an area and move away. They did this in 1675 when soldiers from Golkonda, on the instructions of Madanna, attacked the weaving villages near Karedu, where the Madras merchants had invested a lot of money.

Two factors—the payment by merchants of higher prices to weavers with advances from their own money (which was at risk in unsettled times), while having to supply cloth at previously fixed prices to the English according to strict specifications—led to the merchants complaining of their great losses and their refusal to supply the total demand of the English.[15] An added complaint was that the English ordered only a very small quantity of fine cloth (on which the profit margins of the merchants were higher). The merchants therefore insisted on supplying only fine cloth in payment for European goods—broadcloth, silver, coral and tin—which they were forced to take. There was demand for such goods only in the Golkonda kingdom which also produced the finer textiles.[16]

One of the more noteworthy developments beginning in the later part of the 1670s was a steady shift of the Dutch, for their cloth requirements, from northern to southern Coromandel. This happened even though conditions in the south were far from ideal and there was greater competition for cloth from local merchants who carried on a great trade.[17] The English merchants were also looking increasingly to southern Coromandel for their cloth pro-

14. *Ibid.*
15. *Ibid.*; PC, 21 July 1676.
16. PC, 30 June 1675; 21 August 1677.
17. Letter from Governor Pits at Pulicat to Batavia, 24 November 1681, *DR*, vol. 29, 1681, p. 686. About six months later, another letter again referred to the fact that the Dutch trade was becoming more active in the south, while it was slackening in the north. 29 May 1682, *DR*, vol. 30, 1682, p. 669.

curement, especially as the law and order situation in Golkonda deteriorated.

Kasi Viranna

English trade in the 1670s was dominated by Kasi Viranna. His great power in the cloth trade as well as his considerable influence with the local Golkonda officials like Podala Lingappa, the revenue farmer (and later governor) of Poonamallee, rendered him suspect to many among the English. When Governor Langhorn was accused of accepting a bribe of 20,000 pagodas a year from Kasi Viranna to favour him in his business with the Company, Viranna refuted the accusation by pointing out that he had begun to trade with the Company before Langhorn came on to the scene and that his dealings were not carried on in private. Most of all, he had his reputation in the country to protect.[18]

Langhorn's successor Streynsham Master was also very suspicious of Viranna's influence. He disapproved of the fact that Viranna "had the boldness" to invite William Langhorn to stay at his house for a considerable time whenever Langhorn called on him, which he did quite often.[19] Master succeeded in persuading Kasi Viranna to agree to a rebate of 6½ per cent on the contract price for the total contract of 70,000 pagodas in longcloth and salempores, which he considered a great triumph.[20] This rebate was essentially treated as an implicit interest on the advance, and it was normally fixed at 5 or 6 per cent.

Though Temple (the editor of Master's papers) also rejoices over the fact that Master "had mulcted" the "native merchants whose frauds he had detected",[21] the long-term success of Master's forced reduction of prices is doubtful. To begin with, the dependence on Kasi Viranna and other merchants could not be avoided, because they would be called upon to supply cloth at short notice if the ships returning to England were not fully laden.[22] Further, the local merchants were disinclined to accept large contracts from Fort St George at these rates. In 1679, after four months of negotiations,

---

18. PC, 14 September 1676.
19. Master, *Diaries*, vol. 1: p. 66.
20. *Ibid.*, p. 71.
21. *Ibid.*, p. 130.
22. PC, 19 December 1678; 31 January 1679/80.

Viranna and his merchants were persuaded to accept a contract for only 51.7 per cent of the quantity required by the English (30,000 pieces of ordinary longcloth against 58,000). The rebate was brought down to 6 per cent.

Venkatadri brothers

Kasi Viranna died suddenly in March 1680, and Beri Pedda Venkatadri, the seniormost among the Company's merchants, was appointed as the chief merchant. The extent to which Kasi Viranna had dominated the other merchants during his lifetime became very evident when soon after his death the other merchants complained about their accounts which had not been settled in five years.[23] Though the contracts had been made jointly with all the merchants, and the accounts were also settled collectively with Fort St George, it is clear that the merchants participated in the contract as individuals. Pedda Venkatadri, Chinna Venkatadri, Alangatha Pillai ("Allingall") and, nominally, Kasi Viranna's adopted son Kasi Muddu Viranna (at that time only ten years old) were the principal merchants against whom the other twenty-odd merchants complained. This gave Streynsham Master the opportunity to organise the merchants into a joint-stock company, along the same lines as the Dutch had done at Pulicat, which would provide the entire investment. Fort St George would pay for the cloth as it was brought in, and about seven of the principal merchants were to manage the trade and adjust the accounts.[24]

In spite of stiff resistance from Pedda Venkatadri, the joint stock was constituted with a share capital of 100 shares of 500 pagodas each. A hundred and fifty shares were subscribed, and many more wanted to come in. The group headed by Pedda Venkatadri held twenty-five shares. The other 7 chief merchants had two and three-fourth shares each, and the rest of the merchants held the remaining shares.[25] The complaints of the other merchants against Kasi Viranna and Pedda Venkatadri however continued. The contract used to be shared on a 25:75 basis between Kasi Viranna, Pedda Venkatadri and their group and the other merchants. The latter complained that they

---

23. PC, 21 and 28 June 1680.
24. PC, 30 June 1680.
25. PC, 5 and 10 July 1680.

Textile Trade: Merchant Capitalism at its Zenith

had not been paid the prices given by the Company for the cloth and had been overcharged for the European goods sold by the Company.[26] The chief merchants were thus clearly intermediaries between the Fort St George Council and the other merchants. The Council finally awarded 48,944 pagodas 6 fanams 8 cash as dues outstanding to the other merchants from Pedda Venkatadri and his group.[27]

Pedda Venkatadri and his partners, of course, did not accept either the constitution of a joint-stock company—which would reduce their authority—or this award meekly. Fundamentally, this continued to be an acrimonious personal struggle between Pedda Venkatadri and Chinna Venkatadri, on the one hand, and Streynsham Master, on the other. Master suspected that the continuous harassment which the English at Madras faced from the local governor Podala Lingappa had been caused by Pedda Venkatadri, Chinna Venkatadri and Alangatha Pillai, and he had them imprisoned in the Fort.[28] Pedda Venkatadri was also told that if he and his partners did not settle their dues with the other merchants, they would be forcibly made to pay.[29]

The next day the sons and sons-in-law of Pedda and Chinna Venkatadri left Madras secretly with several artisans and labourers—painters, fishermen, catamaran men and coolies—"upon a combination".[30] Generally they were able to muster the support of various castes of the right side, since the chief merchants were the undoubted leaders of the right-hand caste groups. They went to San Thome (then an independent port) and from there tried to incite people both in Madras and in the surrounding areas to prevent cloth and other supplies from coming into Madras.[31] They also approached Podala Lingappa and Akkanna, the great minister of Golkonda, for help. Akkanna demanded that Pedda Venkatadri should be reinstated as the chief merchant (on the same footing as the late Kasi Viranna), that he and his brother should be made to pay only what was justly due from them, and that the English should return what had been taken from them.[32]

26. PC, 7 October 1680.
27. PC, 26 November 1680.
28. PC, 6 October 1680.
29. PC, 26 October 1680.
30. PC, 27 October 1680.
31. PC, 1, 6 and 22 November 1680.
32. PC, 25 December 1680.

In retaliation, Master decided to take Triplicane, which was under Pedda Venkatadri, directly under the administration of Fort St George and to place Company peons in charge of the town.[33] Finally, when Master was assured by the other merchants that their accounts had been settled and Pedda Venkatadri and his brother produced security for their debts, the brothers were released. However, Master decided that because of their attempts to disrupt the trade at Madras, and because they had appealed to the authorities at Golkonda, the Venkatadri brothers would no longer be Company merchants. They forfeited their 25 per cent share in the joint stock. Further, they were "not to carry rundells nor have other things of honour and respect as formerly", but they could live in the town like any other merchant.[34]

Within a few months, however, Pedda Venkatadri, Chinna Venkatadri and Alangatha Pillai were sent for and asked to return as chief merchants. The Fort St George Council did so because there were "no persons in the country of greater interest and reputation, nor in whom we can confide more". The 25 per cent share of these merchants in the joint stock was restored to them. As a further affirmation of their triumphant reinstatement, three "turbulent" merchants, presumably the most vocal against the Venkatadri brothers, were discharged.[35] The fact that they were recalled almost as soon as Streynsham Master had been relieved as the Governor of Fort St George was not a coincidence. The Fort St George Council was a suitably docile body which would submit to the dictates of the governor. The removal or recall of any powerful governor was usually followed by contentious controversies and investigations into the activities of the said governor.[36]

The careers of Kasi Viranna and Pedda Venkatadri highlight the many facets of the relationship which existed between the English and the local merchants at Madras. Their interaction was not merely confined to trade, with the merchants supplying cloth and buying European goods in return. The merchants were also the intermedi-

---

33. PC, 21 February 1680/1. Triplicane had been farmed by Kasi Viranna on behalf of Fort St George, and Pedda Venkatadri as his successor had also taken charge of Triplicane.
34. PC, 24 February 1680/1.
35. PC, 12 and 14 July 1681.
36. In September 1681, Pedda Venkatadri, Alangatha Pillai and several other residents of Madras gave petitions to the Fort St George Council about several abuses against them by Master who had extorted large sums of money from them. This was followed by a long inquiry, and Master was finally allowed to embark for England in February 1682 after settling Pedda Venkatadri's claims. PC, 19 and 26 September 1681; 8 February 1681/2.

aries between the English and the local government, which was both a reflection and an affirmation of their standing in local society. Kasi Viranna often interceded for the English with Podala Lingappa, the *tarafdar* or revenue farmer of the district of Poonamallee. As a nephew of the powerful brahmin ministers of Golkonda, Madanna and Akkanna, Lingappa was very influential and, if one were to judge by the remarks of the English, very capricious.

Between 1675 when Lingappa came to Poonamallee and 1680 (when Viranna died), Viranna defended the English—who had consistently refused to give the tarafdar the customary ceremonial presents *(tashrif)*—from Lingappa's harassment.[37] Besides this, the merchants also helped the English exercise de facto control over areas neighbouring Fort St George and Madras, by farming the revenues of "towns" like Triplicane.[38] The relations of the merchants with the officials were maintained at a social level—they were entertained at Kasi Viranna's "garden" outside Madras and were given interest-free "loans" which kept Madanna, the divan and Lingappa in good humour.[39] It was this influence that Pedda Venkatadri tried to exploit when he was facing problems with Streynsham Master.

The social status of the merchant capitalists was also reinforced by the privileges which they enjoyed in Madras. These privileges were both economic—the chief merchants paid only half customs on their imports—and social. The symbols of social status, in particular, had great significance in the context of the popular perception of an individual's standing in society. The right to walk with a parasol ("rundell" or roundel), to be carried on a palanquin, to ride a horse or even an elephant, to receive annual ceremonial gifts presented by the Governor of Fort St George every New Year's Day, were all privileges which marked a person as someone of importance. The English were fully sensitive to this. In fact, they were imitating the

---

37. There are several references to the tactics followed by Lingappa to harass the English. On one occasion, he had complained to the governor of Poonamalle, Mirza Muhammad Amin, that the English were adding a strong defensive bulwark to Fort St George. Kasi Viranna intervened and explained that the English had only repaired an old bulwark. PC, 13 April 1678.
38. For those unfamiliar with the history of Madras, it must be explained that many localities of Madras like Triplicane (Tiruvallikkeni), Egmore (Elumbur), Purasavakkam, San Thome, Mylapore, Tiruvottiyur and others, were all originally independent towns or villages. They were gradually incorporated into the city of Madras during the eighteenth and nineteenth centuries.
39. PC, 15 September 1680.

local rulers—who accorded these privileges to their subjects as a mark of honour—when they declared that the discharged chief merchants could not have the distinction of "things of honour and respect". In resisting Master's proposal to curtail their economic power, Pedda Venkatadri and Chinna Venkatadri were equally trying to protect their social status which was of great importance to them. Social authority and economic power were interactive components of the class identity of merchant capitalists.

The recall of Pedda Venkatadri certainly boosted the Company's trade. In spite of the evidence of high volume of cloth investment in 1680 and 1681 (table 6.1), when the Venkatadri brothers were out of the investment, the merchants were supplying less cloth than the English were demanding. In 1681, the merchants agreed to provide only 45 per cent of the quantity required by the Company. In 1682 and 1683, however, the merchants were bringing in cloth faster than Fort St George could pay for.[40]

After Pedda Venkatadri's death in March 1683, Chinna Venkatadri succeeded his brother as the chief merchant. From 1682 the English at Madras also began to make sustained efforts to expand their catchment area for cloth procurement and made overtures to the merchants in Kunimedu and Cuddalore. However, these initial attempts were not really successful since the merchants there either wanted a price higher than what Fort St George was prepared to pay or they wanted to supply too large a proportion of fine cloth, which the English did not want.[41]

Chinna Venkatadri's tenure as a chief merchant was not particularly distinguished. Both cloth procurement and the sale of European goods were poor, partly because Fort St George had decided not to buy cloth or sell European goods in Podala Lingappa's territory. By this counter-offensive—when Lingappa's revenues would fall because of their boycott—the English intended to make him more reasonable in his dealings with them.[42] In general, the unsettled

---

40. PC, 18 November 1682; 6 December 1683.
41. PC, 5, 8 and 12 June 1682; 4 December 1684.
42. This was a retaliation that the English had planned throughout 1684 to protest about the fact that Lingappa, and a subordinate governor in Kovalam, had taken money to ensure that "Interlopers" would not be allowed to trade in the region, but that did not happen. Finally, the embargo was imposed in October 1684 (PC, 2 October 1684). By the following January, the strategy was proved effective when Lingappa's revenues began to suffer and he came to a settlement with the English.

political conditions did not help trade and the ultimate in political disruption took place in 1687 when the Mughal army captured Golkonda. The only event of note concerning Chinna Venkatadri was that just before the fall of the Golkonda kingdom, he rented San Thome—the town, customs, adjacent towns and paddy grounds—from the brahmin governor Madananta Pantulu at Kanchipuram on behalf of the Company.[43]

Sorry state of textile trade

By 1688 the accounts of the joint stock were once again in disarray. The internal disputes among the merchants had begun as far back as 1683. The Fort St George Council, after trying to reconcile their mutual differences, decided not to make a contract with the merchants until they had settled their accounts.[44] The other merchants were opposed to Chinna Venkatadri participating in the joint stock because he was behind with his share of the stock and because of his other disputes with them.[45] In 1688, after five years of disputes, the accounts were finally settled and a new joint stock was formed, with 100 shares of 200 pagodas each and with twelve chief merchants and two heads. Of the other merchants, twenty were to be selected to go into the country to buy cloth.

In spite of all the complaints against him, Chinna Venkatadri and his faction—Alangatha Pillai, Beri Timmappa (Pedda Venkatadri's son), and Kasi Muddu Viranna—were once again in charge of the joint stock.[46] With rather naive surprise the Fort St George Council noted that the capital of the joint stock was not being used as a fund to purchase cloth for the Company. Instead, it was used to finance the private trade of the merchants, and at the end of five years, there was little left except bad debts.[47]

Alangatha Pillai succeeded as chief merchant after the death of Chinna Venkatadri in 1689. During the next six years, partly because of the aftermath of the Mughal invasion and partly because of a severe famine, cloth procurement remained very poor. The English

---

43. PC, 4 August 1687.
44. PC, 22 November 1687.
45. PC, 5 July 1688.
46. PC, 26 July and 19 August 1688.
47. PC, 6 September 1688.

consistently recorded very low export figures from Madras. The merchants complained of severe losses, which were the result of their losses (up to 30 per cent) on European goods and a shortage of weavers who had died in the famine or run away. To entice the weavers to move back, the merchants had been forced to solicit their return by promising them houses, looms, yarn and money as advance, in spite of the hazardous conditions of the day.[48]

The relationship between the merchants and the weavers was not a simple, unidimensional exploitative relationship as is often assumed. It was a complex and multilayered relationship and the level of exploitation had to be tempered with a measure of paternalism. The weaver was still a free agent who had the option of selling to the best paying customer. He optimised his returns according to the prevalent conditions, including the availability and price of yarn and the kind of fabric demanded by different buyers.

The Madras merchants pointed out that in nearby towns the weavers could sell coarser cloth of 12 or 12½ punjams, meant for the Manila markets, at 1 pagoda per piece. Since this was more profitable than supplying cloth with 18 punjams to the English at the prices the latter were willing to pay, the weavers would naturally produce cloth for Manila.[49] This was the dilemma of the merchants—reconciling the conditions in the two different market structures in which they had to function. The Dutch had increased prices by 15 per cent in 1690, and they and the French again increased prices by 20 per cent in 1692. Finally, the English followed suit and raised prices by 8 per cent in 1692.[50]

The Fort St George Council had their own explanation for the sorry state of their textile trade. The merchants were so busy "engaged in lawsuits and controversies amongst themselves", that they could be expected to do little for promoting the interests of the English.[51] Particularly damaging were the disagreements between Beri Timmappa, the nominal head, and Alangatha Pillai, the more experienced and capable partner, which led to the merchants also

---

48. Petition by the Joint Stock Merchants, PC, 1 May 1690.
49. *Ibid.* Similarly, in 1694 the weavers had changed their looms for the Manila musters and would not produce cloth according to English specifications (PC, 5 November 1694). Arasaratnam also stresses the independence of the weavers, however "flimsy and formal". *Merchants, Companies and Commerce,* pp. 268–270.
50. PC, 25 July 1692.
51. PC, 14 June 1694.

being divided into two factions. Besides this, the merchants also continued to quarrel amongst themselves about their accounts. Further, most of the principal merchants were indebted to the joint stock since 1692, which discouraged other merchants. The Fort St George Council viewed the domination of the families of Kasi Viranna and Pedda Venkatadri with concern. Though the standing of these families in local society was high and, consequently, though they were the most capable of maintaining good government among the local people, this also meant that these families had the power to make mischief.[52]

This was an added dimension in the relationship between the English and the merchants, who, because of their recognised social status, were able to mediate between the English (the government) and the indigenous society. This was perhaps why the English still continued with Beri Timmappa and Alangatha Pillai as the chief merchants when the joint stock was reorganised once again in 1694. This was despite their stated intention to do away with the custom of family members succeeding their fathers or brothers.

Other social and economic realities were also recognised in this reorganisation. The competition between the right-hand and left-hand caste groups to defend their social space and to establish their claims to superior status over the other, also extended to their economic activities. The chief merchants and Beri Timmappa's father-in-law, Kitti Narayan (who was the Company's dubash, and thus a person of great influence), all belonged to the right-hand castes—mostly comprising Balijas, Komatis, Mudalis and Pillais, among the merchants. The merchants who carried on most of the business and the contract, on the other hand, were the Beri Chettis who belonged to the left-hand castes. To contain this conflict, at least in the context of the cloth investment, two chief merchants, one representing the right-hand and the other the left-hand caste, were appointed in place of Durgappa, Chinna Venkatadri's son, and Kasi Muddu Viranna who had died.[53] Three weaver merchants were also taken into the joint stock, an indication that class differentiation had emerged within the artisan groups as well.

52. Note by President Higginson about the Company's merchants. PC, 5 November 1694.
53. *Ibid.* Durgappa had little interest in trade and had moved out in 1693 without informing the president. He had been retained in the joint stock only because Beri Timmappa had argued that if he were removed, it would not be consistent with the honour of the family.

In what had become an inevitable characteristic, the accounts of the joint stock were once again hopelessly in a tangle by 1695. The merchants tried to delay the final auditing of the accounts, but ultimately were pressured into doing so at the insistence of the Fort St George Council.[54] The joint-stock merchants and Beri Timmappa both claimed that the other party owed them about 9,000 pagodas.[55] The Fort St George Council finally decided not to buy cloth from the old joint stock for the 1696 contract,[56] but constituted a new joint stock headed by Chikka Serappa, Beri Krishna and Sivataksham Nataraya Pillai. Though the Council ruled that there would be no chief merchant that year,[57] clearly Chikka Serappa who had been the English dubash since 1680, Sivataksham Nataraya Pillai (Alangatha Pillai's brother or son) and yet another member of the Beri family would dominate the other merchants.

The trusting faith with which the English at Madras reconstituted the joint-stock company at periodic intervals does seem remarkable. This did not improve the accountability of the merchants. As the Fort St George Council often acknowledged, entrusting their textile procurement to local merchant capitalists, with an assured status in local society and credibility in the trade and administrative circles of the region, was their best safeguard. Contracts were fulfilled on time even if the chief merchants had to use their own resources, and the English did not have to worry about bad debts. The contrast with the joint stocks organised by the Dutch is thus quite evident, because in the absence of chief merchants, the Dutch did have to face the risk of bad debts.[58]

The English should have forseen that such a dominant class as the chief merchants, with their resources and power, would never function on equal terms with the lesser merchants. The capital stock of the joint stock thus became a source of funds which the chief merchants

---

54. PC, 29 July 1695.
55. PC, 17 February 1695/6. The old joint stock claimed that the Beri family owed them more than 9,000 pagodas. Beri Timmappa gave a thirty-one-page answer, also claiming that the joint stock owed him and his family a similar amount. PC, 3 March 1695/6.
56. PC, 13 April 1696.
57. PC, 14 and 19 May 1696.
58. Arasaratnam, surprisingly, has continued over the years to see the joint-stock companies of both the English and the Dutch as similar organisations. See "Indian Merchants", "Activities of South Indian Merchants", and *Merchants, Companies and Commerce*, pp. 239 ff.

used in their own trade, and the organisation itself served as an additional channel for reinforcing their economic power. The rules of the joint stock only perpetuated these unequal power relations by giving large allowances to the chief merchants and their servants, to which the other merchants finally raised strong objections.[59]

Chikka Serappa

In the textile trade of Madras the years from 1696 to 1703 were clearly the years of Chikka Serappa. Unlike for most of the merchant capitalists of this period, it is difficult to construct a genealogy for Serappa. We first hear of him in 1680 when he was appointed the Company's dubash in Madras.

The Fort St George Council noted that it was necessary to employ a dubash or linguish whose duties would include finding good and able merchants to handle the sale of European goods and to provide cloth.[60] The timing of Serappa's appointment (during Streynsham Master's governorship) and the strictures, in the same consultation, against Beri Timmanna and Kasi Viranna—who had become the "engrossers" of all the trade of Madras, which the Council proposed to prevent by organising the joint stock—lead to the inference that this Serappa was the same Serappa who was the agent of Streynsham Master and was implicated in the latter's extortionate activities.[61]

Serappa successfully extended the procurement area of cloth for Fort St George, so that weaving centres like Udaiyarpalayam and areas in the hinterland further south were incorporated into the textile market of Madras. A new joint-stock company was constituted when Serappa produced a list of 31 merchants who had contributed 83½ shares (8,350 pagodas). Serappa dominated the new joint stock with 25 shares.[62]

The revival of the textile trade perhaps owed as much to Serappa's management as to the fact that Fort St George raised the prices of

---

59. PC, 14 November 1696.
60. PC, 2 September 1680.
61. Charles Fawcett, ed., *English Factories in India*, new series, 1678–84 (Oxford: Clarendon Press, 1955), vol. 4: pp. 47, 49.
62. Each share was for 100 pagodas. Other important merchants were Rayasam Ramappa, the Fort St George dubash, and Nayara Viranna with 10 shares each (PC, 25 July 1698). The Nayara family were prominent ruby merchants and dominated the ruby trade in Madras. The list of merchants also includes Beri Ramanna.

longcloth and salempores by 25 per cent in 1698.[63] After a few very successful years, Serappa left the scene almost as abruptly as he came onto it. In 1703 there was yet one more breakdown of the joint-stock accounts. The merchants were trying, as usual, to delay the sorting of the accounts and the Fort St George Council acted with great severity and "confined" Serappa and the other merchants in a godown.[64] This time one of the problems was that the merchants had been overpaid 20,000 pagodas for the cloth which they had supplied. Serappa and one or two other merchants who acknowledged their liability could not pay the entire amount, but only their share. The Beri Chetti merchants, especially Aiyappa Chetti and Ragga Chetti, refused to pay anything and argued that they supplied cloth to Serappa on a private contract—they had nothing to do with payments by the Company.[65]

After this Serappa was no longer involved in the cloth trade, and by 1711 he was bankrupt and in trouble with the Fort St George Council and the governor. In an almost exact repetition of the Pedda Venkatadri episode, the governor of San Thome, Zaudi Khan, wrote to William Fraser, governor of Fort St George, that he was suprised that Serappa had been turned out of Madras and had had to take shelter in San Thome, because "he was in your predecessor's time the manager of your affairs . . . therefore to use him so now is very improper for 'tis in a great measure owing to him that your place is in so flourishing a condition".[66] The reference to Fraser's predecessor, Governor Thomas Pitt, points to the inference that Serappa was being victimised because of the hostility between Pitt and Fraser. In his years with the English, Serappa had acquired eleven houses and one garden in Madras.[67] It is not clear how Serappa's fortunes had declined to such a disastrous level. But this descent into bankruptcy became a pattern which was replicated again and again with most of the merchant capitalists involved in the textile investments of the English in subsequent years.

63. PC, 1 August 1698.
64. PC, 12 and 16 August 1703.
65. PC, 9 September 1703.
66. PC, 2 May 1711.
67. PC, 3 January 1714/5. An inventory was taken of Serappa's houses and gardens mortgaged to the Company, and it was judged that the mortgage would be enough to cover his debt to the Company which amounted to 8,199 pagodas. PC, 2 and 7 April 1714.

Weavers

By the end of the seventeenth century, the increasing competition among the Europeans for cloth and the exigencies of political instability, which destabilised cloth production, brought home to the English and their European competitors the point that more attention had to be paid to the weavers to ensure regular and adequate supplies of cloth. One way to achieve this was to give incentives to weavers to move to the European port enclaves. In 1690 Governor Elihu Yale persuaded nearly fifty families of the jamawar (janrawar) caste to move to Madras. They were allotted ground to build houses, assured of freedom to practice their religion, and greeted ceremoniously with betel, rosewater and other gifts of honour.[68] Madras thus had three weaver castes—saliyar, janrawar and ponnambalam residing in the city.[69] In 1698, Serappa informed the Fort St George Council that fifty weavers were willing to migrate to Madras on condition that they were given the same incentives.[70]

Weavers were also encouraged to settle in Tevanampattinam with the inducement that they could bring in grain for their own consumption without paying customs duties.[71] Though these measures had attracted many weavers to Fort St David and the number of weavers within the "bounds" had increased to five to six thousand, within a few years the number had dwindled to less than three hundred. The weavers had left, partly because of the attacks by the Mughal forces led by Sulaiman Khan and partly because of the high taxes on betel and tobacco—which were evidently considered as a heavy burden on wage goods—and the inducements offered by the Dutch and the French to attract weavers to their enclaves. In Pondicherry there were about fifteen hundred to two thousand weavers under the French.[72] Again in Madras, when some betilla (muslin) weavers

68. PC, 22 February 1689/90.
69. PC, 19 November 1694; 13 July 1696. The saliyar are a traditional weaving caste, and the janrawar were the jandra caste who specialised in weaving longcloth. (P. Swarnalatha, "The World of the Weaver in the Northern Coromandel, 1750–1850" [Ph.D. diss., University of Hyderabad, 1991], pp. 79, 589. Vijaya Ramaswamy identifies ponnambalam as a master weaver (*Textiles and Weavers in Medieval South India* [Delhi: Oxford University Press, 1985], p. 143), but the consultation clearly says that it is a caste.
70. PC, 17 November 1698.
71. FSDC, 29 June 1696.
72. FSDC, 1 August 1701.

applied for permission to build a new *pettai* (settlement) and to be exempt from various local taxes—scavengers' tax, quit rent, town wall and *talaiyari*'s (head watchman) duties—for three years, this was also accepted.[73]

The anxiety of the Europeans to have captive production of cloth by locally resident weavers is quite understandable, for in the southern region, the total demand for cloth had increased sharply. The English wanted to procure cloth for 100,000 pagodas, while the Dutch had made a total contract for 400,000 pagodas in 1701, their highest in more than half a century.[74] Another way to achieve an assured supply of cloth was a practice referred to as "securing" the weavers' looms.[75] Since the weavers could not be held to advances, the merchants began the practice of depositing 5 pagodas for each loom with the weavers, thereby booking the loom, the money to be delivered in cloth at the final settlement. In 1701, which we have already seen was a peak year for contracts, the English merchants complained that the Dutch—in order to ensure that their very large demand would be fulfilled—had increased the deposit to 10 pagodas. So the English, in turn, decided to increase this to 15 pagodas.[76]

Kelavi Chetti

The twenty years after Serappa's exit from the Madras textile trade (from 1705 to 1725) marked a period of steady increase in the demand for cloth by the English Company, as evidenced by the contract figures (table 6.1). Some of the most remarkable merchant capitalists of our period also came onto the scene now. In 1704 Kelavi (Colloway) Chetti and Venkata Chetti were entrusted with the supply of cloth. They were given an advance by Fort St George, and accounts were to be adjusted as the cloth was brought in.[77] By 1706 Sunku Rama Chetti and his associate Karanappa Chetti were also supplying cloth to Fort St George. From 1706 to 1709, the Fort St George Council was able to forestall any increase in the price of textiles which the Madras merchants were demanding, because the Fort St David

---

73. PC, 9 January 1706/7.
74. FSDC, 2 August 1701.
75. PC, 25 January 1694/5; 1 February 1696/7.
76. PC, 28 June 1701.
77. PC, 3 and 4 July, 1 August 1704.

Textile Trade: Merchant Capitalism at its Zenith

merchants were willing to continue supplying cloth at the old rate. In 1709 the Madras merchants were even persuaded to reduce prices by 5 per cent though cotton prices were high, since the Fort St David merchants had reduced prices by the same margin.[78]

Though the contracted figures for 1710 and 1711 were very high, their realisation in terms of cloth supplied shows quite a different picture. Economic logic could not be defied year after year. In 1710 and 1711, the combination of scarcity (and high prices) of cotton and the insistence of the Fort St George Council on lowering prices—longcloth prices had been bargained down to 29.92 pagodas per score as compared to 31.5 pagodas in 1708—resulted in the short supply of cloth by the merchants. Since the merchants had neither signed a formal contract with built-in penalty clauses nor had they been advanced money by Fort St George, no penalty could be imposed on the merchants for their "failure".[79]

In 1711 Governor Fraser virtually forced the merchants to sign a contract to provide 800 bales with a 2,000 pagoda penalty in case of failure to fulfil the contract,[80] but this contract too was not fulfilled. The Fort St George Council persisted with a further 5 per cent cut in prices in spite of all the factors which would have dictated otherwise—high grain prices and the threat of a famine, high cotton prices, and the high risks in sending money to the hinterland in the generally insecure conditions "[un]der the weak government of the present Mogul".[81] The reduction in price was justified on the grounds that no contract was being signed by the merchants.[82] The ultimate result was that in 1712 and 1713 the merchants would contract for only about 50 per cent of the cloth required by the English.[83] In 1714 Fort St George finally agreed to raise prices by 5 per cent, though Sunku Rama Chetti and Kelavi Chetti had pressed for 8 per cent. They argued that the French were buying cloth for 200,000 pagodas—all procured in places where the English cloth was made—and that the Madras merchants would not get any cloth at the existing rates.[84]

78. PC, 4 March 1708/9; 28 September and 3 October 1709.
79. PC, 6 April 1711.
80. PC, 19 June 1711.
81. PC, 18, 21 and 24 January 1711/2.
82. PC, 23 March 1712/3.
83. In November 1713 the merchants agreed to supply 500 bales, whereas the English wanted 1,000 bales. PC, 3 November 1713.
84. PC, 13 and 23 March 1713/4.

The merchants finally agreed to contract for 1,000 bales, whereas the English wanted them to supply 1,833 bales.

Though the consultations continue to talk of the "joint stock" merchants, it is clear that after the Serappa period, the joint-stock form of organisation (in which several merchants held one or two shares each, while the chief merchants had the controlling interest with 25 per cent of the share capital) had quietly died out. It was replaced by the more traditional partnership form of organisation in which the four merchants, Kelavi Chetti, Venkata Chetti, Sunku Rama Chetti and Karanappa Chetti, had equal amounts of capital invested. At this time, the merchants were procuring cloth with their own money, which meant that any risks of loss in transit or of default were also borne by them. Fort St George was evidently very short of money and owed the merchants large sums for cloth supplied and also for money borrowed from them.[85]

Trade at Fort St David

Fort St David was served by merchants from Cuddalore and Tevanampattinam. "Viabo" Chetti, Viraraghava Chetti, Sivaperumal, Mukaddam Nina, Yerram Raju and Sadasiva Rao were the leading merchants who dominated the cloth trade at Fort St David for several decades. Whether they can be really compared to the Madras merchant capitalists is problematic. In the initial decades, after the establishment of Fort St David, the southern merchants were generally less ready to accommodate themselves to the requirements of the English investments. This in fact was the reason why the attempts of Fort St George in the 1680s to procure cloth from Porto Novo, Kunimedu or Cuddalore did not succeed. Even in 1696 these merchants resisted the efforts of the English to tie them down, through advances for supplying cloth.[86]

Some years later, when the Fort St David merchants wanted the price of cloth to be increased, the President and Council of Fort St George responded by pointing out that the quality of their cloth was inferior to the Madras cloth. The merchants retorted that in that case it would be much better to make all the Company investments in

---

85. In 1712 the merchants were owed 40,000 pagodas on cloth brought in. PC, 18 August 1712.
86. FSDC, 14 May 1696.

Madras.[87] It is possible that the major merchant capitalists of the region were concentrated in Porto Novo which was without a doubt the most important port of southern Coromandel.[88]

From the beginning of the eighteenth century, a noteworthy feature of the trade at Fort St David was that it was dominated by the merchant capitalists of Madras. This was probably due in part to the extra-local links that the Madras merchant capitalists had in other ports and trading centres, which gave them an extended sphere of influence. Partly, it was due to the fact that the Fort St George Council knew them and trusted their business expertise which would serve the needs of the English better. Kitti Venkatapati, the brother of Kitti Narayan who was the dubash of Madras,[89] was appointed the dubash of Fort St David in 1696. Kitti Narayan also took on a part of the Fort St David contract with Mayilappa Chetti in 1706.[90]

Over the years, the merchants of Madras continued to be very prominent in the cloth contracts at Fort St David. By 1714 Sunku Muddu Rama, brother of Sunku Rama Chetti, was being referred to as one of the influential merchants of Fort St David. The brothers together were willing to undertake a contract for 64,000 pieces of cloth. The Fort St George Council decided to accept because the Fort St David merchants had disappointed them for three years

---

87. FSDC, 2 August 1701.
88. The Fort St David Consultations contain several references to the volume of shipping and trade in Porto Novo.

The Dutch observed that between July 1680 and August 1681, twenty-two foreign ships and thirty-five smaller vessels had arrived at Porto Novo. Twenty-nine ships and thirty-five foreign vessels had sailed from there, with a total cargo of 8,800 bales of cloth, 250 chests of copper, 100 bahars of spelter and 80 bahars of tin (24 November 1681, DR, vol. 29, 1681, p. 686).

In 1730, the outgoing Dutch governor van Cloon noted that 3,500 bales of coarse cloth worth 200,000 pagodas were exported each year from Porto Novo to Manila, Mocha, Malacca, Persia, Achin, Pegu and other markets (The Memorie of van Cloon, 1730, p. 37, Dutch Coromandel Records, Tamil Nadu State Archives).

Arasaratnam concludes from this that the trade of Porto Novo had declined in this fifty-year period (1680–1730) (*Merchants, Companies and Commerce*, pp. 174–175), which would seem to be a hasty pronouncement based as it is on only two references. There can be little doubt that at least till the 1730s Porto Novo was the major port of the region, whereas Cuddalore had little shipping other than the boats which shuttled to and from Fort St George.

89. Kitti Narayan was the father-in-law of Beri Timmappa and managed to live down Timmappa's fall from grace in 1696 after he secretly left Madras following the disputes about the joint-stock accounts (PC, 21 April 1696). Kitti Narayan regained his influence with the Fort St George Council in 1698 and continued to be very powerful for nearly two decades after that.

90. FSDC, 27 September 1706.

consecutively. Further, as Sunku Rama Chetti had a great interest in the country as well as a large stock in trade, the Council was sure that the contract would be fulfilled in time.[91] Two other family members, Sunku Narayana and Sunku Venkatachalam, were also Sunku Rama Chetti's correspondents at Fort St David, on whom he used to draw bills of exchange.[92] Kelavi Chetti's brother Muttamar Chetti and Sunku Muddu Rama were soon a part of the joint-stock company at Fort St David. They had paid 400 pagodas each to become shareholders in the company.[93]

Sunku Rama Chetti

For the first twenty-five years of the eighteenth century, Sunku Rama Chetti was the towering figure in the trade of the region.[94] Like all the merchant capitalists who traded with the English, Sunku Rama Chetti was a prominent merchant on the local scene even before he began to be involved in the cloth trade. He used to facilitate the transfer of money from Madras to Fort St David through bills of exchange drawn on his correspondents at Fort St David.[95] He was also an intermediary between Fort St George and the Mughal Nawab Zulfiqar Khan from whom the English were trying to get a *parwana* (letter of authority) to confirm their rights to Fort St David. The Armenian Amirjan at the Nawab's court was paid 10,000 rupees (3,000 pagodas) by Sunku Rama Chetti in 1698 to advocate the cause of the English.[96]

A few years later, in 1702, the Mughal forces under the Nawab besieged Madras in retaliation against the seizure of the ship of the

91. PC, 6 December 1714.
92. PC, 31 January 1714/5.
93. PC, 7 June 1716.
94. It is clear that Sunku Rama Chetti or Sunkku Rami Setti, as he signed himself in the contracts, died some time in the late 1720s and that his brother Sunku Venkatachalam had succeeded him. Sunku Muddu Rama also continued to be a prominent merchant. Since the English records continue to refer to all the successors as Sunku Rama it is difficult to know when Sunku Rama Chetti acutally died. This confusion persists even in T. P. Minakshisundaranar's "Sunkuvar Kutumbam" [The Sunkuvar Family], in *Tamila Ninaittuppar,* T. P. M. Silver Jubilee Volume (Madras: 1954), pp. 117–126 [Tamil]. Minakshisundaranar says that Sunku Rama Chetti died a broken and disappointed man in 1735 (p. 124), but this was evidently one of the successors.
95. PC, 4 October 1695; 20 and 28 July 1705.
96. PC, 20 April 1698.

Textile Trade: Merchant Capitalism at its Zenith

Surat merchant Abdul Gaffur. For a peaceful final withdrawal (after the dispute had been settled in Surat), the Nawab and the Diwan wanted to be given 20,000 rupees and 5,000 rupees respectively.[97] This was paid by Sunku Rama Chetti, and at the end of 1702 he was pressing the Fort St George Council to settle the balance 14,695 rupees which was still owed to him.[98]

Though Governor Pitt strongly suspected the involvement of Sunku Rama Chetti in the caste disputes started by the right-hand castes in 1707,[99] neither Sunku Rama Chetti's trade nor his influence seem to have suffered. In 1717, when another major caste conflict broke out between the right- and left-hand castes, Kelavi Chetti and Kalatti Chetti orchestrated the exodus of the left-hand castes from Madras as a protest. They were then removed from the cloth contract, and Sunku Rama Chetti and Nayara Bali Chetti offered to send money for procuring cloth on the condition that the Beri Chettis would not be allowed to participate in the contract again.[100]

The resources at the disposal of Sunku Rama Chetti can be better appreciated if we look at the money borrowed from him and the other joint-stock merchants between 1717 and 1718.[101]

	Borrowed from:	Amount (pagodas)	Interest (pagoda: fanam: cash)
Dec. 1716– June 1717	Sunku Narayana	10,000	
	Sunku Rama and Kelavi Chetti	20,000	
	Sunku Rama (Fort St David)	13,000	
	Sunku Rama (Fort St George)	18,000	
		61,000	1475:12
Nov.–Dec. 1717	Sunku Rama	45,000	205:20
Dec. 1717– Mar. 1718	Sunku Rama	85,000	1775:16:64

---

97. PC, 6, 20 and 21 February 1701/2; 5 May 1702.
98. PC, 21 December 1702.
99. PC, 27 August 1707. Serappa, Nayara Viranna and Andi Chetti were named as the other instigators.
100. PC, 21 January 1716/7.
101. PC, 15 July and 16 December 1717; 15 May 1718.

Until 1719 Sunku Rama Chetti, as the head of a group of partners or "joint stock", continued to be the sole supplier of cloth to Fort St George. In March 1719, Muttamar Chetti, the brother of Kelavi Chetti, asked to join the cloth trade. Since he had "proved his loyalty" by not joining his brother when the Beri Chettis had left Madras in 1717—and he was also, independently, a rich merchant—he was admitted into the cloth investment by the Council.

Sunku Rama Chetti's partners, especially Gangaram and Bhadraiya, had not contributed their share of the capital when Sunku Rama Chetti had increased the total capital stock to more than 100,000 pagodas. (He had been obliged to do this since the English owed the merchants so much money. Evidently the loans given to the English were against the paid-up capital of the joint-stock company, at least in theory.) Fort St George therefore decided that to have the rich Beri Chettis once again in their trade would be fruitful, since the Chettis could contribute to the enlargement of the stock whenever the Company required credit from the merchants. However, to promote greater competitiveness among the merchants, the Council decided to make two contracts, one with Sunku Rama Chetti and the other with Muttamar Chetti and his son Muttu Venkata Chetti. Their intention was to derive maximum advantage from the rivalry between the right- and left-hand merchants.[102]

The demand for cloth from England continued to increase, and in 1719 the Company ordered Fort St George to procure 7,700 bales—more than double the investment of the previous year. It hardly seems credible that the East India Company could have been so unaware of the ceiling on productive capacity imposed by the existing technology. The Fort St George Council was constrained to observe that even if the merchants were able to procure the much

---

102. PC, 9 March 1718/9. The tactic of dividing the contract between the left- and right-hand merchants was followed by all the Europeans. In Pondicherry, the contract was divided between Sunku Seshachala Chetti and the (left-hand) merchants of the "old" company (*The Private Diary of Ananda Ranga Pillai*, (1736–1761), 12 vols. Vols. 1–3 ed. J. F. Price and K. Rangachari, vol 4–12 ed. H. Dodwell [Madras: Madras Records Office, 1904–1928], vol 1: pp. 4–5, [4 October 1736]; pp. 38–39, [16 May 1738]; p. 224, [16 May 1743]. The Dutch also followed the same practice. Elias Guillot noted: "It must also be taken care that no differences arise between the castes of the right and left hand. . . . And, since the Company's two chief merchants are the most important of those castes and have the most influence, one must not be given the least preference or honour above the other". Memorie of Elias Guillot for his Successor Jacob Mossel, Nagapattinam, 19 September 1738, Dutch Coromandel Records, Tamil Nadu State Archives, Madras, 109–110.

Textile Trade: Merchant Capitalism at its Zenith

larger quantity of cloth demanded, they did not have enough washers to wash and cure so much cloth in one year.[103]

Both sets of merchants refused to sign the contract in 1720. They were also pressing for a price increase, especially in view of the very large quantity of cloth demanded. The Fort St George Council managed to push down the actual price by 5 per cent to the reference price (table 6.1). Shrewdly judging the fierce competition among the merchants to control the major share of the trade, the Council was able to persuade Sunku Rama Chetti and Muttamar Chetti to sign the contract. This was done by pointing to the fact that a third set of four rich merchants—Gangaram, Amaresh Thakkar, Tanja Chetti and Nallamurli Kalatti Chetti—had agreed to sign the contract.[104]

In 1723 Sunku Rama Chetti protested to the Fort St George Council that his share in the Fort St David contract had been reduced, while that of Sadasiva Rao had increased to one-third. Since otherwise Sunku Rama Chetti was very useful to the English, Sadasiva Rao and Yerram Raju's shares were reduced to a quarter each.[105] Yerram Raju's share was soon under Tambu Chetti of Madras. Though the contracts at Fort St David were in the names of Sunku Rama Chetti and Tambu Chetti, several local merchants were incorporated into these contracts.[106]

Tambu Chetti and the textile trade crisis

Another great merchant capitalist of Madras of this period, Tambu Chetti, came onto the scene in the 1720s. His name first appeared in the contract of the left-hand merchants in 1720,[107] and by 1723 he was clearly the head of the group.[108] He had also already acquired a quarter share of the Fort St David contract. But by this time, the combination of a forced lower price and a boom in market demand for cloth resulted in the merchants falling behind on their contracts. In 1723 their contract for 4,069 bales included 1,203 bales of the previous year's contract which were yet to be supplied.

103. PC, 22 June 1719.
104. PC, 9, 10, 17 and 24 November 1720.
105. PC, 19 February 1722/3; FSDC, 25 February 1722/3.
106. PC, 3 March 1725/6.
107. PC, 29 February 1719/20.
108. PC, 19 March 1722/3.

While the merchants were under great pressure to bring in large quantities of cloth, the Fort St George Council complained about the unacceptably high proportion of substandard cloth which was being supplied.[109] The merchants were yet again caught in the irreconcilability of the logics of the two market structures in which they had to function. The English demand was growing year by year and had increased to 4,000 bales. The sorting was also very strict. The merchants explained that while they could supply more cloth, they could not always vouch for the quality. Due to the very high level of demand, they had to give advances to the weavers and, consequently, were forced to take what was supplied, or else lose their money. The merchants could not reduce cloth prices either, because the wages of the weavers had gone up on account of the very large demand for cloth. The prices offered by the English, on the other hand, were lower than even the prices of cloth for the Manila market.[110]

A few months later, the merchants again tried to convince the Fort St George Council that given the market conditions in which the producer had many buyers for his product, they could not insist on the conditionality of quality control—especially when the merchants were already committed under contract to supplying a certain quantity of cloth. The Fort St David merchants even raised the prices paid to the weavers (without an increase in the contract price) in order to improve the quality of cloth.[111] On their part, the Fort St George Council often had to accept the poorer quality cloth. They were also under pressure because of the fact that ships could not be kept waiting without sufficient cargo.[112]

In 1724, the president informed the Fort St George Council that having two sets of merchants had become counter-productive. Instead of giving a competitive edge to their trade, this only meant that they were competing against each other for the same cloth, the supply of which was not sufficient to meet the demand.[113] In 1725, for the first time, the penalty clause in the contracts for non-fulfilment was invoked by the Fort St George Council. From the point of view of

109. PC, 2 January 1723/4.
110. PC, 29 August 1723. Though the references would indicate that these conditions operated only for the Madras merchants, the experience of the Fort St David merchants was no different.
111. FSDC, 10 November 1724.
112. PC, 2 January 1723/4.
113. PC, 4 May 1724.

the merchants, they had been obliged to undertake contracts to provide large quantities of cloth (at prices which were below the market prices), which they had no hopes of fulfilling. From the point of view of the English, the cloth supplied was so poor that the reputation of the English East India Company had suffered in the European markets.

The merchants reluctantly accepted a further contract for 4,000 bales and agreed to take the broadcloth at 30 per cent over the invoice value. In return, the Council reduced their penalty to 30,000 pagodas, instead of the 90,000 pagodas actually applicable, hoping that this would deter the merchants "from any more such vile practices as they have of late been guilty of."[114] A further concession on the penalty was given the following year, but once again only on the same condition—of a forced contract to supply more cloth than Sunku Rama Chetti and Tambu Chetti were willing to accept.[115] Thus each succeeding contract only drew the merchants deeper and deeper into an unredeemable situation.

By 1729, the merchants were once again in arrears and had brought in only 1,300 bales out of the total contract for 3,000 bales. The penalty, however, was not levied because the Fort St George Council viewed that this would go against their own interest in the long run.[116] The Coromandel region experienced a widespread famine between 1727 and 1730. As a result, by 1729 grain prices rose sharply (tables 6.2 and 6.4). This in turn caused a steep increase in wages and textile prices. By 1730 the Dutch raised their prices,[117] and the English finally followed suit with a moderate price increase the same year.

In 1731 Tambu Chetti circulated a detailed note about the progress of cloth investment, which clearly explained the nature of the crisis in the textile trade.[118] In centres like Udaiyarpalayam, where cloth production had not been badly affected, prices were very high. The weavers were able to sell inferior cloth at ports like Nagapattinam, Porto Novo and Tarangampadi at 1.5 pagodas per piece, and the Mocha ships paid 1.625 pagodas per piece. Cloth

---

114. PC, 8 February 1724/5.
115. PC, 3 March 1725/6.
116. PC, 24 February 1728/9.
117. The Dutch increased the prices of cloth in Sadras and in Nagapattinam where the merchants had suffered because wages had gone up due to the high price of foodgrains. Memorie of van Cloon, pp. 16–17, 118, Dutch Coromandel Records.
118. PC, 22 August 1731.

according to the specifications of the English could not be made for less than 2.0625 pagodas per piece (whereas the English were paying only about 1.5 pagodas per piece). Even the cloth for the French, which used to be sold for 1.25 pagodas, was now selling for 2.0625 pagodas.

At other centres like Tindivanam, Viravandi, Acharavakkam, Madurantakam, Tirukkalukunram, Manampadisampakkam and Kaliapetta (in South Arcot and Chinglepet districts), most of the weavers had died or had fled because of the famine. Their numbers had dwindled to between one-third to one-fifth of the original populations. In many other centres, the weavers who remained were not willing to take advances because of the shortage of yarn.

The English finally allowed a higher price in 1733 and again in 1734, but a price of 39 pagodas per score for ordinary longcloth gave Tambu Chetti a margin of barely 1 pagoda per score.[119] In addition to the increased price, the Council also gave concessions like not invoking the penalty clause and giving advances to the merchants (a practice reintroduced in 1731). Most importantly, there was an explicit acknowledgment that the merchants should be expected to make a reasonable profit on the investment they undertook for the English. The latter would have to match the prices offered by the French at Fort St George as well as at Fort St David.[120] Unfortunately, all these steps came too late to really save the merchants of Madras.

This renewed crisis in the textile industry, caused both by the fast growing demand and rise in wages and cotton prices, once again made the English aware of the need to have some control over the weavers in order to have an assured supply of cloth. The president of Fort St George had spoken to the Company merchants about the need "to people our villages with those sort of spinners and weavers who work the Company's sort of cloth". Since weavers worked under shady trees, tree planting was taken up extensively in the villages around Madras.[121] Some months later, in 1734, the weaving village of Chintadripet was established in the area which used to belong to Sunku Venkatachalam.[122] The prevalent famine conditions made this an attractive location for migrant weavers looking for a place where

---

119. Tambu Chetti submitted a detailed list of prices for various types of cloth. PC, 24 January 1731/2.
120. PC, 2 February 1733/4.
121. PC, 7 January 1733/4.
122. PC, 21 October 1734.

they would not suffer from the lack of foodgrains. Fort St David, similarly, attracted many weavers and painters who migrated during the famine.[123]

Sunku Rama Chetti's heirs and partners were not able to recover from several years of overextending themselves in the contracts. In 1733, Sunku Venkatachalam, Sunku Muddu Rama and Nayara Bali Chetti wanted to be excused from paying the penalty for the non-fulfilment of contracts of 1729, which the Fort St George Council insisted on demanding.[124] This was virtually the end of the influence of the Sunkuvar family in the textile trade of Madras. Sunku Rama Chetti's son, Sunku Venkatarama Chetti, however, was again employed in the textile contract in 1744.[125]

Tambu Chetti totally dominated the cloth investments of the English at Fort St George and Fort St David until 1739. However, it is doubtful whether his virtually monopolistic control in these years after eliminating Sunku Rama Chetti improved his financial position. The overall economic conditions were not conducive to a prosperous textile trade. The famine which had haunted the Coromandel region earlier recurred between 1733 and 1738, pushing up the prices of cotton and foodgrains. Textile prices also rose because of the uncertainty engendered by the movement of the forces of the Nawab of Arcot in the region.

In reply to the Fort St George Council's query about the prices he charged, Tambu Chetti stated that the prices that he paid in the country were much higher than the prices he was receiving from the English and adamantly refused to reduce the price that he had quoted.[126] By April 1739 Tambu Chetti had been able to bring in only seventeen bales of cloth,[127] and four months later, he was virtually bankrupt. His brother Tellasinga Chetti took over his contract. Tambu Chetti hoped that with his brother's help, his cloth trade would revive and that he would be able to begin repaying his debt at 5,000 pagodas per year.[128]

In the 1730s, the composition of demand from England began to change to include a higher proportion of fine longcloth. The Fort St

123. FSDC, 31 January 1733/4.
124. PC, 26 September 1733.
125. PC, 20 February 1743/4.
126. PC, 16 February 1736/7.
127. PC, 16 and 19 April 1739.
128. PC, 21 August 1739.

George Council started a new system of entrusting the procurement of specified varieties of cloth to different merchants. This did not really improve the quality or the quantity of cloth procured. As the merchants explained, the weavers would work only if money was advanced to them, and after that it was impossible to force them to keep to quality specifications. The fundamental fact was that the total demand for Coromandel cloth exceeded the supply, which made any punitive action against the weavers impossible.[129]

The system of cloth procurement through merchant intermediaries was followed until 1769 when Fort St George shifted to direct contracts with weavers.[130] This step must be seen in the context of the crisis faced by merchants in the textile trade after 1725, when they found it increasingly impossible to function effectively in the dual, fragmented market structures created by the conditionalities of English contracts. The English decided to bypass the intermediaries to exercise direct control over the producers, whose independence had defied their (the English) attempts at imposing artificial, monopolistic restrictions on the textile market.

Lingi Chetti, the last great merchant capitalist of our period,[131] began to participate in English textile contracts from 1747 by bidding for broadcloth and supplying fine longcloth.[132] He is first heard of in 1733 as a dealer in bullion who used to function as a money changer or shroff for the English.[133] It is very evident that by 1750 he was emerging as the leading merchant for the English, in much the same fashion as Sunku Rama Chetti or Tambu Chetti had in the earlier decades.

Re-examination of two beliefs

At the end of this long chronology of merchants in European textile trade, it would be interesting to re-examine two generally held beliefs

---

129. PC, 4 January 1738/9.
130. Iyer, "Trade and Finance", ch. 4.
131. Lingi Chetti, Tambu Chetti and Sunku Rama Chetti live on in the memory of the people of Madras, since the streets named after them are the main streets in the business district of present-day Georgetown.
132. FSDC, 13 June 1747; 25 February 1748/9. Iyer ("Trade and Finance", ch. 4, app.) lists the main merchants in the textile contracts after 1750, and it is surprising that Lingi Chetti's name does not feature among them.
133. PC, 31 March 1732/3.

about the effects of European textile trade on merchants, in the light of the specific experience of the merchants of Madras and Cuddalore. The first of these was that supplying textiles to the Europeans was a very profitable activity which generated considerable surplus capital for the merchants. The second was that the forced sale of European woollen cloth, especially broadcloth, in part payment for Indian cottons caused the financial ruin of the merchants in the long run.

Forced sale of broadcloth

The second question can be taken up first. The constant struggle of the European companies to reduce their import of bullion in return for textiles, indigo and other commodities for export from India is well documented. Among the Europeans, the Dutch perhaps had the best trade balance because they were able to import spices, gold and copper—commodities with established demand—from their intra-Asian trade into the Coromandel region. But by the early eighteenth century even the Dutch had begun to appreciate that the financing of cloth exports through commodity imports was both cumbersome and less productive in terms of cloth supplies.[134]

The English in Madras were under pressure from the Company throughout the period to finance their local trade through the sale of imported "European" goods, especially broadcloth, silver, coral and tin. In the seventeenth century, the demand for all these was generally poor. Most often, all these goods, especially broadcloth, would be taken by the Madras merchants only at invoice value. After the region came under Mughal rule, the position changed and there was a genuine, if limited, demand for broadcloth. Since the Europeans used broadcloth as ceremonial gifts, they were able to invest broadcloth with a totally artificial value which also created an additional demand for the cloth. Gradually, the merchants were persuaded to take broadcloth at higher than invoice prices, which for most of the years was negotiated at 30 per cent over invoice value (table 7.1).

---

134. In 1730, van Cloon noted that the Dutch had switched to procuring cloth with ready money, as opposed to "the rejected, detrimental method which was in practice in former times", when cloth was paid for with imports. Memorie, p. 12, Dutch Coromandel Records.

Table 7.1: Terms of Sale of Broadcloth at Madras

21	August	1677	Prime cost
19	August	1681	Refused to take European goods
5	October	1704	20 % over invoice
9	July	1705	25 % over invoice
2	September	1706	25 % over invoice
31	July	1707	30 % over invoice
21	January	1709	45 % over invoice
27	September	1710	55 % over invoice
30	September	1713	45 % over invoice
29	June	1715	35 % over invoice
17	March	1716	30 % over invoice
15	July	1717	30 % over invoice
17	July	1718	30 % over invoice
14	September	1719	30 % over invoice
8	January	1722	30 % over invoice
5	September	1722	30 % over invoice
8	February	1725	30 % over invoice
3	March	1726	30 % over invoice
11	February	1727	30 % over invoice
14	July	1729	35 % over invoice
25	May	1731	35 % over invoice
8	January	1733	Tambu Chetti refused the broadcloth
18	October	1736	30 % over invoice
27	March	1738	33 % over invoice
1	November	1740	30 % over invoice

Note: Dates refer to the date of the Public Consultation.

It would seem undeniable that broadcloth was profitable for the Madras merchants. In order to exploit the steady though slow-moving demand to maximum advantage, the Madras merchants wanted to retain a monopoly over broadcloth—thereby ensuring that too many merchants would not flood the market and cause the prices to crash. The Fort St George Council was quite quick to realise this and the profits on broadcloth were treated as an implicit addition to cloth prices.

After 1725, when the merchants' affairs entered a prolonged financial crisis, broadcloth served two purposes. As long as the cloth was given out without advance payment—usually the Fort St George

Council allowed more than a year for payment—the merchants were able to use the money realised on broadcloth sales (up to a total value of 60,000 to 70,000 pagodas) to finance cloth procurement. This virtually became an interest-free advance. The fact that the English also trusted the merchants to this extent added to their creditworthiness.[135] In fact, Tambu Chetti's total debt of 38,000 pagodas to the English was repaid only because he and his brother Tellasinga Chetti were given the monopoly over broadcloth for several years.[136]

High profits of merchants

The notion of high profits earned by merchants in supplying textiles to the European companies was not matched by the actual situation. This is evident from the number of times the local merchants complained to Fort St George about their losses in the cloth trade between 1675 and 1725 (table 7.2), well before the general decline in the textile trade had begun. The pattern of English demand (with too high a proportion of coarse cloth on which the merchants earned very low margins), the constant pressure to reduce prices in an expanding market (where several supply-side factors were also pushing prices up), and finally, the frequent wars and disturbances, all contributed to the losses of the merchants. The Fort St George Council itself frequently accepted that the merchants could not have made much profits on the contracts.[137] The losses, however, became critical for the merchants after 1725. The great increase in demand from the other Europeans—the French, the Danes, the Dutch as well as the Portuguese—created a situation in which demand greatly exceeded supply. The increase in input costs because of a shortage of cotton and grain also contributed to higher prices. Though the English did raise their prices after 1734, this came too late for the merchants to recoup their cumulative losses. Nor could this increase really match the rising prices.

---

135. The Fort St George Council did resort to releasing the broadcloth only on spot payment in the 1730s, but soon gave up the practice because of the damage this caused to the liquidity and creditworthiness of the merchants in local trading circles. PC, 6 May 1736.
136. PC, 10 December 1744.
137. PC, 24 May 1693; 5 April 1701; 18 January 1711/2.

Table 7.2: Calendar of Losses Reported by Merchants, 1675–1725

30 June	1675
5 August	1678
24 July	1679
26 February	1685
21 June	1689
1 May	1690
24 May	1693
5 April	1701
2 August	1701*
5 July	1707*
19 October	1709*
25 October	1711
17 January	1712
13 September	1712
13 March	1714
2 January	1724

Note: Dates refer to the date of the Public Consultation.
* Refers to the date of the Fort St David Consultation.

Continued cloth supply to the English

1675–1725: One of several commercial ventures

The question which then has to be answered is, why did the merchants continue to supply cloth to the English? The explanation lies both in the nature of the activities of the merchant capitalists of the region, and in the exogenous factors which shaped their world. The period from 1675 to 1750, in fact, has to be split into two sub-periods in which the political and economic circumstances were vastly different.

In the earlier period, that is until 1725, undertaking to supply cloth to the English was only one of the many business ventures of the merchant capitalists—all of whom conform to the characteristics of merchant capitalists outlined earlier (see chapter 5). With their extended family linkages, the merchants had trade interests covering a very large region in which they dominated. In addition to blood relationships, these links were also strengthened through marriage. The Beri Timmanna family and the Sunkuvar family were cases in point. Beri Timmanna and Kasi Viranna were not merely business partners but were also related by marriage.[138]

---

138. It was noted on the death of Kasi Viranna's wife that he had married her "out of Timmanna's house". PC, 22 August 1678.

Textile Trade: Merchant Capitalism at its Zenith

Timmanna's nephew Beri Timmappa was married to the daughter of Kitti Narayan, the dubash of Fort St George.[139] The daughter of the other brother, Chinna Venkatadri, was married to Ponkala Viraraghava.[140] Though Beri Timmappa was the last member of the family to have the coveted position of chief merchant, and though he, that is the Beri family, was effectively out of the cloth trade after 1696, the family still maintained a high profile in local affairs. In short, the Beri, Kitti and Ponkala families dominated the trade of Madras down to 1750.

Two grandsons of Beri Timmappa, Narayana (the dubash of Governor Richard Benyon) and his brother Chinnatambi, were entrusted with developing and managing the weavers' village of Chintadripet which was set up in 1734.[141] Another descendant, also Beri Timmappa, was a partner with Lingi Chetti in taking over Tambu Chetti's lease of Tiruvottiyur and other villages from the Fort St George Council in 1741.[142] Kitti Narayan is rarely mentioned in the cloth contracts, but his influence, his ships (*Jayalakshmi* and *Venkatalakshmi*), his trade with Manila and other markets, all are frequently mentioned in the consultations, while the Ponkala family figure prominently in other activities.

Similarly, the Sunkuvar family was found in major centres all along the Coromandel coast, and they also had great influence at the court of the Nawab of Arcot. In fact, when Sunku Rama Chetti first wanted to share in the cloth contracts of Fort St George, the Council was not inclined to deal with him because he was involved in endless financial dealings with persons in the government.[143] His trade links extended throughout the region, and he traded in pepper[144] and cotton from Malabar.[145] His network of agents was also very large and were to be found all along the coast, down to Tarangampadi (Tranquebar).[146]

Besides Sunku Rama Chetti's personal and extensive commercial empire, the Sunkuvar family were very prominent in trade throughout

---

139. PC, 21 April 1696.
140. *Ibid.*
141. Petition of Jaggu and Chengalroy, children of Narayana and Chinnatambi. PC, 24 September 1750. The consultation says that the brothers were the grandsons of Beri Timmanna, which is clearly not correct. Also, Love, *Vestiges*, vol. 2: pp. 502–503.
142. PC, 3 September 1741.
143. PC, 9 August 1707.
144. PC, 2 June 1715; 19 May 1722.
145. PC, 4 April 1728.
146. PC, 1 June 1719.

the Coromandel. Sunku Muddu Rama was the main cloth supplier to the Dutch,[147] while Sunku Seshachala Chetti was involved in cloth trade with the French and had several other commercial interests.[148] Another member of the family, Sunku Lakshmipati (Sunku Seshachala Chetti's brother, perhaps) was a leading merchant of Salem.[149]

All the merchant capitalists were shipowners, trading extensively to Manila, Achin, Pegu, Tennassery and other parts of Southeast Asia and West Asia. In fact, in 1726 when penalties had been levied on Tambu Chetti and Sunku Rama Chetti, they were still sending large consignments of cargo to Basra and Mocha.[150] The diverse commercial interests of the merchant capitalists becomes evident if Ananda Ranga Pillai's activities are noted. He traded in cloth, yarn, indigo and arecanut, and participated in trade ventures to Manila, Mocha and Mascereigne, besides sending his own ship, the *Anandappuravi*, on trading voyages.[151] It can thus be inferred that the involvement of the local merchants in the textile contracts of the European companies was not a major part of their commercial ventures, and that the advantages they gained from being "Company merchants" offset the losses or low returns on the cloth supplies.[152] (A close parallel to this would be the purchase of loss-making industrial units by present-day capitalists for tax relief.) Being "Company merchants" gave them a very clear status in local society.

Madras had rapidly achieved a reputation as the richest town on the coast—Ananda Ranga Pillai called it *"kuberapattinam"* (the city of Kubera, the god of wealth). The French and the English were regarded as autonomous rulers on par with other local rulers and chiefs, and as their merchant representatives, the local merchants gained great credit and commercial advantages. They could avail of the concession on tolls and customs given to the Europeans to carry goods on their own account. Even in Madras, the merchants would

---

147. Memorie of van Cloon, p. 30, Dutch Coromandel Records.
148. Sunku Seshachala Chetti is mentioned very often by Ananda Ranga Pillai, and he was the leading right-hand merchant supplying cloth to the French (*Private Diary*, vol. 1, passim). Also, FSDC, 31 July 1743.
149. FSDC, 17 October 1744.
150. PC, 25 October 1726.
151. Ananda Ranga Pillai, *Private Diary*, vol. 1: p. 325 (16 March 1746).
152. Ananda Ranga Pillai felt that if he were the French Company's courtier, he would earn a profit of 2,000 pagodas per year, while on his private trade, he could earn 6,000 pagodas. *Private Diary*, vol. 2: pp. 155–156 (30 July 1746).

bring in cloth for their personal trade—along with cloth on the Company account—without paying local duties.[153] The total ambit of their interactions with and on behalf of the Europeans enhanced their social status besides strengthening their economic domination—for which the losses on their textile contracts was perhaps a small price to pay.[154]

Post-1725 scenario: European enclaves as inviolate strongholds

The post-1725 scenario was quite different. The nature of the changed economic environment has already been outlined. Politically, the incursions of the Marathas, the widespread disturbances and frequent wars disrupted normal life throughout the region. The people were brutalised, standing crops burnt and villages deserted because of the looting by armies which were rarely paid on a regular basis and were in fact a rapacious armed mob on the loose. In this landscape, Fort St George, Fort St David and Pondicherry had become inviolate strongholds where even the leading residents of Arcot sought refuge.

As early as 1712, when the death of the Mughal emperor Shah Alam was confirmed, "several considerable persons" of Arcot had sent their money to Madras for security.[155] This was re-enacted when the Marathas invaded the Karnatak in 1744.[156] When Chanda Sahib was kept a prisoner at Satara by the Marathas, his wife and family were given protection at Pondicherry by the French. Until the 1720s, whenever the merchants of Madras wanted to protest against some specific injustice, they would leave the town and go to San Thome less than five miles away, but still a flourishing independent port under the Indian rulers. But the great deterioration in law and order throughout the region left the merchants of the colonial ports with almost no safe place to go, and thus increased their dependence on the Europeans.

153. PC, 8 December 1694.
154. This perhaps answers Indrani Ray's comment: "The one problem that keeps on intriguing us is the apparent contradiction between the image of an Indian merchant as an indebted Company middleman and a solvent participant in the Asian trade ventures of Europeans" ("The Multiple Faces of the Early Eighteenth Century Merchants", occasional paper no. 29, Centre for Studies in Social Sciences, Calcutta, 1980, p. 21). Ray does not take into consideration the trade of the merchants on their own account.
155. PC, 7 April 1712.
156. PC, 4 February 1743/4.

Arasaratnam has very strongly disputed the claim of the earlier English historians that the local merchants came to Madras and Fort St David because of the just administration of these city enclaves. He has listed the various abuses of basic liberties, the extortionate practices which the governors of Fort St George resorted to in order to fleece the Madras merchants, and the general level of corruption in English administration which give the lie to this claim.[157]

Ray has pointed out, as has Arasaratnam, that the merchants were definitely subservient to the Europeans,[158] which is well borne out by Ananda Ranga Pillai. The merchants had to approach the Europeans circumspectly and respectfully, maintaining a patron-subordinate relationship, irrespective of the status of the merchant in local society. Ananda Ranga Pillai has also recorded with great bitterness the many instances of gross injustice on the part of the French governors. At one point, he has even commented that under the administration of Dupleix and Madame Dupleix, the city of Pondicherry was going through a very bad astrological phase of a seven-and-a-half-year domination by the planet Saturn.[159]

While in retrospect it is clear that the Europeans were far from being just, able and liberal administrators (and rulers), the merchants' choices cannot be understood without taking into account their perceptions of the French and the English and of the advantages in residing in the European enclaves. Ananda Ranga Pillai's *Diary* is the only contemporary document we have which records the personal point of view of the Coromandel merchant. In spite of his criticisms of the French, it is very clear that Ananda Ranga Pillai felt that he was a loyal French subject. There is no "nationalist" self-awareness in his diary which accepts, without question, the status of the French as rulers on par with any other Indian ruler. Besides, though corruption and extortion were very visible and even rampant in the colonial cities, the merchants were perhaps less open to abuses here than under the local rulers.

The colonial enclaves also provided avenues for the merchant capitalists to enhance their social position. Such avenues were not open to them in indigenous society with its traditional, stratified

---

157. Arasaratnam, *Merchants, Companies and Commerce*, pp. 258–265.
158. Ray, "Multiple Faces", p. 13.
159. Ananda Ranga Pillai, *Private Diary*, vol. 5: p. 294 (6 September 1748).

Textile Trade: Merchant Capitalism at its Zenith

hierarchies. The social aspirations of the merchants and their consciousness of themselves as a social class with specific objectives explain the choices they made in their relations with the Europeans more convincingly than any analysis of them as a purely economic class.

EIGHT

Merchant Capitalists as a Social Class

The evolution of merchant capitalism in the Coromandel was a dual process in which the merchants emerged as a dominant economic as well as social class. In many ways, the affirmation of their status as the dominant class and social elite, and as individual leaders of society, underpinned their economic behaviour. The European cities on the Coromandel coast offered avenues for social advancement to the merchant class. This was in contrast to the traditional towns and market centres of South India with their strong linkages with the rural economy and power structures, where social hierarchies were stratified along the traditional grid of caste and land ownership.

The basis of the merchants' social status was the fact that they provided the interface between the Europeans and local society at all levels. The Europeans needed the merchants to be their intermediaries with local governments as well as the local economy. The people who lived in the European towns also needed the merchants to represent them and to voice their demands to the European authorities. The complex and interactive process by which the merchants established their ascendancy as leaders of society can be analysed by examining their interactions with the local society, the Europeans and the indigenous governments and ruling elites. With reference to another social class, the Tamil peasants, David Ludden has argued that the world of the peasant was shaped by four types of social networks—"kinship, religion, state and market interactions."[1] The world of the merchant was also defined and integrated by the same networks through which the merchants manipulated their own social space.

1. Ludden, *Peasant History*, p. 9.

Social stratification in Tamil society

Society in the Tamil region was stratified along traditional caste lines as well as through a vertical subdivision of castes into right and left "hand"—or perhaps more correctly, right and left side *(valangai* and *idangai)*—castes which was unique to the region.[2] In rural society and economy, this division (with its implicit tension indicated by the binary contraposition of right and left) pitted the land-related castes—the landowners (vellalar) and the agricultural labourers (paraiyar)—against the landless artisan castes (kanmalar).

In urban commercial centres like Madras, contending merchant castes were on both sides of the divide. The right-hand merchant castes comprised Komatis and Balijas as well as vellalar (Mudaliar or Pillai) who had turned to commerce. The left-hand merchant castes were predominantly the Beri Chettis. The Nattukottai Chettis or Nagarattar also belonged to the left hand, but till 1750 they did not enjoy high visibility in Madras, Pondicherry or other major cities.[3]

Within this vertical grouping, the upper castes were the dominant castes in their respective hierarchies which included, on the right side, several other artisan and service castes and, most vocal of all in the caste conflicts, the paraiyar. The left-side castes were numerically fewer, and the main constituents were the kanmalar (blacksmiths, masons, carpenters, goldsmiths and braziers) in addition to the Beri Chettis.

Social status, in popular perception, was determined by the composite interplay of several symbols and factors. One of the most important of these was the exclusive right to physical space. Towns and villages in the Tamil country till recently were clearly segregated into specific quarters allocated to different social and economic groups. The left and right sides were both very jealous of their right to "their" streets, through which their public processions—religious, marriage or funeral—could pass, with their own musicians and

---

2. The ensuing analysis of the right- and left-side castes draws extensively on my earlier study, "Caste Conflict".
3. The recorded and documented history of the Nagarattar's activities does not go beyond the beginning of this century. A collection of temple inscriptions dating back to the seventeenth and eighteenth centuries would indicate that they were primarily concentrated in the hinterland of Madurai, especially near Palani, and were involved in local trade in commodities like salt. "Nagarattar Arappattayangal" ["Nagarattar Temple Inscriptions"], in *Nanipugal Nagarattar* [The Renowned Nagarattar], ed. Iniyavan (Madras: Auvai Manram, 1990), pp. 203–223. [Tamil]

dancing girls in attendance. Most of the caste conflicts, especially in the European port cities, were articulated in the context of preserving the exclusive right of a caste group to urban space, whatever the basic reason for the disturbance.

The merchant capitalists, because of their extensive economic resources and power, were automatically acknowledged as the leaders of their own castes and also of the respective caste sodalities of the right and left sides. By defending the rights of their groups to their respective physical spaces, the merchants were able to validate their position as leaders and create a social space for themselves. They were also able to use the same forms of collective social action to advance their own interests, so that in popular perception there was no dividing line between the interests of the merchants as individuals and the interests of the composite caste groups as a whole.

This becomes very evident if one looks at the major caste disputes which erupted in Madras over the years. The first recorded dispute in Madras occurred in 1652–53 when the chief merchants Seshadri Nayak and Koneri Chetti (of Malaya Chetti's family) claimed to have been insulted by the Beri Chettis and started a riot in the city. Incited by the merchants, the right-side castes armed themselves and attacked the houses and the people of the left-side castes. The conflict ultimately resulted in the division of Madras into two segregated quarters, with Muttialpetta being assigned to the left-side castes and Peddanaikpetta to the right. Though bewildered by the intensity of the dispute, the Agent of Fort St George, Aaron Baker, could still see that the real reason behind the conflict was that the chief merchants wanted to divert the attention of the English from the thousands of pagodas they owed the Company.[4]

Once again, in 1707–8, the caste dispute was ostensibly over the redrawing of the demarcated areas, which the right side claimed was iniquitous and had been contrived by the money power of the left-side Beri Chetti merchants. Kelavi Chetti and Venkata Chetti, at that time dominant in the textile trade, openly stated that the disputes had more to do with their near monopoly over the Company's investments than issues of rights over physical space. Governor Pitt even summoned Chikka Serappa, Nayara Viranna, Sunku Rama Chetti and Andi Chetti who he believed were the instigators of the riots.[5]

---

4. Love, *Vestiges*, vol. 1: pp. 118–125; *EFI* 1651–54, pp. 152–153, 155–156, 258–259.
5. PC, beginning 26 June 1707 through 15 January 1707/8.

It is also clear that the solidarity engendered by a composite caste identity was used by the merchant leaders to muster the support of the people of various castes (belonging to a particular side), on the premise that the prestige of the leader was identical with the prestige of the caste group as a whole. When Pedda Venkatadri's and Chinna Venkatadri's sons and sons-in-law left Madras, the issue was the personal hostility between the Beri brothers and Streynsham Master, the governor of Madras. Yet, the former were able to rally round several service castes—painters, fishermen, catamaran men, coolies and others—who left town with them. Leaving a settlement was the commonest form of popular protest in the region, and thus what was essentially a struggle to protect the trading interests of two individuals, soon assumed the proportions and connotations of a mass movement in which even people belonging to the right-hand castes outside Madras were asked to join.[6]

These right- and left-side caste loyalties did not really weaken or change over time. Several decades later, when Tellasinga Chetti, the brother of Tambu Chetti, went to the Kachchalisvarar temple using a palanquin through the right-side streets, there was a near riot. The left-side castes solidly supported Tellasinga Chetti, seeing this not as a question of personal privilege but as an issue of collective prestige.[7]

These blurred perceptions of individual and class interests could sometimes result in bizarre confrontations. In 1740, there was a major caste dispute in Cuddalore which began with protests about the marriage procession of the daughter of Arasappa Chetti, one of the leading merchants of the town. In the course of the disturbances which followed, the wife of Arunachala Pillai of the right side died. Even as the Fort St David Council was inquiring into the incident, Venkatachalam, one of the local dubashes, left the town with all the paraiyar. He took to roaming around outside the town, threatening dire reprisals on the left-side castes and demanded that the English should accept several conditions before he returned to the town. These conditions if accepted would have greatly increased Venkatachalam's personal consequence. Even though they recognised this, the leaders of the right side demanded that Venkatachalam

---

6. PC, 27 October, 1 and 6 November 1680.
7. PC, 2 and 3 March 1750. For an explanation of the peculiar circumstances of Kachchalisvarar temple, see fn. 12 below.

should be pardoned and permitted to return to town, since he was only representing the interests of the entire caste group and this was therefore a matter of their collective prestige.[8]

Social status also had to be validated in the context of the supra-local solidarity of the caste group. In the caste disputes of 1716–17 in Madras, Kelavi Chetti and Venkata Chetti led the exodus of the left-side castes from Madras because the Komati Chettis had openly broadcast the litany of their caste glories in the local temple, which brought the left-side leaders into disrepute among their caste people everywhere.[9] Aware of the consequences of the exodus of the right-side castes in 1707, the left-side merchants must have known that this step would bring reprisals from the English and that they would lose their status as Company merchants.

One possible explanation for the action of Kelavi and Venkata Chetti would be that the loss of social status of the merchants among their reference group adversely affected their economic position as well. This calculated risk of an en masse exodus was probably both rational and expedient, for though Kelavi Chetti lost the contract with the English, he remained one of the most prominent and wealthy merchants of Madras.

The right-left form of social organisation in an urban economy based on commerce also provided avenues of upward social mobility to the merchants. In general, the appellation "right" was considered to confer a superior status on the right-hand castes in a social value system which equated "left" with unclean and polluted. The traditional left-side group, the kanmalar (in common usage kammalar), tried to counter this by claiming brahmin status and adopting brahmin insignia, and the other left-side castes, especially the Beri Chettis, never accepted the superior caste status of the right-side groups. Yet, the more general perception was that incorporation into the right-side castes indicated upward social mobility. An even higher status was accorded to those who were outside this caste divide, referred to in the English records as "middle" castes. Two prominent families which went up the social ladder can be cited.

Beri Timmanna, who started as a merchant in Madras in the 1640s, was said to belong to the "Percawar" (Perike) caste,[10] a not very high sub-

---

8. FSDC, especially 23, 24, 26 and 30 April 1740.
9. PC, 10 and 20 December 1716.
10. Bundla Ramaswamy Naidoo, *Memoir on the Internal Revenue System of the Madras Presidency*, 1820. Published as Selections from the Records of *South Arcot District*,

caste of Balijas. By 1680, Beri Timmanna's brothers Pedda Venkatadri and Chinna Venkatadri were considered the unquestioned leaders of the right-side castes and could mobilise broad-based support in their struggle against Governor Streynsham Master. About fifty years later, another descendant Gooda Ankanna[11]—the dubash of Richard Horden and later of Governor James Macrae—was a signatory, as a member of the "middle" caste, to a mutual agreement between the right and left castes about the use of the Kachchalisvarar temple.[12] The Beri family had thus successfully made the transition from a "low" Balija sub-caste to the highest rung in the right-left caste ladder.

Ananda Ranga Pillai, the dubash of Dupleix, belonged to the shepherd or *idaiyar* caste. In 1756 we find him explaining the right- and left-caste division to Governor de Leyrit, showing him his hands, and adding his own interpretation that since Krishna was born a shepherd, the shepherds belonged to neither grouping but were a neutral caste.[13] In reality, however, his family were the acknowledged leaders of the right side, and the fact that shepherds were routinely included among the dominant right-side castes in Pondicherry[14] can be attributed to the prestige of Ananda Ranga Pillai and his family, since normally shepherds would not be considered an upper caste.

---

no. 11. (Madras: 1908), app. 1, no. 3, p. 73. Edgar Thurston quotes from the Census Report of 1891: "the Perikes claim to be a separate caste, but they seem to be . . . not a very exalted subdivision, of Balijas. . . . Their hereditary occupation is carrying salt, grain, etc. on bullocks and donkeys in perikes or packs. . . . Some of them have attained . . . considerable wealth, and now claim to be kshatriyas". *Castes and Tribes of Southern India* (reprint, Delhi: Cosmo Publications, 1975), vol. 4: pp. 191–192.
11. Gooda Ankanna, according to the family tree given by Bundla Ramaswamy Naidoo, was a direct descendant of Beri Timmanna, probably through one of his daughters. Ankanna achieved notoriety in 1730, after Macrae left for England, and was accused of having extorted large sums of money from several merchants and traders in Madras. He was fined 20,000 pagodas by the Fort St George Council. PC, 19 May, 2, 16, 20 and 26 June, 16 July 1730.
12. The Kachchalisvarar temple was built by the left-side castes in a garden belonging to Kelavi Chetti in Muttialpetta, but had extended up to the right-side streets, so that the approach was only through those streets. Both sides agreed to give each other access to the temple. The middle castes signed as witnesses to the covenant. PC, 4 November 1728.
13. Ananda Ranga Pillai, *Private Diary*, vol. 10: pp. 42–43 (13 March 1756).
14. There was a long inquiry after the caste disturbances in Pondicherry in 1768, and several witnesses when asked to list the leading right-side castes, routinely included shepherds along with Vellalas and merchant castes. The Tamil transcript is in the Mackenzie Collection. *Idangai Valangai Jatiyar Varalaru* [An Account of the Left- and Right-Hand Castes], R. 7749, Government Oriental Manuscripts Library, Madras. [Tamil]

However, the pre-eminence of the family in Pondicherry society was such that his nephew Tiruvengadam Pillai who succeeded Ananda Ranga Pillai as the head of the family was also appointed as the head of the Tamils or *chef des Malabars* by the French. According to a contemporary observer, Tiruvengadam Pillai was generally accepted as the leader of both the right- and left-side castes. On his death, his son succeeded to the office.[15]

Social status and caste panchayats

Two central institutions of indigenous society were of particular significance in defining and validating the social status of merchants. The first was the institution of caste panchayats which mediated in all disputes. Every caste had an elected head known as the *nattanmai*, and the representatives of all the castes were collectively known as the *mahanattar*. They formed a stratum between the Europeans and the people in Madras and Pondicherry, and served as a conduit for the demands of the English (and the French) as well as of the local people to reach one another.

When Madras was founded, the English had found it expedient to follow the locally prevalent custom of allowing people to live in the town without paying any rent or taxes. As Madras grew and became established, the Fort St George Council was under pressure from the Company to raise more revenues locally, though the Council explained that "in all these countries, there is no such practice" of collecting rents from local residents. Further, the Council said that the imposition of any levies was particularly ill-advised when in neighbouring San Thome, the local authorities had given remission from taxes for three years.[16]

Several attempts by the English to levy taxes on the local people sparked off mass protests, which usually resulted in shopkeepers shutting down their shops and most of the people moving to the temple ("pagoda") while enlisting the support of people in the surrounding regions.[17] Each new move to introduce a new tax, like the proposal to levy quit rents on the people of Madras in 1695, was

---

15. Vira Naykkar, *Irandam Vira Naykkar Natkurippu* (1778–1792) [The Diary of Vira Naykkar the Second], ed. M. Gopalakrishnan (Madras: Narramil Patippagam, 1992), p. 122, 2 March 1785; p. 232, 13 February 1791. [Tamil]
16. PC, 29 February 1676.
17. *Ibid.*; 3 January 1685/6.

met with stiff resistance.[18] Since the caste heads were the leaders of the movements, the English began to co-opt the leaders in the process of collecting the taxes. They did this, for instance, towards the beginning of the eighteenth century (in 1699, 1703–4 and 1706), when they decided to build a protective wall around Madras and levied a tax on the residents to pay for it.

The heads of castes played a crucial role in all such tax levies because they submitted the census of their castes and the assessment they were liable for. They were evidently expected to use their judgment and collect the tax on some basic principles of progressive taxation. But the Fort St George Council, with somewhat ingenuous anger, noted in 1704 that "[n]otorious and egregious villainies" had been committed by the heads of the castes, who had collected the tax with arbitrary iniquity, laying the burden of the tax on the poorest.[19]

In 1706 when the caste heads delayed the assessment and collection of the wall tax, they were jailed ("confined") to compel them to raise the money. The facile assurance from the Fort St George Council was that once they had cleared the account of the town wall, they would pay no more on that account.[20] Some years later, when some form of urban property tax was levied, the heads of the Beri Chettis did not want an enumeration of their property. Instead they offered to pay, as a collective assessment, one-third of the total tax as their share, and an additional 500 pagodas for this privilege (of not being listed).[21]

The mahanattar of Pondicherry were very visible on all ceremonial occasions and called on the governor with presents, to pay their respects.[22] In 1759, when the Pondicherry government was facing a severe financial crisis, the mahanattar were forced by General Lally to raise rupees eight to ten lakhs from the people which the French would borrow at 12 per cent interest. When the caste heads were

18. PC, 14 November 1695.
19. PC, 24 February 1703/4.
20. PC, 12 September 1706.
21. PC, 20 and 27 November 1718. The total value of property in Madras was estimated at 450,000 pagodas, of which the Beri Chettis owned a third.
22. Ananda Ranga Pillai records several routine occasions like New Year's Day, or the Governor's "saint's day" and so on, when such ceremonial visits would take place. In 1747, when the capture of Madras was announced, all the merchants and mahanattar called on Dupleix and presented him with 157 gold mohurs. *Diary*, vol. 3: pp. 385–386, (27 February 1747).

unable to pay 100,000 pagodas, they were imprisoned and threatened that they would be hanged. The local people resorted to the familiar forms of protest by closing shops in retaliation, but ultimately they did not succeed. The heads were treated with great barbarity and were finally persuaded by Ananda Ranga Pillai to sign for 81,000 pagodas to secure their release.[23]

There was also a collective assembly of the heads of castes for the right and left sides, respectively, which adjudicated all the intracaste and intercaste disputes. The assembly was also called upon by the English and the French to mediate in disputes—especially those dealing with property, inheritance and business agreements—which had been referred to the authorities. In such cases, it was more common to select a committee of leaders of the merchant communities who were called upon to adjudicate the disputes,[24] thereby reinforcing the authority and status of the merchants in local society. While there are several references to such panels of arbitration, one famous instance was the property settlement dispute after the death in 1736 of Kanakaraya Mudali, the courtier of the French Company at Pondicherry.[25]

The establishment of the Mayor's Court in Madras offered the Madras merchants a legal channel to settle their business disputes. It comes as no surprise that most of the cases involved the major merchants—Kitti Narayan, Kelavi Chetti, Muttamar Chetti, Venkata Chetti, Ponkala Krishna, Sunku Venkatachalam, Nayara Bali Chetti, Beri Durgappa, Chikka Serappa and Gooda Ankanna, among others. The frequency with which the names of the leading merchants appear

23. Ananda Ranga Pillai, *Private Diary*, vol. 11: pp. 371–372, 374–375, 397–404, 407–408 (August to September 1759). It may be noted that in Pondicherry both rupees and pagodas were prevalent.
　　This scenario was repeated again in 1760 when the heads of different castes were told that they had to pay for the wages of the sepoys at the rate of Rs 353 (evidently 100 pagodas) per 50 sepoys per month, and the leading merchants were told to pay 120,000 rupees. *Ibid.*, vol. 12: p. 20 (18 March 1760); pp. 43, 47 (12 and 14 April 1760).
24. The Mayor's Court Records (Pleadings and Proceedings), Tamil Nadu State Archives, have many references to such arbitration. When the sons of Kitti Venkatapati, the dubash of Fort St David, wanted their uncle Kitti Narayan to account for the property which he held in trust for them, Sunku Muddu Rama, Kelavi Chetti, Chodarmal and Nayara Viraraghava, "eminent merchants of as good character as any in the place", were appointed to audit the accounts and give a verdict. PC, 20 and 28 November, 4 December 1712.
25. Ananda Ranga Pillai (*Private Diary*, vols. 1 and 2) gives an inside view of the process of arbitration, and the manipulations and biases evident in the process.

in the Proceedings of the Mayor's Court indicates that the merchants had enthusiastically embraced the process of litigation. At the same time, it also reduced their influence because disputes which used to be solved by the caste panchayats now tended to be referred to the courts.

It is evident that this was a step undertaken by the English to introduce European civic institutions and norms of governance, as well as to strengthen their own authority by eliminating extra-state legal or adjudicatory institutions which diluted their control over local affairs. Perceiving this, the merchants also made moves to protect their rights to decide intracaste and intercaste disputes. In 1725, the castes gave a petition stating that they were greatly perturbed by the newly instituted Grand Jury and their "foreign methods"—especially the demand that all questions asked by the Grand Jury must be answered and the punishing of theft with death. According to the petition, such alien measures, especially swearing oaths, discredited the local people in the eyes of their castes, and it stated that the people could not live in peace in Madras if they were so going to be harassed by the Grand Jury.[26]

A similar petition was submitted by Tambu Chetti and Sunku Rama Chetti in 1729, though they recanted a year later and alleged that the petition had been masterminded by Gooda Ankanna.[27] The Fort St George Council clearly was not pleased by such petitions. A more detailed petition setting out the matters taken up by the caste panchayats for settlement and the punishments awarded (to those who did not abide by the decisions of the panchayats) was submitted a year later. It asked that the jurisdiction of the caste panchayats should continue as before.[28]

Social status and temples

A second institution of great significance in local society was the temple. We have already discussed that the temple was both a sacred as well as a secular institution—the central agency in social and economic life. Over the centuries, in Tamil Nadu the old political

26. PC, 12 December 1725.
27. PC, 26 June 1730.
28. PC, 10 February 1731/2. Tambu Chetti was the signatory for the Beri Chettis and Ponkala Krishna for the right-hand Velamas.

order changed and new ruling groups and elite came up, but the temples continued to be an important source of legitimacy and authority. On the economic front, large-scale endowments, especially of money, to the temple had virtually disappeared. The role of the temple as a lender of capital also receded, though for most of the smaller merchants in local trade, borrowing from the temple continued to be a source of finance.[29] But the importance of the temple as an institution which conferred legitimacy on its patrons did not diminish over the centuries. For the merchant capitalists, the construction and management of temples established their status on a par with that of the landed elite and marked them out as unimpeachable leaders of local society.

Beri Timmanna had constructed a temple complex in Madras, which the English referred to as the "Gentue pagoda" (the two temples in it being dedicated to Chennakesavaperumal and Chennamallikarjunasvami). This complex was managed by the family members who also collected a small tax paid by all the local residents, including the Muslims, to maintain the temple brahmans.[30] The only exceptions were the Europeans and the Armenians. When Kasi Viranna, in 1676, procured from Golkonda the firman to farm the revenues of Triplicane, for the English, the famous Parthasarathi temple was also included in the charter at Viranna's special request. This temple too was managed by the chief merchants, that is, the Beri family. The revenue from the land near the temple was used for maintaining the temple and its religious services.[31]

On their own initiative, Pedda Venkatadri and Chinna Venkatadri extended their authority to raise resources for the temple by levying other taxes on the local people. Chinna Venkatadri was collecting taxes from shopkeepers, fishermen and the betel and tobacco merchants, which he explained were used for charitable purposes.

---

29. The temple inscriptions after the fifteenth century indicate that the amount of money endowed to the temples tended to be very small. David West Runder shows how the Nagarattar (Nattukkottai Chettiars) used the endowments to the Palani temple for their salt trade. "Religious Gifting and Inland Commerce in Seventeenth Century South India", *Journal of Asian Studies* 46, no. 2, May 1987, pp. 361–379.

30. Kasi Viranna had also built a mosque in Madras which was managed by the Hindu merchants, which generated a great deal of dissension. The Muslim priests protested because the Muslims were paying taxes to maintain the Hindu temple as well as because the management of the mosque was in the hands of the Hindus. PC, 1 and 5 August 1712.

31. PC, 29 December 1692.

Pedda Venkatadri was employing his own choultry accountant ("Conicoply" or *kanakkupillai*) to collect customs duties from the people since the 1660s, which he used for maintaining the right-hand dancing girls. When Master became the governor, he stopped both practices, and the fact that Chinna Venkatadri was imprisoned for his tax-collecting enterprise would indicate that he had not received any official sanction for this from the Fort St George Council.[32] This was undoubtedly one more instance of Master's personal vindictiveness towards the chief merchants who he felt exercised a dangerous amount of power. However, since the collection of money for the maintenance of a temple was recognised as a legitimate function by the English, it would seem that the Venkatadri brothers had exceeded the tolerable limits of independent authority.

Kitti Venkatapati, the dubash of Fort St David, built a temple at Tevanampattinam in 1696, which was seen as a public service since the local temple had been razed by the Muslims about thirty to forty years earlier. Kitti Venkatapati said that the people were willing to pay additional taxes on all goods imported and exported, including paddy, to maintain the temple, which was accepted by the Fort St David Council.[33]

Both the merchants and the English recognised the underlying reality that such tax-levying authority, whether self-appropriated or authorised, established and reaffirmed the status of the individual concerned. So, while the Venkatadri brothers were consciously trying to expand their sphere of influence and authority, Streynsham Master was trying to lessen their status. Governor Elihu Yale also tried to devalue the status of chief merchants Beri Timmappa and Alangatha Pillai in 1692 by taking away from them the function of management of the temples and appointing three other trustees instead. This evidently provoked a sufficiently strong popular protest and the merchants, therefore, were restored to their former positions. The Council, though, warned that it reserved the right to change the arrangement and that the merchants could not collect taxes without prior permission.[34] The stewardship of Beri Timmappa was revoked again in 1696, but he vehemently protested that his family had constructed the Madras temples and were their hereditary trustees.

32. PC, 25 November 1678.
33. FSDC, 10 and 27 August 1696.
34. PC, 29 December 1692.

However, he would agree to hand over the management of the Triplicane temple.[35]

In 1749, all the merchants of Pondicherry, under the direction of Ananda Ranga Pillai, agreed to contribute money towards the construction of the Singarikoyil temple. This was a major undertaking, since they also agreed to build eighteen houses for the brahmins, to repair the tank and the *gopuram* (temple tower) as well as other structures and shrines in the courtyard, to build a new stone *mandapam* (pavilion), and to also make provision for the future maintenance of the temple. Several leading merchants of Pondicherry like Sunku Seshachala Chetti, Salatu Venkatachala Chetti, Alagiya Manavala Chetti and many others, including a Muslim merchant, had agreed to participate in this contribution. This large-scale endeavour happened within a year of the destruction of the Vedapurisvarar temple in Pondicherry by the French, which had shocked the local community. It was probably an attempt by the merchants to regain the prestige which they had lost earlier by not being able to stop the temple destruction by the French.[36]

Other social institutions were also promoted and supported by the merchants. Like the Vellala landowning classes, the merchants also extended patronage to brahmins and set up *agraharams* (brahmin quarters). Ananda Ranga Pillai often refers to his "brahmin village"[37] which he had named after his father Tiruvengada Pillai. In Chintadripet, which was set up as a weavers' suburb in Madras on land belonging to Sunku Venkatachala Chetti, there is still a Sunkuvar agraharam.[38]

In 1676, Kasi Viranna together with Pedda Venkatadri and Chinna Venkatadri endowed an irrigation tank known as Chennapatnamcheruvu in Punganur in Cuddapah district, for which a *dasabandam* (right to use one-tenth of the water) was conferred on them by Prince Chikka Raya Bommiah. The rights of the dasabandam were with the family for more than 150 years.[39]

---

35. PC, 18 April 1696.
36. Ananda Ranga Pillai (Private Diary, vol. 6: pp. 287 ff. [2 December 1749]; vol. 5: pp. 296 ff. [7 September 1748]), gives an account of the destruction of the Vedapurisvarar temple.
37. *Ibid.*, vol. 1: p. 149 (29 January 1741), for one instance.
38. Minakshisundaranar, "Sunkuvar Kutumbam", p. 124.
39. Naidoo, *Memoir*, p. 73.

Merchant capitalists as intermediaries of Europeans

For the merchant capitalists, the dual role they played in the trade of the Europeans provided opportunities for consolidating their social position. They were intermediaries for the Europeans both at the official level (as "Company merchants") and in their private trade (as their dubashes or agents). In the period up to 1750, the high profile and visibility of the merchants in the textile trade tends to downplay the other important aspects of their commercial interaction with the European companies. The company merchants supplied not only textiles, but also other commodities for export like pepper and indigo. They were also the main buyers for the imported commodities, as the Europeans found it better to deal with a few merchants as wholesalers rather than to retail their imports to a larger market. In addition to broadcloth, silver and coral were the other major imports of the English, and Sunku Rama Chetti and Lingi Chetti were important buyers of silver. There were several coral merchants who bought the imported coral in bulk[40] and also ruby merchants who bought the rubies imported from Pegu.[41]

Participation in revenue and measuring farms

Several merchant capitalists who did not enter the textile contracts or the other import-export transactions were very prominent in other kinds of ventures. The Fort St George Council was constantly under pressure from the Company to impose European-style taxes in Madras to raise revenues to the maximum extent. While quit rents or other taxes could only be imposed amidst strong popular pressure, several forms of indirect taxation could be resorted to more easily.

The main taxes which the English relied on were customs duties on all imports and exports and fixed "rents" from the merchants who offered the highest bid for the grant of monopoly rights over certain goods and services. Two of the most taxed goods under the latter arrangement were betel leaves (pan) and tobacco, which were articles of mass consumption. Among commercial services, "measuring" was similarly farmed out, and the bidders or "farmers" were allowed to

---

40. There is still a Coral Merchants Street *(Pavalakkaran Teru)* in Georgetown or old Madras.
41. The Nayara family—Nayara Viranna and several other members—dominated the ruby trade in Madras.

take a fixed fee for every garce of paddy sold from the grain sellers. As the population grew, the tax base also widened, and the farms were let out at increasingly higher rates over the decades.

As nearby "villages" like Egmore, Purasavakkam and others were added to Madras, the revenues of these villages were rented out—usually to the Company merchants, since the English felt that they themselves would be unable to collect the revenue efficiently. Three such revenue farms were given out—one for Egmore, Purasavakkam and Tondiarpet, one for Tiruvottiyur, and the last for what were euphemistically called the "paddy fields" (in reality the salt pans, north of Madras).

Ponkala Krishna was one of the leading merchants who was never involved in the cloth trade, but was quite prominent in the revenue farms. He is first mentioned when he took up the tobacco farm at 7,000 pagodas per year in 1710.[42] The tobacco farm used to be let out at 2,900 pagodas in 1695,[43] but this was increased to 7,000 pagodas in 1705.[44] The merchants who had bid for this in 1695 had been members of the joint-stock company organised by Chikka Serappa. They complained that money from the joint stock had been siphoned off for several years to pay for the farm, so that they had suffered great losses both on the textile trade and on the tobacco farm and had ended up bankrupt.[45] Ponkala Krishna continued in the tobacco farm for several years, earning a reputation as the only merchant who paid the farm dues promptly each month. He finally gave up the farm in 1730 when the Council wanted to increase it to 10,000 pagodas.[46]

Ponkala Krishna also took up the measuring farm at 820 pagodas in 1711.[47] In 1716 he offered to renew the farm, but only at 400 pagodas because of his continued losses, and the Fort St George Council rented it to two other merchants.[48] Within two years, this had to be cancelled because of complaints that the merchants had extorted money from the grain sellers and buyers, in addition to the

42. PC, 4 April 1710.
43. PC, 25 February 1694/5.
44. The increase was partly to compensate for the loss of revenue on betel leaves which were being grown within Madras, so that imports from outside were reduced. PC, 21 December 1705.
45. PC, 14 March 1709/10.
46. PC, 6 April 1730.
47. PC, 17 December 1711.
48. PC, 10 December 1716.

Merchant Capitalists as a Social Class

duty that they were allowed to collect. The measuring farm was restored to Ponkala Krishna,[49] which he gave up five years later when Governor Elwick wanted to raise it to 600 pagodas.[50] In 1722, Ponkala Krishna took over the revenue farm of Egmore and other villages after the Company's chief merchants Kelavi Chetti and Venkata Chetti complained of continued losses because of recurrent droughts.[51] In 1735, Ponkala Krishna's heirs informed the Fort St George Council that they had continued to pay the rents though the revenues had been falling. However, they could not maintain the tank in good repair, as stipulated in the conditions, because there was no money.[52]

Several merchants were involved in such contracts with the English, but Ponkala Krishna's manifold ventures into revenue farming clearly indicate that while the farms augmented the revenues of Fort St George, the merchants themselves made little money on them, especially after 1700. This naturally leads us to ask why the merchants took up the farms, which were successively being put up for very high sums by the presidents of Fort St George. The most convincing explanation is that the Fort St George Council was able to offer inducements to the merchants in the form of "privileges".

The chief merchants received several public honours from the English. They were given honorary presents every New Year's Day. They were allowed to come into the Fort with a roundel (parasol), and to ride in a palanquin. Guns were fired during their family weddings or their funerals. All these priviliges, from which other merchants were excluded, gave them great standing in society. The revenue-farming transactions gave these other merchants the much-desired opportunity to enhance their social status and made even loss-making contracts attractive to them. At Fort St David, Sadasiva Rao discontinued the tobacco farm in 1732 when such privileges were withdrawn, even though he had continued with it for several years despite losses.[53]

---

49. PC, 20 October 1718.
50. PC, 23 and 30 October; 6 November 1723.
51. The lease was not officially in Ponkala Krishna's name, but he had stood security for the other merchants. PC, 9 July 1722.
52. PC, 1 July 1735. This was in response to the admonition by the Council for not maintaining the tank in good repair.
53. FSDC, 29 April 1732.

It is clear that the English and the French modelled themselves on the patterns of behaviour of the Indian rulers whose prerogative it was to award these symbols of status as special honours to select persons. The English were also able to exploit the desire of the merchants to enjoy these honours, which enabled them to attract bidders to the least profitable farms. One of these was the farming of the salt pans ("paddy fields") in the mudflats north of Madras. Taking this up, specifically entitled the revenue farmer to "wear a roundel". In 1717, the salt farm was taken away from Rayasam Papaiya, the dubash of Fort St George, and given to one Venkanna "brahmin". The *kaul* (or agreement) for the salt farm was delivered with the roundel and a kaul for "wearing" it, though the roundel could not be used in the English town, nor in the presence of any member of the Fort St George Council.[54] The same consultation, in fact, clarified that no "black" person whatever could make make use of a roundel without express permission from Fort St George.[55]

Rayasam Papaiya left town in disgrace a few months after this,[56] mainly because he was suspected of having colluded with the Beri Chettis in their agitation. He was taken back into Company service in 1721—in fact as soon as President Collett with his obsessive suspicion of the Beri Chettis left Fort St George. Rayasam Papaiya was reinstated as chief dubash in recognition of his great ability and was given the kaul for the paddy fields and a roundel.[57] In 1728, after his death, his nephew Coolacherla Vyasam gave a petition that his uncle had taken up the farm which used to be let for 40 pagodas at 710 pagodas, in order to please the English and to regain his right to use a roundel. Rayasam Papaiya had steadily lost 300 pagodas per year, so that at the time of his death, his losses had accumulated to more than 2,000 pagodas.[58] This gives us a rough idea of the monetary worth of this privilege to the person concerned.

Even the revenue farms of the villages of Egmore and Tiruvottiyur were taken up by the Company merchants because this enhanced their

---

54. PC, 6 February 1716/7.
55. Thomas Bowrey observed that anybody could use a "cattisol", a bamboo-handled umbrella, but nobody could use a roundel unless he were in a good office, and only a governor could use more than one. *A Geographical Account of Countries Around the Bay of Bengal, 1669–1679*, ed. R. C. Temple (Cambridge: Hakluyt Society, 1905), p. 86.
56. PC, 16 September 1717.
57. PC, 4 December 1721.
58. PC, 9 September 1728.

social standing. There is no instance of these farms ever having yielded a surplus, but, nevertheless, each successive chief merchant would take up the farm to consolidate his position. Lingi Chetti was the last merchant in our period who voluntarily took up the farms of Tiruvottiyur and other villages,[59] tobacco and betel,[60] and the paddy fields and salt pans.[61] The experience of Ananda Ranga Pillai was also quite similar, and he records his great losses in revenue farming which he undertook on the persuasion of Dupleix. On the other hand, only he among the "Tamils" (i.e., the Hindus), and Chanda Sahib's son, and Ali Naqvi among the Muslims could come into Pondicherry on a palanquin.[62]

Merchants as private agents of Europeans

The local merchants also acted as the private agents or dubashes of the Europeans. In Madras, after 1770 they played little role in the Company trade. They became notable in the local trade and society only in their capacity as the private agents of the English, whereas in the earlier period, the private role of these merchants tended to be less visible. From the mid-seventeenth century onward, the merchants built on this relationship with the Europeans to further their economic and social power. Kasi Viranna, Beri Timmanna, Kitti Narayan and Chikka Serappa were notable examples. Beri Timmappa's grandson Narayana, who established Chintadripet, was the dubash of Governor Richard Benyon. He was said to have been a person of great power and influence.[63] Many other agents, who never entered the more public world of contracts, were able to achieve high social status through their power as agents of leading members of the Fort St George Council. The dubashes of the governors—like Markrishna, the dubash of Hastings, and Gooda Ankanna, the dubash of Macrae—had considerable influence and authority which they misused extensively. Both Markrishna and Ankanna were accused of using their powerful position to extort money from the local merchants.[64]

59. PC, 3 September 1741.
60. PC, 7 October 1745.
61. FSDC, 30 November 1749.
62. Ananda Ranga Pillai, *Private Diary*, vol. 9: pp. 55–57 (15 October 1754); pp. 174–175 (21 February 1755).
63. Love, *Vestiges*, vol. 2: pp. 502–503.
64. Many dubashes of governors were publicly accused of extortion almost as soon as their masters stepped down from office. Complaints were made about Govinda, the

Ananda Ranga Pillai had achieved his status in Pondicherry Tamil society as the private dubash of Dupleix. Though not a Company merchant, he was still supplying cloth to the governor of Pondicherry for his private trade.[65] His wealth and standing are indicated by the fact that he was personally assessed for a tax of 400 pagodas, as compared to 1,000 pagodas for the Beri Chettis and 500 pagodas for Sunku Seshachala Chetti, both Company merchants.[66] Ananda Ranga Pillai, nevertheless, hankered for the public recognition of his abilities and the services (rendered to the French), which he would receive by being appointed courtier after Kanakaraya Mudali's death. He felt this should have been his office by right, but which had been given to Kanakaraya Mudali because the latter had converted to Christianity. He did acknowledge that this office otherwise made little difference to him—since his financial position would not really improve and he was already allowed the honours of torches and a palanquin and was even vested with judicial powers.[67]

Merchant capitalists and Indian rulers

Almost all the great merchant capitalists of the time had extensive contacts with the local rulers, which facilitated their trade, allowed them to intercede on behalf of their European masters, and also consolidated their social position. In the earlier period, till the end of the seventeenth century, one mode of such interaction with the rulers was through revenue farming. Chinna Venkatadri was the renter of Sriharikota, while Kasi Viranna was the renter of Armagon (Durgarajapatnam) and Kotapatnam, north of Madras, for which he paid 1,200 pagodas.[68] Since the customs of both the towns amounted

---

dubash of acting Governor Fraser (October 1709 to July 1711), in July 1711 (PC, 16 July 1711); Markrishna, the dubash of Governor Hastings (1720–21), was accused of extortion by Tambu Chetti and Mutta Venkata Chetti and several other leading merchants of Fort St George and Fort St David (PC, 8 September 1722; 26 March 1722/3); by far the longest list of complaints of extortion was against Gooda Ankanna, the dubash of Governor Macrae (1725 to May 1730), almost immediately after the latter left for England (PC, 19 May; 2, 16, 20 and 26 June 1730). It is worth noting that the governors themselves almost never became embroiled in these inquiries and returned to England with their fortunes intact.

65. Ananda Ranga Pillai, *Private Diary*, vol. 1: p. 11 (15 January 1737).
66. In 1740, the courtier Kanakaraya Mudali persuaded Governor Dumas to levy such a tax. *Ibid.*, p. 138 (22 December 1740).
67. *Ibid.*, vol 2: pp. 155–156 (30 July 1746).

to only 960 pagodas, it can be inferred that revenue farming was undertaken not because it gave additional income, but because it conferred social status. In the later decades, we do not hear of the Madras merchants entering into revenue farming, except when they did it in order to bring nearby towns (especially San Thome and Triplicane) effectively under Fort St George.

The private intercourse of the merchants with the local rulers continued in spite of the disapproval of the Europeans, who were suspicious of the independent status that this gave the merchants. The English often used Kasi Viranna's good offices with Podala Lingappa to protect their interests. However, they viewed with disapprobation his personal relations with Madanna, the Golkonda minister, and Podala Lingappa, both of whom called on Kasi Viranna and stayed in his garden.[69] Pedda Venkatadri, when he was reinstated as chief merchant in 1681, was advised "not to live at so high a rate as his predecessor", Kasi Viranna.[70]

The influence that Pedda Venkatadri and Chinna Venkatadri and, some years later, Chikka Serappa had with the local rulers was clear when the latter intervened on behalf of the merchants with Fort St George. Pedda Venkatadri's son, Beri Timmappa, and Alangatha Pillai, when they were chief merchants, had procured parwanas in their own names from the Mughal Nawab Zulfiqar Khan to carry on trade in the Karnatak country. The Fort St George Council took strong exception to this, since the document did not mention that they were Company merchants.[71] When Beri Timmappa had been replaced as the chief merchant, the Fort St George Council received reports that he had an agent at the Nawab's court and was said to have invited the Nawab to besiege Madras.[72] Sunku Rama Chetti's connections with the Nawab of Arcot were also well known.

Ananda Ranga Pillai had close contacts with the Karveti Raja of Bommarajapalayam. In 1746, he received a horse, an embroidered silk-cloth, a sash, a turban, a shawl and a dagger inlaid with precious stones from the Raja as a gift.[73] When a son was born to Ananda

---

68. A Memorial of Streynsham Master's Visit to Masulipatnam, PC, 13, 14 and 15 March 1679.
69. PC, 5 September 1678; 3 January 1678/9.
70. PC, 14 July 1681.
71. PC, 18 January 1693/4.
72. PC, 14 September 1696; 16 August 1697.
73. Ananda Ranga Pillai, *Private Diary*, vol. 2: p. 24 (17 May 1746). Ananda Ranga Pillai records how jealously Dupleix reacted to this. A year later, the Raja gave him

Ranga Pillai in 1748, the *qiledar* (governor of the fort) of Vandavasi sent him as a gift the *sanad* (deed of grant) for a village, worth 100 pagodas, and a dress of honour.[74] He also recorded, with no undue modesty, the political skill and sagacity with which he had dealt with the Nawab of Arcot on behalf of the French over the attack on Madras. In the same tone, Ananda Ranga Pillai noted that the Nawab told his sons that as long as he (Ananda Ranga Pillai) was associated with the French, even the Mughal emperor could not overcome Pondicherry.[75]

These forays by the merchants into the realm of politics and especially their ventures in revenue farming has led Arasaratnam to refer to them as "political merchants".[76] More recently, Sanjay Subrahmanyam has elaborated an analytical framework which is sharply critical of the views of earlier historians, especially Pearson. According to these historians, in India, politics and commerce were unrelated, compartmentalised activities. Citing the example of many rulers and ruling elite—notably the Mir Jumla of Golkonda, Mir Muhammad Saiyid, who had extensive commercial interests—Subrahmanyam argues that these merchants and rulers constituted a class of "portfolio capitalists who were able to straddle the worlds of commerce and political participation".[77] This framework is problematic, to say the least. To begin with, it is based on precisely the same artificial dichotomy between politics and commerce which Subrahmanyam criticises Pearson for. This distinction, which characterised Western social identity, was not relevant in the Indian context. In India, both activities were regarded as integral parts of a composite system, and rulers as well as merchants sought to augment their resources and power through participation in both.

Subrahmanyam's framework further overlooks the fundamental question of the self-perception by which a class identifies itself. The Mir Jumla might have owned ships and had commercial interests, but

---

a village which he could use for making salt. *Ibid.,* vol. 4: p. 137 (13 August 1647).
74. *Ibid.,* vol. 5: p. 8 (4 April 1748).
75. *Ibid.,* vol. 3: pp. 365–382 (26 February 1747).
76. Arasaratnam, *Merchants, Companies and Commerce,* p. 224.
77. Subrahmanyam initially outlined this framework in his *Political Economy of Commerce,* ch. 6, and further elaborated it in Subrahmanyam and C. A. Bayly, "Portfolio Capitalists".

he did not think of himself as a merchant.[78] Equally, even as political a merchant as Chinnanna Chetti knew that he would always be subject and subservient to the whims of the ruling classes. Thus, while the activity spheres might have overlapped, the social divide based on class perceptions was quite clear-cut.

The increasing politicisation of the Coromandel merchants can be explained partly by the enlarged scope of their activities provided by the weakening of the traditional states. This pattern had been evident even at the end of the Chola empire when merchant assemblies began to take more decisions on taxes and assignment of taxes. So, there was nothing different about the way the merchants in later periods also enlarged their spheres of activity in the absence of strong state control. In part, this also stemmed from their need to establish themselves as a dominant social class, on a par with the upper-caste landed elite.

Merchants as patrons of art

The merchant capitalists consistently and consciously followed the behaviour norms of the landowning ruling elite.[79] This is seen in their founding of temples and other socially acceptable institutions. Revenue farms certainly produced little revenue, whether taken from the Europeans or the Indian rulers. But they conferred power and social prestige on the revenue farmers, especially since this activity permitted them to use status symbols reserved for the ruling classes.[80]

One of the most significant aspects of this imitative behaviour was the patronage extended by the merchants to the arts. In the eighteenth

---

78. Subrahmanyam also refers to the other major prince-merchant, the great Sidakkadi or Syed Abdul Qadir Marakkayar of Kilakkarai. I have not included Sidakkadi among the merchant capitalists because it is clear that his main sphere of authority was politics and the source of wealth was his political position, though he was also involved in commerce. For a thorough note on Sidakkadi as patron, politician and merchant, see Rao, Shulman and Subrahmanyam, *Symbols*, pp. 264–304.

79. Susan J. Lewandowski's analysis of the social relations of the merchants is quite similar to this, but she argues that the merchants sought to fill the power vacuum within the city of Madras by aspiring to kingly status ("Merchants and Kingship: An Interpretation of Indian Urban History", *Journal of Urban History* 11, no. 2, 1985, pp. 151–179). It is difficult to agree with this, since royal status had several connotations of divine legitimacy that the merchants would not have aspired to.

80. Most of the revenue farming referred to here was essentially on a very small scale, and it cannot be compared with the kind of revenue assignments made to the English by the Nawab of Arcot in the latter half of the eighteenth century.

century, Vellala landowners were the major patrons of literature and poetry and, in fact, had commissioned several literary works.[81] Ananda Ranga Pillai was also a well-recognised patron of the arts. Poets, impoverished in the absence of princely courts, went to him to sing his praises and received ample rewards for their efforts. The hyperbole that was employed to praise Ananda Ranga Pillai parallels the glorification that used to be lavished on royalty. Ananda Ranga Pillai is addressed in the same terms as kings or princes: as *naradipane* (lord of men), as the ruler of the city of Pondicherry (with its towering buildings, roofed with gold and caressed by clouds), and as the conqueror and ruler of all directions.[82]

Like the Vellala landowning elite, the merchant capitalists had also begun to adopt a highly sankritised tradition of patronage. Ananda Ranga Pillai was not only approached by Tamil poets, but many odes and *champus* (literary pieces in Sanskrit and Telugu) were also written about him. The *Ananda-ranga-rat-chandamu*, which was composed by Kasturirangaiyan of Tiruchirapalli, was set to music and performed in public at the garden adjoining the house of Muttaiya Pillai.[83] Muvala Sabhapati Aiya, a minor composer, also composed a love lyric in the Carnatic classical music mode (known as *padam*) dedicated to Ananda Ranga Pillai.[84]

Later in the eighteenth century, the dubashes of Madras continued the same tradition and extended patronage to several poets. Manali Muttukrishna Mudali, the dubash of Governor Pigot, was the patron of Arunachalakkavirayar who composed the *Ramanatakam* like an opera, set to music. Several other patrons, especially Tottikkalai Vedachala Mudaliar, are mentioned in the *Sarvadevavilasa*, a con-

---

81. A patron named Arunchala Vel (c. 1700) asked Atmanatha Desikar to compose the *Chola-mandala-satakam* to extol the greatness and prosperity of Cholanadu. Karuppa Mudaliar of Mavundur, the son of Kalatti Mudaliar, commissioned Padikkasuppulavar to compose the *Tondai-mandala-satakam* in praise of the Vellalar. Vallam Kacchiyappa Mudaliar was another great patron. (N. V. Jayaraman, *Sataka Ilakkiyam* [Satakam Poetry] (Chidambaram: Manivachakar Nulagam, 1973), pp. 54, 64–65, 72–73. [Tamil]

82. All these poems, by poets like Madurakavirayar, Javvaduppulavar and others, are published in collections of individual verses known as *tanippadal* or *tanichcheyyul*.

83. Ananda Ranga Pillai, *Private Diary,* vol. 2: p. 238 (25 August 1746). Another Sanskrit poem, *Ananda-ranga-vijaya-champu* was composed in 1752 in praise of Ananda Ranga Pillai's father. V. Raghavan, "Notice of Madras in Two Sanskrit Works", in *The Madras Tercentenary volume* (London: Oxford University Press, 1939), pp. 107–112.

84. The padam begins with the words, *Upamugane.* I am indebted to Sri T. S. Parthasarathy for the identification of the composer.

temporary champu kavya in Sanskrit about Madras.[85] The parallel to the ambience of patronage and splendour in which the Vellala ruling classes held court is quite inescapable.

In a reversal of the normal methodology followed in research, we can look to the theory of social classes to support and validate our empirical analysis that the merchant capitalists primarily functioned as a social class who aspired to enhance their social prestige and who progressively adopted a pattern of behaviour modelled on the values of the established landowning elite and ruling classes. Weber's discussion of social classes, in fact, describes precisely such a process of dynamics: of social classes struggling for advantage among a variety of groups to pursue both economic and non-economic interests, when the ultimate objective was not merely to achieve wealth but also power.[86]

Though Weber's theory of social classes continues to be debated by sociologists, the historical experience of the merchant capitalists in the Coromandel supports the hypothesis that the social interests of a class can supersede its economic interests, particulary when its economic position is secure. Time and again, we see the merchant capitalists sacrificing economic interests in the pursuit of social goals. Perhaps, the tragedy and irony was that when they achieved the desired social status, the forces of colonialism and industrial capitalism deprived them of the economic power which underpinned their social ambitions.

---

85. *Sarvadevavilasa*, ed. V. Raghavan (Madras: Adyar Library, 1958).
86. Pete Martin, "The Concept of Class", in *Classic Disputes in Sociology*, ed. R. J. Anderson, J. A. Hughes and W. W. Sharrock (London: Unwin Hyman, 1987), pp. 67–96.

NINE

Conclusion

Merchant Capitalism in India: Two Views

This study started with the premise that the historical evolution of economic institutions in the Coromandel culminated in the formation of a merchant capitalist class. Further, that there was a concomitant development of organisational structures and institutions in the local economy which were the necessary pre-requisites for the economy to move towards commercial capitalism.

While several historians and economists have stressed the importance of the development of commerce and urbanisation in effecting long-term transformation as an economy matures to industrial capitalism (Pirenne, Braudel, Sweezy), the application of this analysis to non-Western European economies has been minimal. For those who work on merchant capitalism in India, Perlin's polemical essay becomes a pathfinder.[1] The main thread of Perlin's argument is that non-European economies also underwent stages of development parallel to, but *independent* of the processes in Europe and not merely in response to the worldwide ramifications of industrial capitalism. He writes:

> I argue that India, like Europe, was affected by profound and rapid change in the character of its societies and economies, and state-forms, from at least the sixteenth century, and secondly that a fundamental aspect of that development was a local merchant capitalism which emerged independently of that in Europe, but within a common international theatre of societal and commercial changes.[2]

1. Frank Perlin, "Proto-Industrialisation and Pre-colonial South Asia", *Past and Present* 98, 1983, pp. 30–95.
2. *Ibid.*, p. 33.

Conclusion

This phase, characterised by home-based handicraft production on a commercial scale, Perlin chooses to call "proto-capitalism" (in preference to the more common appellation "proto-industrialisation"), within which the institutions of commercial capitalism emerged. Commercial capitalism, Perlin goes on to say, stands for "the commercial and financial developments associated with towns, ports, traders and manufacturing regions, while at the same time being incorporated as an essential motor of the wider changes proto-capitalism suggests."[3] The proto-capitalist stage involves, among other changes, monetisation and also an overall shift to market relations, whereby peasants and artisans were incorporated into market relations and the proto-capitalist economy.

A. I. Chicherov has also argued that the Indian economy displayed many characteristics of merchant capitalism. Chicherov's rather chaotic methodology which treats a history of more than three hundred years as a homogeneous temporal unit and his indiscriminate juxtaposition of data relating to diverse parts of the country at diverse points of time to build up a composite picture obviously presents major problems. But his insights into the processes of change are both relevant and intuitive, though not methodologically sound.[4]

Chicherov points out that several preliminary changes took place in the Indian economy which moved it further on the path of evolution. Of these, the important ones were: the transformation of artisans into commodity producers, with ties to the market outside the village community and the consequent erosion of village self-sufficiency; the development of small-scale commodity production, both home-based and by professional artisans; market exchanges and commodity-money relations; the deepening of the social division of labour and markets (as a consequence of the development of productive forces in the crafts) which overcame the limitations of caste-based production; urbanisation; and the emergence of an integrated national market. All these processes culminated in the evolution of merchant capitalism which would set the stage for the emergence of capitalist relations in production through the gradual subjection of the producer by the merchant capitalist.[5]

3. *Ibid.*, p. 59.
4. A. I. Chicherov, *India: Economic Development in the Sixteenth—Eighteenth Centuries* (Moscow: Nauka Publishing House, 1971).
5. This can be contrasted with Marx's implicit assumption that the producer remained independent of commercial capital. See ch. 1.

The broad schema of economic change outlined by Chicherov and Perlin's arguments have much in common. Perlin, however, emphasises as a hypothesis that the economic evolution of non-European economies was not qualitatively different from the pattern in Europe, and nor did fundamental changes take place in the former only in response and as a reaction to their contacts with the Europeans. This, however, is not the primary focus of this study. The basic proposition of this study admittedly is that the evolution of merchant capitalism in the Coromandel, the region under study, was characterised by the same processes of institutional and structural changes which were evident in Europe. However, it also argues that these processes were shaped by the sociocultural institutions and ethos which were specific to the region, so that there is a regional identity to the process which overlies the commonality of evolutionary changes.

Trade and mercantile activity in the Coromandel

The development of trade and mercantile activity in the Coromandel comprised two distinct strands. The first was the evolution of trading as a specialised function, distinct from production; the second was the development of a hierarchy of markets, which integrated the economy both spatially and functionally.[6] The most specialised classes of merchants traded in the highest-level markets, whereas the village markets were frequented by undifferentiated producer-traders. Commodities—agricultural products, raw materials, manufactured products and luxury consumption goods—and trade flowed to and from the villages, local market towns, urban centres and ports in ever-widening networks, served by the producer-trader, the itinerant pedlar merchants and merchant capitalists with international trade links. The region was characterised down the ages by the contemporaneous coexistence of non-specialised and specialised trading and by precapitalist and capitalist relations.

The chronological outline of the history of merchants in the Coromandel clearly indicates the gradual evolution of new institutions and changes. Even two thousand years ago, the Coromandel had a distinct history and tradition of maritime trade as well as interregional trade.

---

6. Francis Buchanan's travel account gives a vivid description of the network of markets in South India. *A Journey from Madras,* 3 vols. (London: W. Balmer and Co, 1807).

Conclusion

This trade was supported by a degree of commercial production, urbanisation and a distinctly urban class of merchants. The medieval period was the really formative age in the development of trade, preceded by the development of agriculture, village organisation and local administrative bodies. The gradual evolution of the temple which integrated the secular with the sacred, agrarian and urban society, and agricultural and mercantile interests was of critical importance in the history of the Coromandel. The growth of temples also promoted urbanisation, and the management of temple resources led to the popular adoption of commercial principles like the creation of a corpus fund, lending money on interest, and so on. Corporate bodies of merchants also became involved in temple administration, while guilds protected the interests of the individual merchants.

By the early sixteenth century, the Coromandel region had been incorporated into the world of the Indian Ocean maritime trade. The scattered evidence of the presence of the Coromandel merchants in various parts of Southeast Asia gave way to a pattern of merchant diaspora. All along the ports of call (of coastal shipping) from Western Asia to Southeast Asia, Coromandel merchants had settled down and were actively engaged in trade. The trade links with Southeast Asia remained particularly strong, with cotton cloth from the Coromandel becoming a staple in the overseas markets of these regions.

The arrival of the Europeans in this trading world did not usher in any dramatic changes. The preconditions for merchant capitalism were already present in the economy, and the Europeans, in fact, entered the local economy and trade circuits through the intermediation of the merchant capitalists. This in itself was not unique to the Coromandel, since in Gujarat and Bengal, also, the same pattern was manifest. What was unique to the Coromandel was the creation of European port enclaves and the effect, if any, this had on the merchant capitalists. The rapid expansion of the European demand for cotton textiles from the Coromandel was also a factor which had an impact on the local economy—especially in terms of integrating the textile-producing hinterland with overseas markets, as well as incorporating the weaver/producer into market processes.

Commercial practices

The last eighty years of the period of this study, 1670 to 1750, sees merchant capitalism at its zenith in the region, supported by many complex organisational structures and commercial practices.

Partnerships

As regards the trading organisation, the guild had given way to partnerships. Most of the merchant capitalists traded together as partners, as was very evident in the textile trade. In the several unsuccessful "joint stock companies" organised by the English, the chief merchants effectively ran the company as a partnership trading venture. Merchant capitalists generally resisted the pressure from the Europeans to form more broad-based associations which would dilute their control and economic power. The Dutch governor, van Cloon, noted in 1730 that the "new company" at Nagapattinam which was formed for supplying cloth to the Dutch with a capital stock of 8,000 pagodas was more nominal than real. Sunku Muddu Rama Chetti, the chief merchant, had contributed the entire capital, and the other merchants shown as shareholders or partners were, in fact, his employees.[7]

While the partnerships among the merchants supplying textiles to the English tended to be long-term arrangements, merchants would also come together for specific ventures. In 1724 and 1725, Ponkala Krishna and three other merchants, each with a 25 per cent share, bought coral from Nathaniel Elwick, governor of Fort St George. Six years later, the accounts were settled and the profits divided among the four.[8]

Trading on respondentia

For overseas trading, the most favoured method was trading on respondentia. Even merchants who had their own ships opted for sending goods or money on respondentia arrangements. The money or goods were deposited with the ship's captain or supercargo, who would use the money or the sales proceeds of the goods in port-to-port trading. The "risk" was repaid with a higher than normal rate of interest and fell due when the ship returned to harbour. It is evident that the interest varied according to the destination of the ship, since the risk also increased or decreased correspondingly. In fact the following table shows that even in lower-risk voyages across to Burma, the risk would go up according to the season.

---

7. Memorie of van Cloon, p. 30.
8. Pleadings in the Mayor's Court, 18 April 1732. Case of Ponkala Krishna, merchant, against Devaraya, "Conicoply" of Madras.

Conclusion

Table: 9.1: Respondentia Interest Rates at Madras in Early Eighteenth Century

Sind	25 %	1 August 1706*
Tonquin	25 %	22 March 1717
Maldives	15 %	8 May 1717
Junkceylon	26 %	12 September 1727
Ceylon	15 %	10 October 1727
Pegu	15 %	(Little Monsoon)
	30 %	(Great Monsoon) 22 August 1732
	18 %	19 June 1733
Macao	18 %	12 May 1742

Source: All the dates refer to the dates of the Mayor's Court Records: Proceedings for the period 1717–1727 and Pleadings for 1732 and after.
* PC of the same date.

There were obvious advantages to the system, in that the trading in Asian ports would be done by persons with many years of experience in intra-Asian trade, while the merchants who had the capital would finance the voyage. The interest rates in Madras ranged around 8 to 9 per cent, and it can be assumed that a voyage to Ceylon or Pegu could be completed within three to six months, so that the additional interest went to cover the risk of total loss.

One of the problems with respondentia arrangements was that ships, on returning from a voyage, would be taken to ports other than where the respondentia was arranged, in which case, technically, the amount did not fall due. In 1727, James Hubbard filed a case in the Mayor's Court that Chinna Kutti Chetti had taken money from him on respondentia to go to Ceylon. On his return, however, he had disembarked at Porto Novo and therefore was not returning the amount.[9] Another problem with respondentia was that in spite of defaulting on payment for previous voyages, the supercargoes of ships were able to raise money for new voyages, creating a problem of a multiplicity of claimants. Normally the respondentia bonds were registered, and the English announced that creditors had to renew the bonds in order to claim on voyages for which they had not contributed.[10]

Direct subscription to voyages

Merchants could also directly subscribe to voyages. In 1726, several merchants of Madras subscribed to a voyage to China and received

9. Mayor's Court Proceedings, 10 October 1727.
10. PC, 12 and 21 February 1727/8.

a dividend of 17.3 per cent.[11] Ananda Ranga Pillai also traded on French ships to Mocha and other Asian markets on the same basis, though he normally used to send consignments of goods rather than money. For the China voyage, the local merchants of Madras had contributed more than 10,000 pounds, which indicates that the merchants had enough liquid resources to put into such ventures.

Active credit market

There was an active credit market in Madras. Merchants normally borrowed from one another at fixed rates of interest. The normal terms were that the borrowed sum and the interest on it would have to be paid in monthly instalments, and if the payment was defaulted any month, the entire sum would fall due.[12] The local merchants evidently did not feel the need for any more institutionalised credit facilities, like banks, to serve their credit needs. After 1700, the interest rates in Madras normally fluctuated between 8 and 9 per cent, which was lower than the rates prevailing in other parts of India. In Surat, for instance, the interest rate ranged between 12 and 24 per cent per year. The English perhaps managed to maintain interest rates at a slightly lower level than would otherwise have prevailed, but it would seem that the lower rate was not really an artificially fixed rate. In 1686, the English had failed to get money at 9 per cent and had had to accept that money could be raised only at 12 per cent.[13] This, in fact, came soon after an unsuccessful attempt to establish a bank in Madras, when merchants were invited to deposit money at 6 per cent.[14] It has to be inferred that by the beginning of the eighteenth century, the credit market had eased considerably in Madras and the interest rates had, as a consequence, come down.

Insuring ships in overseas trade

There is also an interesting reference to the practice of insuring ships setting out on voyages. A ship going to Perah had been insured for 1,500 pagodas, with the condition that the insurance cover was valid until the ship returned to Madras. The ship, however, had to make

11. PC, 26 August 1726.
12. Mayor's Court Pleadings, 9 November 1731.
13. PC, 19 October 1685; 21 October 1686.
14. PC, 21 June 1683; 8 January 1684/5.

an unscheduled stop at Tennassery where it was destroyed by fire and the insurers refused to pay the claim. The merchants who had insured the ship argued that by custom, the insurance cover was valid only when the ship was sailing and not when it had anchored at a port, especially one which was not on the specified itinerary. Otherwise, they argued, "every leaky old vessel has only to insure" and afterwards claim that it was destroyed at a port. The court decided in favour of the insurers.[15] Insurance, though not heard of otherwise, was clearly a common practice and there were merchants who specialised in providing insurance.

Changing power relations in the Coromandel: Indian state in retreat

European influences seem to have had little impact on the evolution of these commercial practices. Partnership trading, overseas trading, credit markets and other practices like insurance had all developed in response to the needs of the local mercantile community and their activities. What then was the impact, if any, of the Europeans on the system?

For much of this work, we have taken the forms of government and state as a given, the implicit understanding being that for all states, commerce was primarily a revenue-generating activity. It is clear that from the earliest times, the government assumed the basic responsibilities of protecting property, maintaining law and order and ensuring fair trade practices (through, for instance, official checking of weights and measures). Raychaudhuri's argument that local trade in the Golkonda kingdom suffered because of an extortionate and rapacious administration may hold good for short periods in some localities, but the freedom of merchants and artisans to move around precluded the state from being overexploitative. Efforts to repopulate deserted settlements by promising less taxation and better treatment are recorded several times down the centuries, indicating that while exploitation did take place, it was contained by the freedom of the people to move away to other areas in what had become the most standard form of popular protest.

15. Mayor's Court Pleadings, 5 June to 1 December 1744.

It would seem incontrovertible that the European port cities introduced a new power equation in the region. One of the clear symptoms of the weakening of the state was seen in the debasement of local coinage. In the Coromandel, both the English and the Dutch had been allowed to mint local coins since the 1620s by the nayakas and later by the Golkonda authorities. After the Mughal conquest, special firmans were issued to the English in 1692 by which they were permitted to mint *mohurs,* rupees and pagodas. The dies for the coins were sent with the firman, and the musters had to be sent back for inspection.[16] Thus, though the Mughals had relaxed their strict rule by which coins could be minted only in the imperial mints, they still considered it the responsibility of the state to maintain the value of money.

By 1736 there were widespread complaints that the pagodas from the government mints were much debased.[17] This was probably one of the effects of the severe financial crisis which the Nawab of Arcot was facing. The same year, he had graciously sent a firman to the French at Pondicherry permitting them to mint rupees for which the French had paid him a handsome sum.[18] By 1739, the complaints about the pagodas from the country mints increased, and the falling value of money had begun to hinder the smooth functioning of trade.[19] The official or current pagodas were discounted by 11 per cent against the pagodas minted at Madras of 80½ touch.[20] In 1741, in order to maintain the value of the pagoda, Fort St George decided to issue a new pagoda (of 76–78 touch) marked with a star. The value of the Arcot pagoda had fallen even lower and was discounted at 15 per cent against this "new star money" or star pagoda,[21] which soon became the only accepted currency throughout the region, displacing the official coinage.

This was just one facet of the changing power relations in the Coromandel, as the Mughal state was disintegrating. With growing political instability, the European towns, especially Madras and

16. PC, 19 April 1692.
17. PC, 13 December 1736.
18. This firman, which was received by the French with great ceremony, cost them 48,000 pagodas (144,000 rupees) in "gifts" to the Nawab and other influential men at Court. Ananda Ranga Pillai, *Private Diary,* vol. 1: pp. 3–4 (10 September 1736).
19. PC, 2 April 1739.
20. PC, 2 July 1740.
21. PC, 7 and 9 April; 14 June 1741.

Pondicherry, became sanctuaries for the merchant classes and occasionally even for the ruling classes. The French and the English might have been corrupt and extortionate, but the merchants still perceived that they were better off in these port enclaves. This had long-range implications and repercussions on the further expansion of merchant capitalism beyond our period. The experience of southern Coromandel thus does not corroborate either the hypothesis of the stability offered by a strong, centralised Mughal state, or of the supposed viability of successor states. The region was, on the contrary, characterised by a power vacuum which had become evident as the three post-Vijayanagar nayaka kingdoms collapsed, and was one whose historical experience was quite distinct from that of Gujarat and Mughal north India.

Textile trade in crisis

The sudden expansion in the demand from Europe for cotton textiles, especially Coromandel textiles, also intensified the ongoing process of market integration. As the merchants undertook to supply very large quantities of cloth, they began to look further and further inland for their cloth requirements, so that production centres in the hinterland like Udaiyarpalayam and Salem began to be linked to the export markets. These links also strengthened the functioning of internal trade, and inland market centres began to handle larger volumes of trade. Lalapet, for instance, became a major cotton-yarn market, which used to supply yarn to Pondicherry and Madras. Lingayat merchants from Karnataka ("Lingam and Canary") used to bring down yarn worth 130,000 to 150,000 pagodas to Lalapet for the annual fair, which would then be transported to the seaports.[22]

The weavers were also drawn into these market networks. Contrary to the general perception that they were completely exploited and subjugated to merchant control, they acted as independent decision-making agents in markets with a multiplicity of demand. Take the weaver who produced cloth for export. The preferences of different overseas markets were quite specific with reference to patterns, quality, texture, and so on. As the overseas markets expanded, the weaver made decisions which were optimal from his

---

22. PC, 7 January 1733/4. Ananda Ranga Pillai also often refers to Lalapet as a major market centre.

point of view, given the prevailing conditions, like the availability and price of yarn, the price of foodgrains and other factors, and the merchants had to contend with this reality. In the face of constant pressures to keep cloth prices down, the merchants informed the English that when foodgrain prices were high, cloth prices would be high because wages/returns to the weaver would have to be high, and if they lowered the prices, they would not get any cloth at all.

The ultimate result of the boom in European demand was that coupled with the local conditions which made foodgrains and cotton scarce, the entire region could not produce enough textiles to meet this demand. For the merchants who had to agree to supply the demanded quantities on contract, this spelt financial disaster—none of the merchant capitalists after 1725 emerged from the textile trade without becoming bankrupt. As we leave the scene in 1750, the merchant capitalists, though still viable and visible, were slowly beginning to go into oblivion.

This scenario was re-enacted in the different textile-producing regions of India to a remarkable degree. The story was the same everywhere—the merchants were unable to fulfil their contracts for supplying cloth because of disruptions in the manufacture of textiles and were becoming hopelessly indebted to the English East India Company.[23] The shortfall in supply led the European companies—the English in particular—to resort to "'captive' trading" (in effect combining commercial interests with political power) to exercise direct control over the producer in order to ensure an uninterrupted and adequate supply of cloth.[24] In Bengal and southern Coromandel, this strategy led to the elimination of merchant intermediaries by the end of the eighteenth century and carrying out of

---

23. For Gujarat: Lakshmi Subramanian, "Calicoes and Companies in Western India" (paper presented at a seminar on Textiles as a Medium in Cultural Exchange, Max Müller Bhavan, Hyderabad, November 1995).

For Bengal: Hameeda Hossain, *The Company Weavers of Bengal* (Delhi: Oxford University Press, 1988).

For Masulipatnam (northern Coromandel): P. Sudhir and P. Swarnalatha, "Textile Traders and Territorial Imperatives: Masulipatnam, 1750–1850", *Indian Economic and Social History Review* 29, no. 2, 1992, pp. 145–169.

24. Dietmar Rothermund explains 'captive' trading as follows: "The merchant who is not only sure of recurrent transactions but of an increasing or stable demand under conditions of scarcity or uncertainty as far as the supply is concerned will try his best to capture the sources of supply ... and establish relationships with the suppliers which attach them to his interest". *Asian Trade and European Expansion in the Age of Mercantilism* (Delhi: Manohar, 1981), p. 9.

Conclusion

procurement transactions directly with the weaver. In northern Coromandel, however, merchants continued as suppliers, though the English company sought, through regulations, to impose legal and binding contracts on weavers to ensure continuous and full supply.[25]

These experiences of the different regions of India show that the long-term ramifications of such a sustained expansion of exports on the local economy cannot be explained only through an analytical framework of "export-led growth" (Om Prakash), though this was a partially valid explanation for the medium term, nor through the incorporation of the role of other endogenous economic factors like productivity, demographic change and urbanisation (Sanjay Subrahmanyam). The reality was far more complex, and a key variable in understanding the processes was the changing power relations between the European companies and local merchants on the one hand, and the local governments, on the other, as well as amongst the European companies themselves.

Unique features of the Coromandel region

Importance of maritime trade

In the long mercantile history of the Coromandel, there were certain features which were unique to the region. The first was the importance of maritime trade in the local economy. From the earliest times, the trade of the region looked outward to overseas markets. The central place of maritime trade in the commerce and cultural ethos of the region is exemplified by coins stamped with ships, temple sculptures depicting ships, literature with maritime trade as the central theme, and a popular perception that crossing the seas was the road to prosperity.

While economic historians attempt to analyse the theoretical underpinnings of this trade and its impact on the local economy,[26] local society in the Coromandel practically understood that trade resulted in higher standards of consumption by integrating markets and making available goods and commodities from other regions as well as from distant foreign places. Trade was thus held in high

---

25. Sudhir and Swarnalatha, "Textile Traders", p. 153.
26. Subrahmanyam, *Political Economy of Commerce*, ch. 7.

esteem, in contrast to the hostility with which it was perceived in other civilisations, especially the West.

Merchants as a socio-economic class

Down to the eighteenth century, didactic poetry eulogised merchants as a thrifty, careful class. Their main activities were buying and selling and moneylending, and if they were extremely careful with money, they also donated generously for good causes. In order to trade, they travelled far distances, over treacherous seas and mountains, and would even acquire influence and control over kings who ruled over extensive kingdoms.[27] This is reflected in the self-perception of merchants who ultimately tried to validate themselves not merely as an economic class, but primarily as a social class.

This treatment of merchants as a socio-economic class rather than viewing them through caste identities may answer, in some part, Burton Stein's criticism that for most social scientists, "caste remains the totalised and essentialised conception of Indian sociology." To some extent, Stein lays the blame for this on historians who "have failed to challenge the ideological hegemony of caste and religious communalism by showing that socio-economic classes have as much historical antiquity as caste as it is known now."[28] The degree to which the class phenomenon as opposed to caste phenomenon is operative in Indian society remains a vexed question in Indian sociology.[29] A further category is "community", and this leads to the question as to whether community is coterminous with class or caste.[30]

---

27. In the genre of literature known as *satakams* (usually comprising a hundred verses), there are individual verses devoted to specific topics, one of which, invariably, is merchants. I have referred to *Kumaresasatakam* by Gurupadadasar, *Arappalisurasatakam* by Ambalavanakkavirayar and *Tiruvenkatasatakam* by Narayana Bharati, all dating to the eighteenth or early nineteenth century.
28. Burton Stein, "Towards an Indian Petty Bourgeoisie: Outline of an Approach", *Economic and Political Weekly* 26, no. 4 (Review of Political Economy), 1991, pp. PE 9–10.
29. I am grateful to Professor N. Subba Reddy for his efforts to enlighten me on this question. The confusion which remains is entirely my own responsibility. For an overall discussion, see Yogendra Singh, *Indian Sociology* (New Delhi: Vistaar, 1986), pp. 45–62.
30. N. R. Sheth, "Theoretical Framework for the Study of Indian Business Communities", in *Business Communities of India*, ed. Dwijendra Tripathi (New Delhi: Manohar, 1984), pp. 9–26.

Conclusion

All these are categories of social identification as well as social stratification, and the analysis of a social group under any of these categories depends on the way the category itself is defined. For instance, D'Souza has argued that "the ideal-typical concepts of caste and class are the same", and that "both caste hierarchy and class hierarchy are basically determined by the same variables as occupational prestige."[31] With respect to the Indian merchants, Chicherov treats them largely as a class, while Gadgil has argued that though businessmen belonging to different communities did "operate as a single pressure group", they "did not show a similarity of behaviour patterns or a degree of social cohesion which would justify their being called members of one business class."[32]

To what extent did the merchant capitalists of the Coromandel region exhibit the social cohesion and solidarity which justifies treating them as a socio-economic class? It is quite clear that there were many spheres of social interaction which were governed by their caste identity. Caste panchayats decided various issues and disputes relating to custom, usage, rules of inheritance, division of property, and so on. The vertical bifurcation of South Indian society into right- and left-side caste sodalities and the vigorous affirmation of the rights and privileges of their respective groups by the merchants adds yet another dimension to the issue of caste versus class identity. Though, overtly, the parameters of the right- and left-side caste disputes were set by normative notions of caste honour and relative positions in a caste-based hierarchy, through these disputes the merchants were also manoeuvring to establish their status as a dominant class in society.

The economic factor, however, was obviously more important than caste in determining social status in the colonial cities. This is evident by the fact that the acknowledged leaders of local society were from the merchant communities rather than from the ritually superior castes like the brahmins. Also, many merchant families from lower castes were, by virtue of their commercial fortunes, the pre-eminent class in society (for instance, the Beri family in Madras

---

31. V. D'Souza, *Inequality and its Perpetuation* (New Delhi: Manohar, 1991), pp. 78–79.
32. D. R. Gadgil, "Origins of the Modern Indian Business Class", (reprinted) in *Writings and Speeches of Professor D. R. Gadgil: On Social and Economic Problems*, ed. Sulabha Brahme (Pune: Gokhale Institute of Economics and Politics, 1981), p. 313.

and Ananda Ranga Pillai's family in Pondicherry). Further, class solidarity rather than caste identity was the decisive factor in guiding the merchants' behaviour. In their textile contracts, the merchants rarely allowed the caste factor to override their economic interests, and in spite of the right-left rivalry, neither group of merchants would be pressured into reducing prices to undercut the other. There are several instances when they united as a class to support other members of the community who might be in trouble with the English.[33]

Even as the merchants were expanding and strengthening their economic status, they were also looking to establish themselves as the acknowledged leaders of society. This could be achieved only in the European port cities (with their economies built on commerce), since in traditional society the links with the rural economy always assigned the dominant status to the landowning elites. The actions of the merchants, their interactions with the rest of society and their behaviour patterns were all in conformity with their need to establish their identity as a social class. The ultimate justification for treating them more as a social than as an economic class rests on their own behaviour of subordinating their economic interests to advance their social ambitions. The irony was that even as the merchant capitalists were achieving the desired social standing, their economic status which was the foundation of their social goals was already beginning to show the first signs of disintegration.

---

33. In 1714, merchants of both sides stood surety for Chikka Serappa when he was in disfavour with the English and was being dunned for the money he owed them (PC, 18 December 1714). On two occasions, once in 1678 (PC, 21 November 1678) and again in 1742 (PC, 18 January 1741/2 and 21 May 1742), the merchants threw their weight behind errant shroffs whom the English wanted to punish.

GLOSSARY

adaikkalam	under the protection of
adappam	ceremonial betel bearer to Vijayanagar king
adichetti	leading (original?) merchants
aduttavan	assistant in business (among Nattukkottai Chettiars)
agraharam	a brahmin quarter
ammanai	a narrative song sung by girls while playing
angadi	market
anjinan-pugalidam	sanctuary
aputrikadandam	cess levied on the childless
aruvai vanikan	cloth merchant
Ayyavole	a famous merchant guild, also referred to as Disai-Ayirattu-Ainnurruvar (the Five Hundred of a Thousand Directions)
bahar	a unit of weight, usually 400 pounds
Balija	a right-hand merchant caste, *kavarai* in Tamil
bendahara	prime minister (Malay)
Beri Chetti	a left-hand merchant caste
betilla	muslin woven in the Coromandel
brahmadeya	a village granted to brahmins
candy	a unit of weight, usually 500 pounds
cash *(kasu)*	a copper coin, 80 cash = 1 fanam
champu, champu kavya	a literary form, in prose and verse, in Sanskrit and Telugu
chauri	a ceremonial fan, made of long white hair
chetti	a trader
chitrameli-periyanadu	a supralocal association; a guild of merchants dealing in agricultural produce
choultry	in Madras a public building or resting place, from Tamil, *chavadi*
Cocanada	red-tinged cotton grown in north coastal Andhra Pradesh
Conicoply	see *kanakkuppillai*
corge	a score (20 pieces) (origin not clear)

Glossary

dasabandam	grant allowing the use of one-tenth of the water in return for maintaining an irrigation tank
devadana	agricultural land donated to temples
devakarmi	temple officials
dipantirattil viyaparigal	overseas merchants
Disai-Ayirattu-Ainnurruvar	see Ayyavole
doab	the region between two rivers
dubash	lit. interpreter; in the Coromandel, local merchants who were agents and men of affairs for Europeans
eaglewood	an aromatic wood, from *agil* or *agar*
erivirapattinam	a higher-order market centre; also, a town defended by armed merchants
fanam *(panam)*	a gold coin, 36 fanams = 1 pagoda (in Madras, until the 1750s)
firman	grant, permission
garce	see *karisai*
gopuram	a tower at the entrance of a temple
idaiyar	shepherds
idan palisai	interest on capital
idangai	left side, left hand
ilakkasu	a gold coin of Sri Lanka
ippar	one of the three classes of merchants mentioned in the ancient Tamil texts
jamawar/janrawar/ jandra	a weaver caste
kaikkolar	a weaver caste, originally warriors in the Chola armies
kalanju	a gold coin
kanakkuppillai	accountant ("Conicoply" in English records)
kanmalar/ kammalar	five artisan castes, of the left hand
karisai	garce, in English; a volumetric measure, 400 *marakkal* = 1 *karisai*
karugar	artisans, weavers
kasu	in the medieval period, a gold coin; later a copper coin. See also cash

· 184 ·

Glossary

kaul	an agreement
kavarai	Tamil word for Balijas
kavippar	one of the three classes of merchants mentioned in the ancient Tamil texts
kling	term for Tamil merchants in Malacca and other Southeast Asian ports
Komati	Telugu vaisya, right-hand merchant caste
kudirai-chetti	merchants dealing in horses
mahanagaram/ managaram	higher-order market town; refers only to Tanjavur and Kanchipuram
mahanattar	collectively, representatives of all the castes
maha-sartha-vaha	great caravan leader
malai-mandalam	the hill regions (of the west)
Manigramam	a merchant guild
mandapam	a pavilion
marakkal	mercall, in English; a volumetric measure, 8 *padi* = 1 *marakkal*, 400 *marakkal* = 1 *karisai*
measure	see *padi*
mercall	see *marakkal*
mohur	a gold coin, in Mughal India
mudal	capital
mudalali	owner of capital, owner of an enterprise
nadu	a local peasant region; also its corporate assembly
nagaram	a town; the corporate assembly of a town; a market centre
nagarattar	members of the nagaram assembly
Nagarattar	Nattukkottai Chettiars
nakhuda	captain of a ship
nanadesi	lit. from several countries
Nanadesi	guilds of merchants in international trade, sometimes also as a description of Ayyavole merchants
nanadesipattanam	lit. a town for nanadesi merchants; sanctuary
nattanmai	elected head of a caste panchayat
nattar	collectively, the members of a nadu assembly
nayaka	lit. leader; military chief under Vijayanagar, especially of Tanjavur, Madurai and Gingee

Glossary

nilaip-poliyuttu	a deposit earning a permanent interest
padam	a love lyric in Carnatic classical music
padi	measure, in English; a volumetric measure, 8 *padi* = 1 *marakkal*
pagoda (varahan)	a gold coin worth 9 shillings or 3.5 rupees or 4.2–4.5 guilders
palayakkarar	see *palayam*
palayam	small principalities, ruled by military chieftains known as *palayakkarar* (poligar)
palisai	interest (money)
panam	see fanam
pangali	partner in business
paradesi/Paradesi	same as *nanadesi*/Nanadesi, foreign merchants
paraiyar	untouchable caste of agricultural labourers, of the right hand
pardao	Portuguese unit of money
parwana	letter of authority
pattanasvamigal	heads of the merchant communities
perangadi	main market
perunkudi	one of the three classes of merchants mentioned in the ancient texts
perunteru	main commercial street
pettai	local market; also locality
podiyan	boy being trained in business (among the Nattukkottai Chettiars)
ponnambalam	a major weaver caste
prasasti	laudatory invocation about donors in temple inscriptions
punjam	yarn count
qiledar	governor of fort
rakshai	under the protection of
roundel, *rundell*	parasol
sabha	the corporate assembly of a brahmin village
sabhaiyar	members of a *sabha*
saliya-nagarattar	cloth merchants
saliyar	a major weaver caste
sanad	a deed of grant
sandai	local fair

Glossary

sankarappadi-nagarattar	oil merchants
sarvamanniyam	land grant, free of tax
satakam	a literary work with a hundred verses
shahbandar	a port official
shroff	a money changer
sri-karyam-arayginra	supervisors of temple officials and accounts
sungachchavadi	customs checkposts
sungam	customs
talaiyari	a head watchman
tambulakarandavahin	same as *adappam*
tarafdar	a revenue farmer, local governor
taragar	a broker
tashrif	presents given on ceremonial occasions
tulaippon	a gold coin, probably punched
ur	a non-brahmin village; its corporate assembly; also, a small town
urar	members of the *ur* assembly
uravar	local merchants
vadugar	Telugu- and Kannada-speaking people from the north
valangai	right side, right hand
vaniyanagarattar	wider association of oil merchants
varahan	see pagoda
velir	minor chieftains, of the Sangam period
vellalar	landowning castes
vishayattar	usually *padinen-vishayattar*, the 18 regional officials
yavana desa	Western countries

APPENDIX

List of Presidents/Agents/Governors of Fort St George (Madras)

Francis Day	1643–44
Thomas Ivie	1644–48
Henry Greenhill	1648–52
Aaron Baker	1652–55
Henry Greenhill	1655–59
Thomas Chamber	1659–62
Edward Winter	1662–65
George Foxcroft	1665*
Edward Winter	1665–68
George Foxcroft	1668–72
William Langhorn	1672–78
Streynsham Master	1678–81
William Gyfford	1681–87
Elihu Yale	1687–92
Nathaniel Higginson	1692–98
Thomas Pitt	1698–1709
Gulston Addison	1709
William Fraser	1709–11**
Edward Harrison	1711–17
Joseph Collett	1717–20
Francis Hastings	1720–21
Nathaniel Elwick	1721–25
James Macrae	1725–30
George Moreton Pitt	1730–35
Richard Benyon	1735–44
Nicholas Morse	1744–46
Charles Floyer	1747–50[+]
Thomas Saunders	1750–[+]

Fort St George was a presidency till 1655, when it reverted to an agency. In 1668 George Foxcroft became the first governor and president.

* Coup by Edward Winter in 1665 who forcibly seized the governorship, until orders came from London in 1668 relieving him.
** Acting governor, after the death of Addison.
[+] After the capture of Madras by the French, Fort St David became the governor's headquarters.

BIBLIOGRAPHY

Primary sources

INSCRIPTIONS (PUBLISHED)

South Indian Inscriptions, Archaeological Survey of India.

Vol. I. Trans. and ed. E. Hultzsch. Madras, 1890.
Vol. II, pts. 1-3. Trans. and ed. E. Hultzsch. Madras, 1891-95.
   pt. 4. Trans. and ed. V. Venkayya. Madras, 1913.
   pt. 5. Trans. and ed. H. Krishna Sastri. Madras, 1919.
Vol. III, pts. 1 and 2. Trans. and ed. H. Hultzsch. Madras. 1899, 1903.
   pts. 3 and 4. Trans. and ed. H. Krishna Sastri. Madras, 1920, 1929.
Vol. IV. Ed. H. Krishna Sastri. Madras, 1923.
Vol. V. Ed. H. Krishna Sastri. Madras, 1925.
Vol. VI. Ed. K. V. Subrahmanya Aiyer. Madras, 1928.
Vol. VII. Ed. K. V. Subrahmanya Aiyer. Madras, 1932.
Vol. VIII. Ed. K. V. Subrahmanya Aiyer. Madras, 1937.
Vol. XII. Ed. V. Venkatasubba Ayyar. Madras, 1943.
Vol. XIII. Ed. G. V. Srinivasa Rao. Delhi, 1952.
Vol. XIV. Ed. A. S. Ramanatha Ayyar. Delhi, 1962.
Vol. XVII. Ed. K. G Krishnan. Delhi, 1964.
Vol. XIX. Ed. G. V. Srinivasa Rao. Delhi, 1970.
Vol. XXII. Ed. G. V. Srinivasa Rao. New Delhi, 1983.
Vol. XXIII. Ed. G. V. Srinivasa Rao. Delhi, 1979.
Vol. XXIV. (Srirangam Inscriptions). Ed. H. K. Narasimhaswamy. New Delhi, 1982.
Vol. XXVI. Ed. P. R. Srinivasan. New Delhi, 1990.

South Indian Temple Inscriptions. Ed. T. M. Subramaniam. 3 vols. Madras: Government Oriental Manuscripts Library, 1953-57.

V. Rangacharya. *A Topographical List of the Inscriptions of the Madras Presidency Collected till 1915, with notes and references.* 3 vols. Madras: Government Press, 1917.

ARCHIVAL RECORDS, TAMIL NADU STATE ARCHIVES, CHENNAI.

Public Consultations, Records of Fort St George. (1672-1750)
Fort St David Consultations, South Arcot District Records. (1696-1750)

Bibliography

The Mayor's Court Records
   Original Mayor's Court, 1689, 1716–1719.
   Pleadings in the Mayor's Court, 1719–1750.
   Private Account Books.
Dutch Records
   Abstracts of all the contracts . . . made . . . or obtained from various native sovereigns in the name of Governors General and Council for India, representing the General Dutch East India Company [Translated from Corpus Diplomaticum Neerlando Indicum].
Dutch Coromandel Records
   The Memorie of Laurens Pit, 1663.
   The Memorie of Cornelis Speelman, 1665.
   The Memorie of D. van Cloon, 1730.
   The Memorie of Elias Guillot for his Successor Jacob Mossel, Nagapattinam, 19 September 1738.

OTHER PUBLISHED SOURCES, INCLUDING LITERARY WORKS

Ambalavanakkavirayar. *Arappalisurasatakam.* [Tamil]
Ananda Ranga Pillai. *The Private Diary of Ananda Ranga Pillai* (1736–1761). 12 vols. Vols. 1–3 ed. J. F. Price and K. Rangachari, vols. 4–12 ed. H. Dodwell. Madras: Madras Records Office, 1904–1928.
Barbosa, Duarte. *The Book of Duarte Barbosa.* 2 vols. Trans. and ed. M. L. Dames. London: Hakluyt Society, 1918.
Bowrey, Thomas. *A Geographical Account of Countries Around the Bay of Bengal, 1669–1679.* Ed. R. C. Temple. Cambridge: Hakluyt Society, 1905.
Buchanan, Francis. *A Journey From Madras.* 3 vols. London: W. Balmer & Co., 1807.
Chau Ju Kua. *His work on the Chinese and Arab Trade in the Twelfth and Thirteenth Centuries, entitled Chu-fan-chi.* Trans. and annot. F. Hirth and W. W. Rockhill. St Petersburg: Imperial Academy of Sciences, 1911.
Dagh Register gehouden in't Casteel Batavia (1624–1682). 31 vols. The Hague: Nijhoff, 1888–1919.
English Factories in India (1618–1669). 13 vols. Ed. William Foster. Oxford: Clarendon Press, 1906–1927.
English Factories in India (1670–1684) (new series). 4 vols. Ed. Charles Fawcett. Oxford: Clarendon Press, 1936–55.
Fitch, Ralph. *Purchas, His Pilgrimes.* Vol. 10. Glasgow: University of Glasgow, 1905.
Gurupadadasar. *Kumaresasatakam.* [Tamil]
Idangai Valangai Jatiyar Varalaru [An Account of the Left- and Right-Hand Castes]. R. 7749. Government Oriental Manuscripts Library, Madras. [Tamil]

Bibliography

Love, Henry Davidson. *Vestiges of Old Madras, 1640–1800*. 3 vols. London: John Murray, 1913.

Manimekalai of Sittalai Sattanar. 7th ed. Ed. U. V. Swaminatha Iyer. Madars: U. V. Swaminatha Iyer Library, 1981. [Tamil]

Master, Streynsham. *The Diaries of Streynsham Master, 1675–1680*. 2 vols. Ed. R. C. Temple. London: John Murray, 1911.

Moreland, W. H., ed. *Relations of Golkonda*. London: Hakluyt Society, 1931.

Naidoo, Bundla Ramaswamy. *Memoir on the Internal Revenue System of the Madras Presidency*. 1820. Published as *Selections from the Records of South Arcot District*. No. 11. Madras: 1908.

Narayana Bharati. *Tiruvenkatasatakam*. [Tamil]

Nilakanta Sastri, K. A. "Two Negapatam Grants from the Batavia Museum". In *Indian Historical Records Commission, Proceedings and Meetings*. Vol. 14, 1937.

Pattuppattu [The Ten Songs]. Commen. Nachchinarkkiniyar and ed. U. V. Swaminatha Iyer. Madras: U. V. Swaminatha Iyer Library, 1974. [Tamil] (Poems used in this work)

Maduraikkanchi by Mankudi Marutanar

Mullaippattu by Napputanar

Nedunalvadai by Nakkirar

Pattinappalai by Kadiyalur Uruththirankkannanar

Perumpanarruppadai by Kadiyalur Uruththirankkannanar

Sirupanarruppadai by Nallur Nattattanar

Periplus of the Erythrean Sea. Trans. and ed. Wilfred H. Schoff, 1912. Reprint, New Delhi: Oriental Reprint, 1974.

Pires, Tome. *The Suma Oriental of Tome Pires*. Trans. and ed. Armando Cortesao. London: Hakluyt Society, 1944.

Polo, Marco. *The Travels of Marco Polo*. Ed. M. Komroff, rev. from Marsden's trans. New York: Modern Library, 1953.

Tanichcheyut-chintamani [A Treasury of Verses]. Madurai: Vivekabhanu, 1908. [Tamil]

Tanippadal Tirattu [An Anthology of Verses]. Madras: Poompuhar Publishers, n.d. [Tamil]

Sarvadevavilasa. Ed. V. Raghavan. Madras: Adyar Library, 1958. [Sanskrit]

Silappadikaram of Ilango. 5th ed. Text and commen. Adiyarkkunallar. Ed. U. V. Swaminatha Iyer. Madras: U. V. Swaminatha Iyer, 1950. [Tamil]

Varthema, Ludovico di. *The Travels of Ludovico di Varthema*. Trans. John Winter and ed. George Percy Badger. London: Hakluyt Society, 1863.

Vira Naykkar. *Irandam Vira Naykkar Natkurippu* (1778–1792) [The Diary of Vira Naykkar the Second]. Ed. M. Gopalakrishnan. Madras: Narramil Patippagam, 1992. [Tamil]

Bibliography

Yule, Henry, and A. C. Burnell. *Hobson-Jobson: The Anglo-Indian Dictionary*. New ed. Ed. W. Crooke. 1903. Reprint, Delhi: Munshiram Manoharlal, 1968.

Secondary sources

Abraham, Meera. *Two Medieval Merchant Guilds of South India*. Delhi: Manohar, 1988.

Ambirajan, S. "The Changing Attitudes towards Business in India: A Long View". *South Asia* 12, no. 1 (new series), 1989, pp. 1–27.

Amir Ali, N. A. *Vallal Sidakkadiyin Valvum Kalamum* [The Life and Times of the Patron, Sidakkadi]. Madras: Islamic Studies Cultural Centre, 1983. [Tamil]

Appadorai, A. *Economic Conditions in Southern India, 1000–1500 A.D.* 2 vols. Madras: University of Madras, 1936.

Appadurai, Arjun. "Right and Left Hand Castes in South India". *Indian Economic and Social History Review* 11, nos. 2–3, 1974, pp. 216–259.

Arasaratnam, S. "Aspects of the Role and Activities of South Indian Merchants, c. 1650–1750". In *Proceedings of the First International Conference of Tamil Studies*. Vol. 1. Kuala Lampur: International Association of Tamil Research, 1966.

———. "Indian Merchants and their Trading Methods (circa 1700)". *Indian Economic and Social History Review* 3, no. 1, 1966, pp. 85–93.

———. "Politics and Society in Tamil Nadu, 1600–1800: A View in Historical Perspective". In *Proceedings of the Third International Conference of Tamil Studies*, pp. 180–198. Paris: International Association of Tamil Research, 1970.

———. "The Politics of Commerce in the Coastal Kingdoms of Tamil Nadu, 1650–1700". *South Asia* 1, no. 1, 1971, pp. 1–19.

———. *Merchants, Companies and Commerce on the Coromandel Coast, 1650–1740*. Delhi: Oxford University Press, 1986.

Bagchi, Amiya Kumar. "Merchants and Colonialism". Occasional paper no. 38, Centre for Studies in Social Sciences, Calcutta, 1981.

Baker, C. J. *An Indian Rural Economy, 1880–1955*. Delhi: Oxford University Press, 1984.

Basu, Susan Nield. "The Dubashes of Madras". *Modern Asian Studies* 18, no. 1, 1984, pp. 1–31.

Bayly, Susan. *Saints, Goddesses and Kings: Muslims and Christians in South Indian Society, 1700–1900*. Cambridge: Cambridge University Press, 1992.

Bibliography

Belshaw, Cyril S. *Traditional Exchange and Modern Markets.* New Delhi: Prentice Hall, 1969.

Braudel, Fernand. *The Wheels of Commerce.* Vol. 2, *Civilization and Capitalism, Fifteenth to Eighteenth Century.* Trans. Sian Reynolds. London: Fontana, 1982.

Brennig, J. J. "The Textile Trade of Seventeenth Century Northern Coromandel: A Study of a Pre-modern Asian Export Industry". Ph.D. diss., University of Wisconsin, 1975.

———. "Joint-Stock Companies of Coromandel". In *Age of Partnership,* ed. Blair B. Kling and M. N. Pearson, pp. 71–96. Honolulu: The University Press of Hawaii, 1979.

The Cambridge Economic History of India Vol. 1. Ed. Tapan Raychaudhuri and Irfan Habib. Indian Reprint. Delhi: Orient Longman, 1984.

Champakalakshmi, R. "Urbanisation in Medieval Tamil Nadu". In *Situating Indian History,* ed. Sabyasachi Bhattacharya and Romila Thapar, pp. 34–105. Delhi: Oxford University Press, 1987.

———. "Urban Processes in Early Medieval Tamil Nadu". In *The City in Indian History,* ed. Indu Banga, pp. 47–68. New Delhi: Manohar Publications and Urban History Association of India, 1991.

———. "State and Society: South India, circa A.D. 400–1300". In *Recent Perspectives of Early Indian History,* ed. Romila Thapar, pp. 266–308. Bombay: Popular Prakashan, 1995.

———. *Trade, Ideology and Urbanization: South India, 300 B.C. to A.D. 1200.* Delhi: Oxford University Press, 1996.

Chandra, Moti. *Trade and Trade Routes in Ancient India.* New Delhi: Abhinav, 1977.

Chaudhuri, K. N. *The Trading World of Asia and the English East India Company, 1660–1760.* Cambridge: Cambridge University Press, 1978.

———. "Markets and Traders in India during the Seventeenth and Eighteenth Centuries". In *Economy and Society,* ed. K. N. Chaudhuri and C. J. Dewey, pp. 143–162. Delhi: Oxford University Press, 1979.

———. *Trade and Civilisation in the Indian Ocean.* New Delhi: Munshiram Manoharlal, 1985.

Chicherov, A. I. *India: Economic Development in the Sixteenth–Eighteenth Centuries.* Moscow: Nauka Publishing House, 1971.

Cipolla, Carlo M. *Before the Industrial Revolution.* New York: W. W. Norton & Co, 1976.

Curtin, Philip D. *Cross-Cultural Trade in World History.* Cambridge: Cambridge University Press, 1984.

Das Gupta, Ashin. *Indian Merchants and the Decline of Surat, c. 1700–1750.* Wiesbaden: Franz Steiner Verlag, 1979.

———. "Indian Merchants in the Age of Partnership, 1500–1800". In *Business Communities of India,* ed. Dwijendra Tripathi, pp. 28–39. New Delhi: Manohar, 1984.

Bibliography

D'Souza, V. *Inequality and its Perpetuation*. New Delhi: Manohar, 1991.

Dobb, Maurice. *Studies in the Development of Capitalism*. Paperback ed. London: Routledge and Kegan Paul, 1963.

Elliot, Walter. *Coins of Southern India*. 1886. Reprint, Delhi: Cosmo Publications, 1975.

Encyclopaedia of Tamil Literature, The. Vol. 1. Madras: Institute of Asian Studies, 1990.

Feldbaek, Ole. *India Trade under the Danish Flag, 1772–1808*. Scandinavian Institute of Asian Studies Monograph Series, no. 2. Copenhagen: Studentlitteratur, 1969.

Furber, Holden. *Rival Empires of Trade in the Orient, 1600–1800*. Minneapolis: University of Minnesota Press, 1976.

Gadgil, D. R. "Origins of the Modern Indian Business Class". Reprint. In *Writings and Speeches of Professor D. R. Gadgil: On Social and Economic Problems*, ed. Sulabha Brahme, pp. 311–370. Pune: Gokhale Institute of Economics and Politics, 1981.

Glamann, Kristof. *Dutch-Asiatic Trade, 1620–1740*. Copenhagen: Danish Science Press, 1958.

Gurukkal, Rajan. "Forms of Production and Forces of Change in Ancient Tamil Society". *Studies in History* 5, no. 2, 1989, pp. 159–175.

Habib, Irfan. *The Agrarian System of Mughal India*. Bombay: Allied Publishers, 1963.

———. "Potentialities of Capitalistic Development in the Economy of Mughal India". *Enquiry* (new series) 3, no. 3, 1971, pp. 1–56.

———. "A System of Trimetallism in the Age of the 'Price Revolution': Effects of the Silver Influx on the Mughal Monetary System". In *The Imperial Monetary System of India*, ed. J. F. Richards, pp. 137–170. Delhi: Oxford University Press, 1987.

Hall, Kenneth R. *Trade and Statecraft in the Age of Colas*. New Delhi: Abhinav Publications, 1980.

———. "Price Making and Market Hierarchy in Early Medieval South India". Reprint. In *Money and the Market in India, 1100–1700*, ed. Sanjay Subrahmanyam, pp. 57–84.

Hasan, Aziza. "The Silver Currency Output of the Mughal Empire and Prices in India during the Sixteenth and Seventeenth Centuries". Reprint. In *Money and the Market in India, 1100–1700*, ed. Sanjay Subrahmanyam, pp. 156–185.

Hicks, John. *A Theory of Economic History*. London: Oxford University Press, 1969.

Hilton, Rodney, ed. *The Transition from Feudalism to Capitalism*. Verso ed. London: Verso, 1978.

Hossain, Hameeda. *The Company Weavers of Bengal*. Delhi: Oxford University Press, 1988.

Bibliography

Iniyavan, ed. *Nanipugal Nagarattar* [The Renowned Nagarattar]. Madras: Auvai Manram, 1990. [Tamil]

Iyer, Lalitha. "Trade and Finance on the Coromandel Coast, 1757–1853." Ph.D. diss., University of Hyderabad, 1993.

Jayaraman, N. V. *Sataka Ilakkiyam* [Satakam Poetry]. Chidambaram: Manivachakar Nulagam, 1973. [Tamil]

Jha, D. N. "Merchants and Temples in South India". In *Essays in Honour of S. C. Sarkar*, ed. Barun De, pp. 116–123. Delhi: People's Publishing House, 1975.

Kanakasabhai, V. *The Tamils Eighteen Hundred Years Ago*. 1904. Reprint, New Delhi: Asian Educational Services, 1989.

Karashima, Noboru. *South Indian History and Society: Studies from the Inscriptions, A.D. 850–1800*. Delhi: Oxford University Press, 1984.

———. *Towards a New Formation*. Delhi: Oxford University Press, 1992.

Lee, Orient. "Mutahir, a Tamil Prime Minister of Malacca". In *Proceedings of the Second International Conference of Tamil Studies*, vol. 2: pp. 328–332. Madras: International Association of Tamil Research, 1968.

Leur, J. C. van. *Indonesian Trade and Society*. The Hague: W. van Hoeve, 1953.

Lewandowski, Susan J. "Merchants and Kingship: An Interpretation of Indian Urban History". *Journal of Urban History* 11, no. 2, 1985, pp. 151–179.

Ludden, David. *Peasant History in South India*. Delhi: Oxford University Press, 1989.

Mahadevan, I. "Tamil Brahmi Inscriptions of the Sangam Age". In *Proceedings of the Second International Conference of Tamil Studies*, vol. 1: pp. 73–106. Madras: International Association of Tamil Research, 1968.

Mandel, Ernest. *Marxist Economic Theory*. Trans. Brian Pearce. London: Merlin Press, 1968.

Martin, Pete. "The Concept of Class". In *Classic Disputes in Sociology*, ed. R. J. Anderson, J. A. Hughes and W. W. Sharrock, pp. 67–96. London: Unwin Hyman, 1987.

Marx, Karl. *Capital*. Penguin ed. Intro. Ernest Mandel. 3 vols. Trans. David Fernbach. London: Penguin Books, 1976–81.

Mazumdar, R. C. *Corporate Life in Ancient India*. Reprint. Calcutta: Firma K. L. Mukhopadhyaya, 1969.

McPherson, Kenneth. *The Indian Ocean: A History of the People and the Sea*. Delhi: Oxford University Press, 1993.

Meilink-Roelofsz, M. A. P. *Asian Trade and European Influence in the Indonesian Archipelago between 1500 and 1630*. The Hague: Martinus Nijhoff, 1962.

Minakshisundaranar, T. P. "Sunkuvar Kutumbam" [The Sunkuvar Family]. In *Tamila Ninaittuppar*, T. P. M. Silver Jubilee Volume, pp. 117–126. Madras: 1954. [Tamil]

Bibliography

Mukund, Kanakalatha. "The Role of Merchants in India's Pre-industrial Economy". In *Studies in Trade and Urbanisation in Western India*, ed. V. K. Chavda, pp. 135–154. Baroda: M. S. University, 1985.

———. "Coromandel Trade and Economy in the Seventeenth Century: Some Insights from Dutch Records". Paper presented at the seminar on Non-English European Sources of Indian History, Nehru Institute of Social Sciences, Pune, March 1994.

———. "Caste Conflict in South India in Early Colonial Port Cities, 1650–1800". *Studies in History* 11, no. 1, 1995, pp. 1–27.

Nagaswamy, R. "South Indian Temple: As an Employer". *Indian Economic and Social History Review* 2, no. 4, 1965, pp. 367–372.

———. "Leaves from the History of Tranquebar". *The Hindu*, 10 October 1993.

Nainar, Muhammad Hussain. *Sidakkadi Vallal* [The Patron, Sidakkadi]. Madras: [N.p.], 1953. [Tamil]

Nilakanta Sastri, K. A. "The Economy of a South Indian Temple in the Cola period". In *Malaviya Commemoration Volume*, ed. A. B. Dhruva, pp. 305–320. Benares: Benares Hindu University, 1932.

———. *A History of South India*. 4th ed. Madras: Oxford University Press, 1975.

———. "A Tamil Merchant Guild in Sumatra". In *India and South East Asia*, pp. 236–245. Mysore: Geetha Book House, 1978.

———. *The Colas*. Reprint. Madras: University of Madras, 1984.

Nilakanta Sastri, K. A., and N. Venkataramanayya. *Further Sources of Vijayanagar History*. Vol. 1. Madras: University of Madras, 1946.

Pearson, M. N. *Merchants and Rulers in Gujarat*. Berkeley: University of California Press, 1976.

Perlin, Frank. "Proto-industrialisation and Pre-colonial South Asia". *Past and Present* 98, 1983, pp. 30–95.

Polanyi, Karl. "Marketless Trading in Hammurabi's Time". In *Trade and Market in the Early Empires*, ed. Karl Polanyi, C. M. Arensberg and H. W. Pearson. Glencoe: Free Press, 1957.

———. "The Economy as Instituted Process". In *Trade and Market in the Early Empires*, ed. Karl Polanyi, C. M. Arensberg and H. W. Pearson. Glencoe: Free Press, 1957.

Prakash, Om. *The Dutch East India Company and the Economy of Bengal, 1630–1720*. Delhi: Oxford University Press, 1988.

Ptak, Roderick, and Dietmar Rothermund, ed. *Emporia, Commodities and Entrepreneurs in Asian Maritime Trade*. Stuttgart: Franz Steiner Verlag, 1991.

Raghava Aiyangar, M. "The Ancient Dravidian Industries and Commerce". In *Tamilian Antiquary*, ed. D. Savariroyan. Vol. 1, pt. 8. 1910. Reprint, Delhi: Asian Educational Service, 1986.

Bibliography

Raghavan, V. "Notice of Madras in Two Sanskrit Works". In *The Madras Tercentenary Volume*, pp. 107–112. London: Oxford University Press, 1939.

Raju, Sarada. *Economic Conditions in the Madras Presidency, 1800–1850*. Madras: University of Madras, 1942.

Ramaswamy, Vijaya. *Textiles and Weavers in Medieval South India*. Delhi: Oxford University Press, 1985.

Rao, Velcheru Narayana, David Shulman, and Sanjay Subrahmanyam. *Symbols of Substance: Court and State in Nayaka Period Tamil Nadu*. Delhi: Oxford University Press, 1992.

Rawlinson, H. G. *Intercourse between India and the Western World*. 2d ed. New York: Octagon Books, 1971.

Ray, Indrani. "The Multiple Faces of the Early Eighteenth Century Merchants". Occasional paper no. 29, Centre for Studies in Social Sciences, Calcutta, 1980.

Raychaudhuri, Tapan. *Jan Company in the Coromandel, 1605–1720*. The Hague: Martinus Nijhoff, 1962.

Rothermund, Dietmar. *Asian Trade and European Expansion in the Age of Mercantilism*. Delhi: Manohar, 1981.

Rudner, David West. "Religious Gifting and Inland Commerce in Seventeenth Century South India". *Journal of Asian Studies* 46, no. 2, May 1987, pp. 361–379.

Sarkar, Jagdish Narayan. *The Life of Mir Jumla*. Calcutta: Thacker, Spink & Co., 1951.

Sathianathier, R. *Tamilaham in the Seventeenth Century*. Madras: University of Madras, 1956.

Sathyanatha Aiyar, R. *History of the Nayaks of Madura*. Madras: Oxford University Press, 1921.

Schumpeter, Joseph A. *History of Economic Analysis*. London: George Allen & Unwin, 1954.

Sheth, N. R. "Theoretical Framework for the Study of Indian Business Communities". In *Business Communities of India*, ed. Dwijendra Tripathi, pp. 9–26. New Delhi: Manohar, 1984.

Spencer, George W. "Temple Money-lending and Livestock Redistribution in Early Tanjore". *Indian Economic and Social History Review* 5, no. 3. 1968, pp. 277–293.

———. "When Queens Bore Gifts: Women as Temple Donors in the Chola Period". In *Srinidhih: Perspectives in Indian Archaeology, Art and Culture*, ed. K. V. Raman et al., pp. 361–373. Madras: New Era Publications, 1983.

———. *The Politics of Expansion*. Madras: New Era Publications, 1983.

Srinivasachari, C. S. *Ananda Ranga Pillai, the Pepys of French India*. Madras: P. Varadachary & Co., 1940.

———. *A History of Gingee and its Rulers*. Annamalainagar: Annamalai University, 1943.

Bibliography

Stein, Burton. *Peasant, State and Society in Medieval South India*. Delhi: Oxford University Press, 1980.

———. "Coromandel Trade in Medieval India". In *All the King's Mana: Papers in Medieval South Indian History*, pp. 220–248. Madras: New Era Publications, 1984.

———. "Towards an Indian Petty Bourgeoisie: Outline of an Approach". *Economic and Political Weekly* 26, no. 4 (Review of Political Economy), 1991, pp. PE 9–20.

———. *Vijayanagara*. The New Cambridge History of India, vol. 1–2. Cambridge: Cambridge University Press, 1989.

———. "Vijayanagara and the Transition to Patrimonial Systems". In *Vijayanagara: City and Empire*, ed. Anna L. Dallapiccola and Stephanie Z. A. Lallemont, vol. 1 : pp. 73–87. Stuttgart: Steiner Verlag, 1985.

Subrahmanya Aiyer, K. V. *Historical Sketches of Ancient Dekhan*. 1917. Reprint, New Delhi: Cosmo Publications, 1980.

Subrahmanyam, Sanjay. *Improvising Empire*. Delhi: Oxford University Press, 1990.

———. "Aspects of State Formation in South India and South East Asia". *Indian Economic and Social History Review* 23, no. 4. 1986, pp. 357–377.

———. "The Coromandel-Melaka Trade in the Sixteenth Century". In *Improvising Empire*, pp. 16–45.

———. *The Political Economy of Commerce: Southern India, 1500–1650*. Cambridge: Cambridge University Press, 1990.

———, ed. Introduction to *Money and the Market in India, 1100–1700*. Oxford in India Readings: Themes in Indian History, pp. 1–56. Delhi: Oxford University Press, 1994.

———. "Precious Metal Flows and Prices in Western and Southern Asia, 1500–1750: Some Comparative and Conjunctural Aspects". Reprint. In *Money and the Market in India*, ed. Sanjay Subrahmanyam, pp. 186–218.

Subrahmanyam, Sanjay, and C. A. Bayly. "Portfolio Capitalists and the Political Economy of Early Modern India". *Indian Economic and Social History Review* 25, no. 4, 1988, pp. 401–424.

Subramanian, Lakshmi. "Calicoes and Companies in Western India". Paper presented at a seminar on Textiles as a Medium in Cultural Exchange, Max Müller Bhavan, Hyderabad, November 1995.

Sudhir, P., and P. Swarnalatha. "Textile Traders and Territorial Imperatives: Masulipatnam, 1750–1850". *Indian Economic and Social History Review* 29, no. 2, 1992, pp. 145–169.

Swarnalatha, P. "The World of the Weaver in the Northern Coromandel, 1750–1850. Ph.D. diss., University of Hyderabad, 1991.

Thurston, Edgar. *Castes and Tribes of Southern India*. 7 vols. Reprint, Delhi: Cosmo Publications, 1975.

Veluthat, Kesavan. *Political Structure of Early Medieval South India*. New Delhi: Orient Longman, 1993.

Venkataramayya, K. M. *Tanjai Marattiyar Kala Arasiyalum Samudaya Valkkaiyum* [Politics and Social Life under the Marathas in Tanjavur]. Tanjavur: Tamil University, 1984. [Tamil]

Verhoeven, F. R. J. "Notes on the Tamil Community in Dutch Malacca". In *Proceedings of the First International Conference of Tamil Studies,* vol. 1: pp. 156–163. Kuala Lampur: International Association of Tamil Research, 1966.

Vijayanagara Sexcentenary Commemoration Volume. Dharwar: Vijayanagara Empire Sexcentenary Association, 1936.

Vriddhagirisan, V. *The Nayaks of Tanjore.* Annamalainagar: Annamalai University, 1942.

Warmington, E. H. *The Commerce between the Roman Empire and India.* Rev. ed. New Delhi: Vikas, 1974.

Winius, George D., and Marcus P. M. Vink. *The Merchant-Warrior Pacified.* Oxford India Paperbacks. Delhi: Oxford University Press, 1994.

Yogendra Singh. *Indian Sociology.* New Delhi: Vistaar, 1986.

INDEX

Abraham, Meera, 11, 37, 39
Aiyappa Chetti, 120
Akkanna, 111, 113
Alagiya Manavala Chetti, 156
Alangatha Pillai ("Allingall"), 110, 111, 112, 115, 118, 155, 163
  as chief merchant, 115–117
Amaresh Thakkar, 129
Ananda Ranga Pillai, 140, 142, 152, 156, 161, 162, 163–164, 166, 174
  family of, and social mobility, 149–150
Andi Chetti, 146
Anjuvannam, 30
Anwaruddin, 104
Appadorai, A., 10
Arasappa Chetti, 147
Arasaratnam, S., 8, 74, 79, 142, 164
Arcot, Nawab of, 101, 104, 126–127, 163, 164, 176
Ariyanatha Mudaliar (of Madurai), 54
Armagon, 64, 162
Asian trade. *See* Indian Ocean: trade
Ayyavole, 30, 36, 37, 39–40

Baker, Aaron, 68, 69, 146
Baker C. J., 43
Balija, 44, 68, 117, 145
Barbosa, Duarte, 48–50
Bayly, C. A., 9
Benyon, Richard, 161
Beri Chettis, 44, 68, 117, 120, 128, 145, 146, 148, 151, 160, 162
Beri Chinna Venkatadri. *See* Venkatadri, Chinna (Beri)
Beri Durgappa, 117, 152
Beri Pedda Venkatadri. *See* Venkatadri, Pedda (Beri)
Beri Timmanna, 69, 70–71, 105, 106, 119, 138, 161
  family moves up the social scale, 148–149
  temples constructed by, 70, 154

Beri Timmappa, 115, 139, 155–156, 163
  as chief merchant, 116–118
Beri Venkatanarayana, 105
Bhadraiya, 128
Boxer, C. R., 7
brahmadeya, 26, 27
Braudel, Fernand, 5, 8, 168
Brennig, J. J., 9, 74
broadcloth sales, 96–97, 131, 135–137
brokers *(taragar)*, 19, 38, 50

caste
  census, in Madras, 151
  vs. class, 180–182
caste conflict
  in Cuddalore, 147
  in Madras, 67–69, 98, 127, 146–148
caste panchayats, 150. *See also maha-nattar*
  role of, 151–152, 153
castes, right- and left-hand, 68, 117, 128, 145. *See also* caste conflict
  collective assembly of, 152
  social mobility of, 148–150
  solidarity and identity of, 147
  textile contracts divided between, 128
Champakalakshmi, R., 11, 14, 25, 29, 30
Chanda Sahib, 104, 141
Chau Ju Kua, 40
Chaudhuri, K. N., 5, 7, 48, 78, 79, 83
Chettiars (Nattukottai), 40–41, 145
Chicherov, A. I., 169–170
chief merchants
  necessity for, 72, 105–106
  organisation of cloth procurement by, 107
Chikka Serappa, 94, 96, 146, 152, 158, 161
  as chief merchant, 95, 118, 119–120
Chinnanna Chetti, 64, 65–66, 73, 165
Chintadripet, 132, 139, 156, 161
chitrameli-periyanadu, 29
Cloon, D. van, 172

Index

Collett, Joseph, 160
"Colloway" Chetti. *See* Kelavi Chetti
Coolacherla Vyasam, 160
credit market (in Madras), 174
Cuddalore, 93, 95, 97, 114, 147

Danes
  in the Coromandel, 57, 58, 64
  exports by, 100, 137
Das Gupta, Ashin, 9
Disai-Ayirattu-Ainnurruvar. *See* Ayyavole
Dobb, Maurice, 3
Dost Ali, 104
dubashes, 69, 161–162
  as patrons of art, 166–167
Dupleix, Francois, 101, 142, 161, 162
Dutch
  and Chinnanna, 65–66
  exports, 72, 91, 93, 94, 96, 98, 100, 105, 106, 108, 122, 137
  form joint-stock companies, 73–74, 105
  imports, 96, 135
  and Malaya Chetti, 62–65, 72
  at Pulicat, 57–58
  offer inducements to weavers, 121
Dutch East India Company, 9

Elwick, Nathaniel, 159, 172
English
  early settlements, 57–58
  and the Madras merchants, 67–71, 112 ff.
erivirapattinam, 28
European port cities, 141, 176–177
European trade
  impact of, 51–52
Europeans
  and merchant capitalists, 60 ff.
  response of local merchants and rulers to, 58–59, 63–64
  rivalry in the Coromandel among, 57–58
  as rulers, 140–142, 160

famines, 66–67, 85, 94, 100, 115, 123, 131, 132–133
farming of taxes and revenues
  by merchant capitalists, 64, 113, 162–163

in Madras
  betel leaves, 157, 161
  measuring duty, 157–159, 161
  salt pans (paddy fields), 158, 160, 161
  tobacco, 158, 161
  village revenues, 158, 159, 160–161
  in Pondicherry, 161
Feldbaek, Ole, 7
Fitch, Ralph, 50
Fort St David, 95, 97, 100, 101, 124–126, 147, 155, 159. *See also* Cuddalore; Tevanampattinam
Fort St George. *See* Madras
Foxcroft, Henry, 71
Fraser, William, 120, 123
French
  exports, 94, 98, 100, 101, 123, 137
  inducements to weavers, 121
  at Pondicherry, 142
  role in local power struggles, 104, 141
Furber, Holden, 7

Ganga Ram, 128, 129
Gingee, 43, 54, 103
Glamann, Kristof, 7
Golkonda
  conquest of Coromandel by, 67
  poor state of administration in, 92
Gooda Ankanna, 149, 152, 161
Greenhill, Henry, 68, 69, 70
guilds. *See* merchant guilds

Habib, Irfan, 3, 77
Hall, Kenneth, 11, 28, 37
Hastings, Francis, 161
Hicks, John, 4
hierarchy of settlements, 28
Horden, Richard, 149

Indian Ocean
  as a holistic region, 8
  trade in, 6, 7, 40, 48–49, 58, 171, 173–174
insuring of ships, 174–175
interest rates
  in the medieval period, 38
  in the 17th and 18th centuries, 173, 174

Index

joint-stock companies
  controlled by merchant capitalists, 115, 118, 158, 172
  died out in Madras, 124
  disputes over accounts of, 115, 116–117, 118, 120
  under the Dutch (see Dutch: form joint-stock companies)
  under the English, 73–74, 110–112, 115–117, 118
  resistance to, 110–111

Kachchalisvarar temple, 147
kaikkolar, 44
Kalatti Chetti, 127
Kanakaraya Mudali, 152, 162
Kanchipuram, 20, 24
  as *mahanagaram,* 38
kanmalar (kammalar), 44, 145, 148
Karanappa Chetti, 122, 124
Karashima, Noboru, 10, 43
Karur. *See* Vanji
Karveti Raja of Bommarajapalayam, 163
Kasi Muddu Viranna, 110, 115, 117
Kasi Viranna, 70–71, 92, 105, 106, 107, 112, 113, 119, 138, 154, 156, 161, 162, 163
  as chief merchant, 109–110
  disputes over accounts after death of, 110–111
Kaveripattinam. *See* Puhar
Kayal, 40, 48
Kelavi Chetti (Kalavai or "Colloway" Chetti), 96, 122–124, 127, 146, 148, 152, 159
Kitti Narayan, 117, 125, 139, 152, 161
Kitti Venkatapati, 125, 155
Komati, 44, 62, 117, 145
Koneri Chetti, 65, 67, 146

Lakshamma Nayak, 63, 65
Lally (General), 151
Langhorn, William, 107, 109
left-hand castes, 117, 145. *See also* Beri Chettis; castes
  leave Madras, 127, 148
Leur, J. C. van, 7
Lingi Chetti, 134, 139, 157, 161
Ludden, David, 144

Macrae, James, 149, 161
Madanna, 92, 108, 113, 163
Madras, 67
  early years, 67–69, chs. 6–8, conclusion
Madurai, 19, 20, 21, 24, 42
  nayaka kingdom of, 43, 54–56
mahanattar, 150
  of Pondicherry, 151–152
Malacca, 48, 49–50, 52, 58, 61
Malaya Chetti, 60, 62–65, 72
managaram (mahanagaram), 28, 38
Manali Muttukrishna Mudali, 166
Manigramam, 30, 35–36, 37, 39
Manila, trade to, 116, 130, 140
Manimekalai, 14, 24
Marathas
  conquest of Tanjavur by, 103
  invasions by, 101, 141
maritime trade (of Coromandel), 6, 13–14, 46, 49–50, 170–171
  expansion of, in medieval period, 39–40
markets
  areas designated as, 38–39
  evolution of, 5–6
  hierarchy of, 11, 170
  marketless trade, 4–5
  nature of, 5
  physical structure of, 5
  role of, 4
  segmented, 93
  structurally fragmented, 76, 130
  in urban centres in the Sangam period, 17, 18
Markrishna, 161
Marx, Karl, 2–3
Master, Streynsham, 109–111, 112, 113, 114, 119, 147, 149, 155
Masulipatnam, 9, 58, 62
Mayor's Court (in Madras), 152
Meilink-Roelofsz, M. A. P., 7
merchant capital, role of, 2–3
merchant capitalism, 1–2
  evolution in India, 169–170
merchant capitalists (after the 17th century)
  behaviour patterned on landowning elites, 165
  as caste leaders, 146, 153

· 202 ·

Index

merchant capitalists (after the 17th century) *(contd.)*
  and changing environment
    before 1725, 138–141
    after 1725, 141–143
  characteristics of, 60
  as a class, 60, 114, 143, 144, 165, 181
  in Company trade and European private trade, 157
  in crisis, 102, 178
  as dubashes, 161–162
  and European companies, 72
  family networks of, 138–140
  and Indian rulers/ruling classes, 113, 162–164
  of Madras and Fort St David, 124–126, 129
  as patrons of art, 165–167
  relationship with the English, 112, 117
  and social institutions, 156
  social leadership of, 70, 182
  and social mobility, 148–150
  social status of, 113–114, 117, 142
  tax and revenue farming by, 64, 113, 157–161, 162–163
  tax collection by, 154–156
  and temple construction and management, 154–156
  and textile trade, 137–138
  trade in Asian ports, 139, 140
merchant guilds, 11, 18, 29–30
  as differentiated groups, 30–31
  of merchants in overseas trade, 44–45
  and nagarams, 36–37
  in Southeast Asia, 39–40
  tax collection by, 36–37
merchants
  as a differentiated class, 61–62, 170
  under European rule, 142 ff.
  in historiography, 7, 179–180
  in the medieval period
    as donors to temples, 32–33, 34
    migration and trading networks of, 35
    relations with corporate assemblies, 35
  portrayed in poetry, 16–17, 180
  in the Sangam period, 16–20
  in the Vijayanagar period
    offered specific inducements, 44–45
    settlements in Southeast Asia, 50–51, 171
    and temples, 45–46
    trade in Malacca, 48–50
    trade in other Southeast Asian ports, 49
    trade networks in Asian trade, 48–50
Methwold, William, 62
middle castes, 148, 149
Mir Jumla (Mir Muhammad Saiyid), 67, 164
monetisation
  in the medieval period, 38
  in the Sangam period, 19
Motupalli, 44
Mughal
  conquest of Coromandel, 103–104, 115
  embargo, 96–97, 126–127
  poor state of administration under, 98, 141, 176 177
Mughal state and successor states, 9
Muhammad Ali, 104
Muttamar Chetti, 126, 128, 129, 152
Muttu Venkata Chetti, 128

nadu, 11, 26, 28
Nagapattinam, 58, 66, 73, 131, 172
nagaram, 11, 28
  functions of, 28
  relationship with merchant guilds, 36–37
  three stages in the expansion of activities of, 29
nagarattar, 28
Nallamurli Kalatti Chetti, 129
Nanadesi, 30, 44. *See also* Ayyavole
Narayana (grandson of Beri Timmappa), 139, 161
nattanmai, 150
nattar, 28. See also *mahanattar*
nayaka kingdoms, 43, 54
nayaka rule
  creation of *palayam*s, 54–56
  end of, 103
  expansion of trade under, 44
  political instability in 17th century under, 55–56

Index

Nayara Bali Chetti, 127, 133, 152
Nayara Viranna, 146
Nilakanta Sastri, K. A., 10, 21, 27, 39
Nizam-ul-mulk, 104

*palayam*s, creation of. *See under* nayaka rule
paraiyar, 145
partnership trading, 172
Pattinappalai, 15, 16, 22
Pattupattu, 14
Pearson, M. N., 52, 164
Perike, 149
Periplus of the Erythrean Sea, 17
Perlin, Frank, 9, 168–170
Piranmalai inscription, 37
Pirenne, Henri, 3, 168
Pires, Tome, 48, 51
Pit, Laurens, 73
Pitt, Thomas, 120, 127, 146
Podala Lingappa, 93, 109, 111, 113, 163
Polanyi, Karl, 4
political merchants, 164
Polo, Marco, 40
Pondicherry (Puducheri), 8, 58, 63, 97, 98, 101, 121, 142, 149–150, 151, 156, 162, 176
Ponkala Krishna, 152, 172
  as tax and revenue farmer, 158–159
Ponkala Viraraghava, 139
popular protest, forms of, 141, 147–148, 150, 155, 175
portfolio capitalists, 11, 164–165
Porto Novo, 93, 97, 124, 125, 131
ports
  of the Coromandel, 46–47, 48
  in the Indian Ocean, 48, 49–50
Portuguese in the Coromandel, 52, 54–55, 57–58, 100, 137
Prakash, Om, 8, 78, 179
price rise, general
  theory of, 8, 77
prices
  in the Coromandel, 79 ff.
    of cotton, 83–84, 86, 91, 95, 96, 97, 98, 99, 105, 123, 133
    of paddy, 83–86, 95–96, 98, 101, 123, 131, 133
    of silver, 77, 88–89
  of textiles, 67, 79, 81–83, 89–102, 109, 116, 123–124, 129, 130, 131–132, 133
  factors influencing, 78–79, 101–102
proto-capitalism, 169
Puducheri. *See* Pondicherry
Pudukkottai, 30
Puhar (Kaveripattinam), 15, 21, 24
Pulicat, 46, 48, 57, 58
  decline in the 16th century, 52, 58

Ragga Chetti, 120
Ramanathapuram, Setupati of, 55–56
Ramappayyan Ammanai, 56
Ray, Indrani, 142
Rayasam Papaiya, 160
Raychaudhuri, Tapan, 9, 74, 175
respondentia trade, 51, 172–173
right-hand castes. *See also* castes
  caste composition of, 117, 145
  leave Madras, 111
  in Pondicherry, 149–150
Rome, 13, 16. See also *yavana*

sabha, sabhaiyar, 28
Sadasiva Rao, 124, 129, 159
Sadras (Sadraspattinam), 46
Salatu Venkatachala Chetti, 156
saliya-nagarattar, 29, 30
San Thome, 52, 58, 64, 104, 106, 111, 115, 120, 141, 150, 163
sankarappadi-nagarattar, 29, 30
Sarvadevavilasa, 166
Seshadri Nayak, 66, 67, 68, 70, 146
Silappadikaram, 14, 18, 24
Sivakataksham Nataraya Pillai, 118
social class, 167, 180–182
social network, 144
social status
  and physical space, 145
  and public honours and privileges, 113–114, 159–160, 161
southern Coromandel, 6, 10
Speelman, Cornelis, 73
Spencer, George W., 32, 39
star pagoda, 89, 176
state
  role of, 175–177
  segmentary, 10

Index

Stein, Burton, 10, 43, 180
Subrahmanyam, Sanjay, 8, 10, 11, 52, 164, 179
Sunku Lakshmipati, 140
Sunku Muddu Rama (Chetti), 125, 126, 133, 172
Sunku Narayana, 126, 127
Sunku Rama Chetti, 96, 100, 101, 122, 123, 124, 125, 126–129, 131, 139–140, 146, 153, 157, 163
Sunku Seshachala Chetti, 140, 156, 162
Sunku Venkatachalam (Chetti), 126, 132, 133, 152, 156
Sunku Venkatarama Chetti, 133
Sunkuvar family, 138, 139–140
Sweezy, Paul, 3, 168

Tambu Chetti, 99, 100, 101, 129, 131, 132, 137, 153
Tanja Chetti, 129
Tanjavur
  as *mahanagaram*, 38
  nayaka kingdom of, 43, 54
  under Maratha rule, 103
taragar. See brokers
taxes
  under Europeans, 121, 150–151
  in the medieval period, 36–37
  remission of, to promote trade, 44, 150, 175
Tegnepatnam. See Tevanampattinam
Tellasinga Chetti, 133, 137, 147
Temple, R. C., 109
temples in the medieval period
  construction of, 26–27
  donations to, 31–34
  multiple roles of, 27
  resource management by corporate bodies, 28, 36
  and urbanisation, 27–28, 171
temples in the Vijayanagar period
  redefinition of role of, 45
temples after the 17th century, 153 ff.
  construction and management by merchant capitalists, 154–156
  reduced endowments to, 154
Tevanampattinam (Tegnepatnam), 57, 63, 73, 121. See also Fort St David

textile contracts (English)
  directly with weavers, 134, 178–179
  and Indian merchants, 80, 83, 134, 136–137, 178–179
  penalty clauses in, 130–131
  reverted to a single contract, 130
  two contracts for greater competitiveness, 128
textile production centres, 131–132
textile trade
  changing pattern of demand from England, 133–134
  Coromandel textiles in Southeast Asian markets, 58
  in crisis, 132, 177–179
  Danish exports, 100, 137
  Dutch exports (see Dutch: exports)
  English exports, 91–102
  European trade handled by chief merchants, 71–72
  extension of textile procurement areas, 114, 119
  French exports, 94, 98, 100, 101, 123, 137
  impact of growing European demand, 8, 91, 99, 122, 128, 130–131, 171, 177–178
  under joint-stock companies, 72–74, 110–112, 115–117, 118
Tiruvengadam Pillai, 150
trade of the Coromandel
  at the beginning of the 17th century, 58
  maritime trade, 6, 170–171, 179
  in the medieval period
    development of trade, 25–26, 27–28
    maritime trade, 39–40
  in the Sangam period, 13 ff.
    coastal trade, 15, 16
    maritime (overseas trade), 13–14, 15–16
    overland trade, 15, 16
    presence of foreign merchants/foreigners, 19, 21
    role of the state, 21–23
    trade in agricultural products, 16
    trade in urban centres, 17, 18
  in the Vijayanagar period, 46 ff.
    maritime trade, 46, 47, 49–50

· 205 ·

Index

trade of the Coromandel *(contd.)*
   in the Vijayanagar period *(contd.)*
     and political instability, 56
     staple commodities, 47
Triplicane, 112, 154, 156, 163

ur, urar, 28
urban space, segregation of, 38–39, 69, 146
urbanisation
   in medieval period, 25, 27–28
   in the Sangam period, 20–21

vaniya-nagarattar, 29
Vanji (Karur), 20
Varthema, Ludovico, 48
vellalar, 145
Venkata II, 55
Venkata (brahmin merchant), 67, 69
Venkata Chetti, 122, 124, 146, 148, 152, 159
Venkatadri, Chinna (Beri), 105, 110, 111, 112, 114, 139, 147, 149, 154–155, 156, 162, 163
   as chief merchant, 114–115
Venkatadri, Pedda (Beri), 105, 110, 114, 147, 149, 154–155, 156, 163
   as chief merchant, 110–113
   recalled, 112, 114

Vijayanagar
   as a feudal state, 10
   as a patrimonial state, 10
Vijayanagar rule in the Coromandel
   creation of nayaka kingdoms under, 42–43, 54
   emergence of local power centres in 16th century under, 54–55, 75
   expansion of trade under, 44
   migration of Telugu-speaking people under, 43
   mobilisation of resources under, 43
Vijayaraghava Nayaka of Tanjavur, 66
Visvanatha Nayaka of Madurai, 54

weavers, 17, 44, 71, 73, 92, 93, 99, 107–108, 116, 117, 121–122, 130, 132–133, 134, 177–178
   inducements to move to European port towns, 121–122, 132–133
weaving castes, 121
Weber, Max, 167
Winter, Edward, 70–71

Yale, Elihu, 121, 155
yavana, 15, 21. *See also* Rome
Yerram Raju, 124, 129

Zaudi Khan, 120
Zulfiqar Khan, 126, 163